JOE KAPP

"THE TOUGHEST CHICANO"

A LIFE OF LEADERSHIP

JOE KAPP

"THE TOUGHEST CHICANO"

BY JOE KAPP

with J. J. Kapp,
Robert G. Phelps,
and Ned Averbuck

Illustration by Emi (Kapp) Carter

ISBN 13: 978-1-63489-289-6
eISBN: 978-1-63489-291-9

Library of Congress Catalog Number: 2019914641
Printed in the United States of America
First Printing: 2019
23   22   21   20   19   5   4   3   2   1

Cover design by Dan Pitts
Interior design by Patrick Maloney

807 Broadway St. NE, Suite 46
Minneapolis, MN 55413
wiseink.com

To order, visit itascabooks.com or call 1-800-901-3480. Reseller discounts available.

To my mother, Florencia Eufracia Garcia Kapp.

CONTENTS

PROLOGUE

"There is no most valuable Viking, there are only forty most valu-
able Vikings ... forty for sixty ... I just can't accept this."

—Joe Kapp, December 1969,
refusing the Most Valuable
Viking Award at the team banquet

"On the surface, 'forty for sixty' is just a slogan or motto. Another
team can shout these words and still be defeated every time it takes
the field. Without the values of the forty players, forged together
in the blast furnace of the sixty minutes, it's all just talk. Teams
are built on achievable goals, endurance, common sacrifice, sweat,
effort, and proper use of skills and strategy. Players and teams that
are not honest with themselves or who look for the easy way cannot
possibly understand the true meaning of forty for sixty."

—Joe Kapp

Those are the words of my father, Joe Kapp, the man *Sports Illustrated*
called "the Toughest Chicano" in its July 20, 1970, cover story. Pop,
as we call him, was as tough as anybody, but he has a huge heart too.
He loved his teammates, football fans, and Cal, and he never met an
underdog he didn't want to help. In fact, Pop is donating the proceeds
from this book to help fund scholarships for the Joe Kapp & Family
Scholarship for first-time Latinos and Latinas attending his alma mater, UC Berkeley.

Off the field, nobody loved his family more than my father. He taught us everything he learned from his unprivileged youth on the move and from leading Cal to the Rose Bowl, the BC Lions to a Grey Cup championship, and the Vikings to their first Super Bowl. He also shared the wisdom he learned from coaching the Cal Bears to a most improbable win in the big game against John Elway and Stanford in 1982 with "the Play." For his entire life, Pop left it all on the field for all those counting on him to do his best. It wasn't always by the book, and wasn't always pretty, but Pop never cared about that stuff. Doing your best mattered. Teamwork mattered. Enjoying the ride together mattered. Celebrating victory and sharing a loss as a team mattered. Living life authentically and fearlessly mattered. Most of all, loving your family and friends mattered. He has always been my hero and my inspiration to help the indigent accused as a career public defender in Santa Clara County, California.

Today, Pop is still the same man in his heart, but he has paid a terrible price for his sacrifices on the football field. He suffers from Alzheimer's disease, caused by repeated concussions suffered from fighting for every inch, on every play, every time. The man who once read defenses at the line of scrimmage, found the magic words to inspire his heroic teams, and protected his family now struggles to remember things most of us take for granted, like what town he lives in or the names of his grandchildren. Yet Pop has no complaints, no self-pity, and no regrets. The way he keeps his chin up with gratitude for the blessings afforded to him in the twilight of his life is more heroic than anything he did on a football field.

Looking back on his life as I helped to write this book, what became clear is that whatever Pop achieved during his migratory life, one thing remained constant: he is a guy who was always willing to fight all out for his family, teammates, or a cause that was just. He was never afraid of long odds. That is the essence of toughness and leadership. He won some. He lost some. Maybe to some critics, he's an unfinished hero. But that's what makes him unique, what makes him an unconventional father and a great leader. That's why he was such an inspiration to me, my brother and sisters, and all those who followed him. Whatever the circumstances, he never quit on himself or anybody counting on him. As he has said recently, even in his compromised state, "I think that my teammates knew I had their back, and they also knew I had their front!"

This book embodies that spirit and is a labor of love on the part of many. It began with my father's hand along with the help of several others, most notably his lifelong friend and Cal basketball teammate Ned Averbuck. Included in this book is Pop's and Ned's effort commenced in 1989, an in-depth project called "Forty for Sixty" that serves as a game-by-game analysis of the 1969 Vikings NFL Championship team. When dad's memory started to fade, I picked up the ball and ran with it. Finally, Robert G. Phelps, my longtime friend as well as a sports writer and screenwriter, stepped up to help us push it into the end zone. The one thing we all share is our love for Pop. We all want the world to know and enjoy his unique life and learn whatever lessons he has to share. This book is Pop's love letter and thank-you to everyone who supported him and his teams during his amazing run. We did our best. We hope you enjoy reading as much as we did bringing it home to you. You are our teammates and most valuable players in *Joe Kapp, "The Toughest Chicano": A Life of Leadership*. You, me, we, us, together!

—J. J. Kapp

AN INTERVIEW WITH ALAN PAGE

Alan Page and Joe Kapp were teammates from 1967 to 1969, the Minnesota Vikings' most formative years. As charter member of the Vikings defensive front known as the Purple People Eaters, Page went on to exemplary success in professional football, including nine Pro Bowls, six First Team All-Pro Selections, League Most Valuable Player, and Hall of Fame induction.

In the early 1970s, Page was the Vikings union representative and was a named plaintiff in the landmark case of *Mackey v. NFL*. In 1978, while still a player, Page earned his law degree and was admitted to the Minnesota State Bar. Page served as a justice on the Minnesota Supreme Court from 1992 to 2015. Alan remains active in the Page Education Foundation, which he founded with his wife Diane Sims Page in 1988. The foundation has awarded over $12 million in grants to nearly 7,000 students, who in turn have given more than 420,000 hours of their time mentoring and educating young children.

Page and Kapp are friends and were teammates and fellow litigants. Here, Page reflects on the strength, character, and legend of Joe Kapp.

J. J. KAPP: What were your impressions of Joe Kapp when you met him in 1967?

ALAN PAGE: Joe was clearly a person with a big heart who understood what team was all about. All of us have big egos, but his was directed at figuring out the best way we could be successful on the field rather than how important he was himself.

J. J. KAPP: Was Joe a tough quarterback?

ALAN PAGE: Joe was about doing anything and everything to win, such as throwing his body around, unlike most quarterbacks. He would accomplish things through sheer force of will. He was willing to sacrifice while not being dumb about it, but he would put his shoulder down and get the first down if that is what the team needed.

J. J. KAPP: What were Joe's strengths as a leader?

ALAN PAGE: Joe led by example, which is what real leaders do. When you see someone give it their all, it makes it so that you want to give your all. Or, at least, it makes you understand that this is what it takes, and if this person is willing to sacrifice, why shouldn't I too? You could trust Joe. Joe would do what he said he was going to do, and he would give what he said he was going to give. In this world, if you can't trust people, there isn't much there. In both word and deed, you knew who he was and what he was going to do.

J. J. KAPP: How did Joe affect the Vikings' culture change?

ALAN PAGE: In 1967, the players were more interested in the fight than in winning. Fighting with opponents after the play or arguing with officials can be entertaining, but it doesn't accomplish the goal of being a good football team. Over time, Bud Grant changed the focus from the fight to the game. During the time of refocus, I remember how intent Joe was on doing whatever it took to win. In that regard, he reminded me of Jim Marshall. Both men brought a spirit, a sense of purpose, and an intense focus on playing well. Joe was a fighter and a brawler, but he was focused on accomplishing the task at hand. If you were not about being as good as you could be or doing what you had to do to win, he didn't have much time for you.

J. J. KAPP: What did you think about Joe suing the NFL and challenging league rules that restricted virtually all player movement in 1971?

ALAN PAGE: I thought it was brave and courageous. I'm not sure I would have had the courage to do it. What Joe Kapp stood for was doing the right thing. I was impressed. Today, the players get a much larger portion of the revenue generated by the game. From that standpoint, things have improved dramatically. Joe Kapp was an important piece of that. In the end, the benefits players enjoy today come on the backs of people like Joe, who had the courage to stand up for what he thought was right.

J. J. KAPP: What was Joe's biggest impact on the Vikings?

ALAN PAGE: He brought us together as a team. When he coined the phrase "forty for sixty," it encapsulated who he was as a football player. His effort to make sure everyone understood that we are all in this together and that we have to work together—and because he did it by example—that says everything there is to say. I was honored to be a part of that. In essence, who he was and what he did as a football player made us better than the sum of our parts. I was heartbroken when he left. His spirit and focus were magic. He may not have thrown the prettiest passes, he may not have been the fastest runner, he may not have been a lot of things—but when things got tough, he was there for everybody.

CHAPTER ONE

THE PUNCH

I've never liked bullies. Maybe it's because we were a working poor family when I was a kid. But bullies are the matador's red cape to this Chicano. On Friday, November 25, 2011, I was a seventy-three-year-old man in Vancouver, British Columbia. I didn't know much about YouTube, but the school of hard knocks was about to give me a quick lesson. The Canadian Football League was hosting its ninety-ninth Grey Cup, the league's championship game. The weekend kicked off with a banquet to honor some retired players, including my old friend and BC Lions Team Captain Norm Fieldgate. The purpose was to raise money for Dire Straits, a charitable organization for retired players. The Blake Law Firm invited me to join the festivities. A great cause for a great guy. I accepted, no questions asked. I invited my son J. J., forty-eight, and his son Frank, fourteen, to come to the game on Sunday. It would be a fun family weekend to enjoy the game and good times with old friends. It would also give J. J. and Frank a taste of my years in the CFL before they were born.

But there's always a catch. Angelo Mosca would be there. He was seventy-three like me, but he had a limp and depended on a metal cane to get around. As I was about to learn, his other medical problem was a chip on his shoulder. It goes back to 1963, when he was a defensive lineman on the Hamilton Tiger-Cats. Mosca was hated throughout the league for his dirty play. He was so hated that an opposing player once jumped offsides to kick him right in "los huevos"—an action that received a standing ovation from every CFL team during film sessions in preparation for Hamilton. We would call this the action of an enforcer. Angelo getting kicked in the balls was the genesis of Burt Reynolds throwing the ball at Ray Nitschke's groin in the original *The Longest Yard* motion picture.

I never liked Mosca. In 1963, our BC Lions squared off against his Hamilton Tiger-Cats for the fifty-first Grey Cup. Our star running back was my friend Willie Fleming. If you wanted to beat us, you had to stop Willie. Everybody knew that, including Mosca. On one play as Willie swept toward the sideline, a Tiger-Cat wrapped him and pulled him down out of bounds by his ankle. The play was dead. Willie was flat on his stomach. Then Mosca dropped the bully's calling card on him, a late hit. Mosca torpedoed him and knocked him out of the game. I ran up and cussed Mosca out in three languages. I hoped he would take a swing at me so we could get a penalty and get him thrown out of the game, but it didn't work. Mosca stayed in the game, and we lost, 21–10. The cheap shot has never been forgotten.

We got our revenge against Mosca's Tiger-Cats the next year in the Grey Cup. It was an easy day for me as a quarterback—it was our game from the start. Some days are like that. We whipped them up front. Pete Ohler's touchdown pass to Jim Charpin on a fake field goal, Ron Morris's and Bill Munsey's catches, and Willie's runs left me without much to do on the way to the 34–24 Grey Cup victory.

I don't like bullies. I hate cheap shots. But I am a fighter—a fighter who now sat at the same round banquet table as Mosca almost fifty years later. The organizers may have thought bringing us together would be a great draw and good publicity for the charity, but I didn't like sitting at the same table as Mosca. I saw him mouthing "Fuck you" to me from across the table. His back was to the stage and I was facing the stage. He was impossible to ignore.

We were both introduced and asked to step up to the riser. I decided to make a peace offering out of the flower centerpiece. This was an attempt at humor, but I didn't want to distract from the noble purpose of the banquet. As it was, my peace offering was not as well thought out as it should have been. But even a guy like Mosca would take it in fun, right? I made the offering—and he took a swing at me! I swung back. Mosca whipped his metal cane at me with everything he had. I countered with a right cross square in the jaw. He went down, backpedaling off the back of the riser, almost taking down the Winnipeg Blue Bombers banner with him. Then I kicked him in the ass. So much for the positive publicity.

I had survived Mosca's cane. I was doing all right until I tripped over a suitcase in the hotel lobby and twisted my knee. It swelled up as big as a watermelon. When J. J. and Frank arrived Saturday, they had to tape my knee so I could go watch the Grey Cup the next day. My wife Jennifer told J. J., a deputy public defender, that I was in a fight, and he immediately said, "Mosca." Yes, the bully's name is infamous in the Kapp family. In fact, during his career as a public defender, J. J. had a picture of me sticking my finger in Mosca's chest on the field after he hit Willie. J. J. kept this as a reminder that we don't tolerate bullies. After hearing about the fight with Mosca, J. J. went into criminal defense mode to protect me. We were confident it was self-defense, but he's seen stranger cases filed during his career. There was some debate as to whether this old quarterback should grant any interviews about my exchange with Mosca. Finally, we granted an interview with National Canadian broadcaster Brian Williams. Like most football fans in western Canada, we knew that in some way when Mosca hit the canvas at the banquet, the wrong he committed forty-eight years earlier was avenged.

When we got back to California, we learned about the video of the rumble on the riser. It got over a million YouTube hits, almost as many hits as I took in my playing days. But at least the world saw that bullies couldn't be tolerated. And bullies can't be glorified either. *Dr. Phil* put the hard sell on me to come on the show with Mosca, but I declined. I told them that *Dr. Phil* is for people with problems—I didn't have a problem. Mosca did the show, I think to promote his book, *Tell It to My Face*. I told him by punching him in the face.

CHAPTER TWO

OUR HARDSCRABBLE HOME LIFE

My mother, Florencia Eufracia Garcia, was born in 1920. To me, she was "the Toughest Chicana." One of nine kids, she grew up near the tiny northern New Mexico town of Clayton. When Flo was twelve years old, her mother, father, older brother, and older sister all suffered food poisoning from eating home-canned chili peppers. Within one week, one by one, they all died. Her family decimated, Flo was raised by five other siblings and relatives.

She married my father, a charming alcoholic named Robert Douglas Kapp, a.k.a. R. D. He was the son of German immigrants. The Kapps were among the only Anglos in the town of Springer, New Mexico, where my father grew up. He spoke fluent Spanish and was a natural-born salesman who loved to gamble. As a kid in Springer, R. D. helped the milkman with deliveries. The milkman was also the bootlegger. My father started taking sips of wine and liqueur at an early age and didn't stop drinking until ten or fifteen years before he died. Alcoholism had a profoundly negative impact on my father's life and the life of our family.

I was born on March 19, 1938. That's Saint Joseph's Day, the celebration of the husband of the Blessed Virgin Mary. But life was no holiday for us. Mom was only seventeen and delivered me in an adobe house on Alto Street in Santa Fe, New Mexico. At that time, it wasn't unusual for kids to be born at home in that part of the country. The hospitals were small, and most people did not have any health insurance. We did not have the money for a hospital stay. According to my mother, when she started having contractions, she told my father to go get the doctor. He did, and the doctor arrived just in time to deliver me.

The source of heat in our adobe house was a potbellied stove. It was normally fueled with coal. When the coal ran out, my mother sent my dad out to find some wood. One night he returned with three twelve-foot two-by-fours he had "acquired" from a construction site. Because the only saw he owned was a hacksaw, he would cut halfway through and then break off a section for the fire. When the wood from the construction site dried up, he came home with old tires to cut up with his hacksaw. As they were for many in the Dust Bowl, things were pretty challenging for our family.

When you do not have a way to make a living and survive, you head to the place with the most potential. For us and so many others from the Plains and Southwest, that place was California. In 1940, my father hopped a boxcar and headed for California, hoping to find steady work. It would be the first of many moves in my childhood. After R. D. arrived in Los Angeles, he sent the money back to Santa Fe to pay for a train ticket for my mom and me.

Over seventy years later, in 2014, I returned to Union Station in downtown Los Angeles as a Megabus passenger. Ironically, I ended up in the very same place where my migratory life started. I was in Los Angeles to attend a special screening of *Through the Banks of the Red Cedar* at USC. It was a documentary about one of my favorite old Vikings teammates, the great Gene Washington, and other African American football players who migrated from segregated Texas and integrated into Michigan State University. The film was made by his daughter, Maya, and should be seen by everyone.

Back in 1940, my family moved to San Fernando, about twenty miles north of Los Angeles. This was the first of numerous moves for a better job or a better place to live, usually triggered by some catastrophic event involving R. D.'s drinking. His life was punctuated by screwups and arrests. He was like a guest star on a TV show: he would drift in and out of our lives. Through it all, my mother was the rock. She provided for us with her meager waitress wages, sent us to school in clean clothes, and insisted on me being a good speller and getting good grades. I was forced to grow up fast, especially after my younger brothers and sisters were born. Mom needed me to be a leader to help us get by.

I attended kindergarten through third grade in San Fernando. We lived in a small house that was once the gatehouse to the larger house owned by the Sierra family. Mission Boulevard was the boundary between the cities of Los Angeles and San Fernando, which had no sidewalks. As a small boy I did not really appreciate the significance of living in a neighborhood without sidewalks. Eventually, I learned that meant we lived in the barrio section of town. My parents spoke Spanish at home, so I learned Spanish. However, my mother discouraged me from speaking Spanish in public—she knew that English was the language to compete in the world.

The Sierras were the well-to-do family in our neighborhood who owned a restaurant and bar. Otherwise, it could be a rough neighborhood. There were lots of gang fights, and occasionally there was a knifing or shooting. I remember seeing the blood on the street in front of the Sierras' bar. I still did not have a sense that we lived in a tough neighborhood. We lived next door to the Vicos, a kind and generous Yugoslav family. Their son, George, was a Major League Baseball player for the Detroit Tigers. Mrs. Vico always baked cookies. The Sierras were Spaniards. Like many people from New Mexico, we identified with our Spanish ancestry, and not necessarily with Mexican culture. The Pachucos and Zoot Suiters in San Fernando and Los Angeles at that time looked foreign to us, but they were part of the neighborhood.

New Mexico seemed foreign too. My only real childhood memories of the state were from a return trip to Springer after we had moved to San Fernando. We had gone back by train to visit my Aunt Betty. We stayed in their house, which did not have indoor plumbing at the time. To help heat the house, we were sent off to pick up chunks of coal that fell off the steam engines at a bend in the tracks. It was also the first time I had ever seen snow in real life. It was really easy to see the black chunks of coal in the white snow along the side of the tracks.

As a little kid in San Fernando, I liked school, and I liked sports even more. Because this was before Little League existed, if sports weren't organized through the school, we organized them ourselves. At a very early age we learned to think for ourselves on the field, which would prove valuable throughout my career.

Mr. Sierra also showed me something I would never forget, something that I would carry with me my whole career. Mr. Sierra was a big fan of horse racing. He took us to the Santa Anita racetrack, where we watched the sport of kings. It was at Santa Anita that I first heard that unmistakable and exhilarating roar of the crowd as the horses rounded the Club House turn and headed down the home stretch. I knew then that the roar of the crowd was something special. It was a calling.

That sort of glamor wasn't found in our home, though. We didn't have a lot of money. I remember eating a lot of homemade tortillas and beans, or, for a change, beans and tortillas. All our neighbors were in the same boat as us—except for the Sierras. I never felt deprived, though. Despite my dad's drinking problems, he was a great cook at home. We loved to eat his sopapilla.

During World War II, he took his cooking skills into the United States Army. He was stationed in the Philippines, where he narrowly missed front line duty, not once but twice! At his first stop, they needed a cook, so he was not sent to the front. Then he found what he thought was abandoned flat, tepid beer. He took it. Unfortunately, that beer belonged to the lieutenant, who loved his beer flat and warm, not stolen. How the hell was an alcoholic like R. D. supposed to know the lieutenant liked his beer flat and warm? That misunderstanding got R. D. sent to the front. Luckily for him, his duty was to return captured Japanese POWs to the rear. He was spared frontline combat.

While we were in San Fernando, my sister Joanie was born in 1943, and my brother Larry in 1945. It felt like the family was stable. I spoke Spanish with my mom and dad, but by the time Joanie and Larry came along, my mother was even more insistent that we speak English. Consequently, the rest of my siblings did not learn to speak Spanish fluently. The Spanish-speaking school was only one block away, but my mother insisted that I walk eight blocks to O'Melvaney School, the English-speaking school. She recognized that if I were to have upward mobility, I would need to speak and succeed in an Anglo school.

During my father's transport duty in the Army, he learned that mom needed money for a medical procedure. He "borrowed" a fifty-pound sack of sugar, sold it on the black market, and sent the money home. Of course, he got caught and got shipped to the front, but by the time he got there the war was over!

We enjoyed good times in San Fernando. I remember going on a trip to Tijuana and riding a pony and seeing bullfights. The family would take trips to the Santa Monica pier in our Whippet automobile. But the good times in San Fernando didn't last. The Kapp family was on the move again.

When R. D. returned from the Army, he found a job selling cookware and Saladmasters for the Wearever Company. We moved to Salinas, a small California city about twenty miles northeast of Monterey. We lived in what I now affectionately call a gated community. This was a subsidized Quonset hut housing project for GI families, likely a converted military installation. Many families with kids lived there. We had a three-bedroom unit, a big step up for the family.

My sisters Linda and Susie had joined the family by this time. Linda was born in 1947, and Sue in 1950. Linda and Susie were tough Chicanas too. After raising families of their own, they heroically did all the hard work of caring for my mother in her last years without complaint. My mom worked at a good coffee shop. She was a lioness—she taught me to stand up for myself and my loved ones, speak the truth, and take the consequences, good or bad. My dad was a great door-to-door salesman. For all his faults, he taught me how to get along with people; to see the world through their eyes; to look at them directly, smile, and speak from the heart. Dad did especially well in the Spanish-speaking neighborhoods because he spoke beautiful Spanish. He was just a natural pitchman. I think the Latinas liked the blond-haired, blue-eyed salesman who spoke perfect Spanish. They never would have believed this was the same guy who got arrested for a DUI after running back to our Quonset hut and filling his mouth with garlic salt, hoping to kill the alcohol on his breath.

In our community, most of us were sports fans, but none of us had a television. We followed sports by listening on the radio, watching Saturday matinee newsreels, or by looking at the televisions in the window of the furniture store. Friday Night Fights sponsored by Pabst Blue Ribbon Beer were a highlight of the week. Joe Louis, Rocky Marciano, and Sugar Ray Robinson were our favorite boxers. Track and field and horse racing were also popular. Our main source of fun, though, was playing sports.

I got hooked on boxing. Our community had a basketball gym as well as a boxing ring, which is where other fighters helped me learn. At Cal, I used to work out with the boxing team, and the coach, Ed Niemer, said that I could have been a great boxer if I focused on it. I was always very coachable because my mom was adamant that I respect and listen to elders and teachers, and I'm glad I did. I never started fights, but I wouldn't back down from defending myself or a teammate. Plus, it helped me land one square on the chin of Angelo Mosca almost sixty years later.

I attended grades four through nine at Sherwood School and El Sausal Jr. High in the Alisal district of Salinas. We had no organized sports, so we chose up sides and created our own games, and we had to be resourceful because we couldn't afford sporting equipment. Sometimes we used lettuce heads instead of footballs. And if we did have a football, it didn't always have laces. This might explain why I was never too concerned with using the laces to pass when I was a pro. The great benefit is that you can get the ball out quicker if you are not worried about throwing with the laces.

I loved organizing games for my own participation but also for my younger siblings and neighbors. We invented a game like baseball that was my favorite. We would throw a ball against a giant concrete electric-transformer building. My siblings say the Olympic-style games I helped to organize were a highlight of their childhoods. It was a good thing too, because my parents counted on me to take care of them when they were at work.

The beginning of my sporting life in Salinas reflects a quote I love. In Cormac McCarthy's novel *Blood Meridian*, a character named Judge Holden says, "Men are born for games. Nothing else. Every child knows that play is nobler than work. He knows too that the worth or merit of a game is not inherent in the game itself but rather in the value of that which is put at hazard." This quote says so much about man's inherent violence and competitiveness. Sports provide a healthy, consensual outlet for these drives, especially football. The game tests a player's heart, mind, and body. As I wrote with Jack Olsen in a 1970 *Sports Illustrated* article titled "Man of Machismo," "Many believe winning is the ultimate measure of success, but that's a lie. The ultimate measure of success is doing your best. If you're doing your best, you will enjoy it."

In our Salinas neighborhood, we settled disputes on the field. Cheaters were not tolerated. On rare occasions there was some street justice, but we used our fists. Weapons were never used or even displayed.

We had diversity within the confines of our gated community. In general, racial tension was not an obvious problem, but there were two distinct groups—Okies and Latinos. I was a Mexican and a German. With my name and appearance, I was identified more as a gringo than as a Latino. But what you looked like didn't matter to me—I cared about what kind of person you were, and especially what kind of teammate you were. Did you pull your weight? Did you give your all for the team? Did you help others to do their best? Everybody on a team has an important job to do. Playing football, I wasn't concerned with the skin color of a lineman or what side of the tracks he grew up on. I was more concerned about whether he could stop a defensive end from throwing me into the cheap seats. Growing up in Salinas did help me to appreciate people from the inside out.

But I didn't get along with everyone. In grade school, a bigger kid called me "a dirty Mexican." I fought him and didn't win, but I did get a few licks in. Not much later, Bob Sartwell took my ball away and rolled it down the hill when we were on the playground. I went home and cried on my mother's shoulder, but I got no sympathy. She was raising five kids on a waitress's pay and exuded fearlessness and courage, and she demanded the same of us. She told me to go right back out and settle it. I did, but without a fight. I used to think that this was a violation of the code of machismo, but now I think it was a time when I stood up for myself.

Bob and I became friends. He was my teammate on all the school teams at Sherwood Elementary, El Sausal Junior High School, and Salinas High School, where we both made the varsity basketball team as sophomores. However, Bob and I did compete against each other in the church basketball league. I played for our neighborhood team at St. Mary's Catholic Church. Bob played for our biggest rival, the Baptist Church. St. Mary's team was competitive against the Baptists—we even recruited Jim Langley from downtown. Jim and I would grow up to play on Cal's basketball team. He went on to become the golf pro at the Cypress Course in Pebble Beach. Jim was the kindest, most Christian person I have ever known.

Playing against Bob when he was on the Baptists, I learned that he was an enforcer, not a bully. There is a difference. An enforcer cares about justice, fair contests, and his teammates. A bully cares about power, glory, and winning at all costs. The enforcer truly enjoys the physical sacrifice and challenge of mixing it up with a potentially stronger and more intimidating opponent. In football and other contact sports, you need a few enforcers on your team to compete with the bullies. Bob Sartwell was an enforcer. He became a successful high school teacher and football coach in Cupertino, California. I heard from a Vietnam War helicopter gunship crew chief that Bob's high school football training camp was tougher than US Army basic training! Bob has my respect and remains my dear friend to this day.

One of my best friends was Everett Alvarez. We were altar boys together; I had a hard time getting him to sample the Holy Wine. He was morally and academically sound, and I looked up to him. He set the bar high for both of us. When we were not in mass or at school, we were playing ball. Like all kids, we loved things besides sports too, like racing bikes and pretending we were cowboys or jet pilots.

Everett's dad was a drinker like my dad, but he seemed to be much steadier and worked in the trades as a carpenter. Everett became a Navy jet pilot and was the first American pilot shot down in Vietnam. Everett was in a POW Camp for nine years, and he is the longest-held POW in American history. After his release, he went on to a distinguished career in public service, including high-ranking positions in the Peace Corps and Veterans Administration. The newest high school in Salinas was named Everett Alvarez High School. He and I remain in touch, and he is an inspiration and true American hero to all of us.

In seventh grade, our homeroom teacher Mrs. Brunelli took us on a field trip to the University of California in Berkeley. Walking through Sather Gate onto campus and past Memorial Stadium was like walking into the center of the universe. The view from the Campanile Tower out toward the Golden Gate and all the way to Hawaii knocked me out. Prior to this, all I knew were barrios, lettuce fields, and Quonset huts. Everett was impressed too. He asked Mrs. Brunelli, "What do we need to do to study at this university?"

She said, "You need AP classes."

My question was different. "What do you need to do to play football for the Golden Bears?" Everett and I had separate priorities at the time. But as always, Everett's focus put me on the right track. I would start taking AP classes, even though I had just learned what they were. That short trip arranged for us by Mrs. Brunelli changed my life forever. I knew I had to get into the University of California. All of us would eventually go to college. Everett went to Santa Clara University and Bob Sartwell went to College of the Pacific, now UOP.

Tenth grade would be my last year in Salinas. Growing up in this competitive town was good for me. I learned early in life that if you don't stand up for yourself, you get squashed. I learned through playing sports that if you don't play by the rules, you're a dishonest person. I learned the value of a victory. A cheated win is no victory at all. I learned never to back down if the fight is just.

My sister Joanie, an astute mother herself who was usually right, believed that I was drawn to confrontation because our mother was mistreated at work. As a waitress, mom had a tough job and met some tough customers. I do think she would have knocked the shit out of any man who tried to sexually harass her. But Joanie was right: my mother had to take many challenges head-on to raise five kids essentially on her own. There is no doubt I have lived my life by her example. Because my father was not around a lot growing up, my mother often relied on me to take care of my younger sisters Linda and Susie and my brother Larry. I tried to live up to my mother's standards. I stood up for my younger siblings. I was their big brother, a big brother born for games. I've always been aggressive and competitive. It's in my blood.

CHAPTER THREE

MY NEW HOME IN NEWHALL

We moved back to Southern California because my parents somehow bought a small Spanish-style house in Van Nuys about twenty miles northwest of downtown Los Angeles. R. D. had secured a good job at Lockheed. He had a knack for making great recoveries. Mom stayed with him, in spite of his drinking and gambling on cards and cock-fights, because she always felt that he was good with the kids and a loving father, at least when he wasn't a really bad drunk.

I went to Van Nuys High School and was looking forward to playing as many varsity sports as I could—football, basketball, baseball, and track. Basketball was my favorite and best game at that time. I used to shoot baskets for hours and hours. I have always said to people, including my kids, that if you want to get better at sports, you have to practice. If you want to be a good shooter in basketball, you have to shoot a million shots. It is the same for passing a football. In a way, our economic disadvantages afforded me the opportunity to excel in sports. Because we had no money for toys or television or piano lessons, shooting baskets and throwing a football were inexpensive forms of recreation and entertainment. I wanted to be ready to excel for my new high school, so I practiced all the time. Then I got the bad news: according to the rules and regulations at Van Nuys High, if you played football, you could not play basketball! This was a crisis to me. My dreams were going down in red tape. Now what?

Luckily, I had an unlikely champion. My aunt Odelia Atler lived in Newhall, California, a small agricultural town about forty-five minutes from Van Nuys. It's now surrounded by Santa Clarita and the Magic Mountain Amusement Park. Aunt Odie had serious health problems. I was always welcome to help care for her boys Jimmy, Fred, Chris, and Ted. I spent summers and holidays with the Atlers helping out any way I could.

While I was staying with them I met George Harris, the principal of William S. Hart High School in Newhall, who gave me a job. He assigned me to work with Charlie Dillenback, who ran the Buildings and Grounds Department for the High School. I became the man with the hoe, and I hoed a lot of weeds. While working at the stadium during the first summer in Newhall, I met Mr. Al Lewis, the school's football coach. Coincidently, he lived in Van Nuys too.

I called Coach Lewis for help with my basketball crisis. Immediately, he invited me to attend Hart and play for him. I accepted; the basketball crisis was settled. I commuted to Hart with Coach Lewis until I moved in with the Atlers. But my family had its own crisis. At Lockheed, R. D. was found sleeping off a hangover in the back of a plane he was supposed to be helping assemble. He lost his job. We lost our house in Van Nuys. This kicked off a series of tough times and moves for the rest of my family.

But I avoided those tough times: I got to stay with the Atlers, play sports, and finish high school at Hart. I have always felt a certain amount of guilt for that, but the family was always extremely supportive. Coach Lewis did many things for me, but perhaps the most significant thing was to make me the quarterback of the football team. I had always been the quarterback until tenth grade in Salinas, where they played me at end. By the time I got to Hart, I was not sure where I fit on a football team—but Coach Lewis was not confused. From the very beginning, he had confidence in me. His unfailing confidence bolstered my belief in myself. He was my champion.

I spent a lot of time studying the game with Coach Lewis. As his quarterback, he taught me his system and expected me to call plays accordingly, and I worked to honor his trust in me. He was my second father. For whatever reason, he believed in me. He used to start his pregame speeches by reminding us that it didn't matter whether we were playing for money, marbles, or chalk—the game demanded you give your best. That included playing by the rules. The way he taught us always stuck with me. To give less than your best or to cheat dishonors yourself, your teammates, and the game itself. Coach Lewis expected his players to honor the game at all times. He was an old-school gentleman and the fiercest competitor I ever knew. If he was my second father, then the teams at Hart High were my extended families. I felt camaraderie and kinship playing sports. The structure, stability, and camaraderie of team life under Coach Lewis replaced something that was sometimes hard to come by in my childhood. A team is a family, and a family is a team.

Our tailback was a guy named Gary Yurosek. He later changed his last name to Lockwood and became an actor. He starred in the film *2001: A Space Odyssey*, among others. Gary taught me a lesson that would be driven home on many occasions when I worked in Hollywood: actors need their proper dose of attention. Gary felt that he should be getting the ball more. I disagreed and explained that I was calling the plays that our coach wanted me to call. I wouldn't give in because it was what was best for the team. The argument got hot, and it brought a challenge to fight.

I've always loved Westerns, and now I was about to star in my own standoff. Gary and I agreed to meet on the hill behind the high school after practice. I arrived on foot and waited for Gary for what felt like forever. Then a brand-new Chevrolet rolled up. Gary got out slowly and strode over to me, and we stood nose to nose. I braced for battle. He looked me straight in the eye and declared, "We don't need to fight." I was relieved. Maybe Gary just wanted to see if he could bully me, or maybe he saw the light. Gary was the son of a wealthy farmer and was established in the town and at school. I was the new guy. Had

I backed down from his challenge, the wrong guy would have led our team. That was, and always will be, something worth fighting about. You do what's best for the team, period. Coach Lewis knew what was best for our team. I wasn't going to be bullied into forsaking his trust in me.

Our football team was pretty good, but our basketball team was better. We were well coached by Bill Beany and Al Lewis. I played forward and was the league-leading scorer. I could handle the ball and shoot from the outside. In my senior year, we were Ventura League Champions, beating Ventura High School by a score of 47–46 for the first time in many years.

In a game against Santa Paula High School, I almost caused a riot. At Santa Paula, my opposite number was hanging back and picking cherries all night. In other words, he was hanging out under the basket waiting for the bomb and an easy score, rather than playing defense. I had to get physical with him, but I was a little late—make that really late! We crashed into the wall under our basket. The spectators in the gym exploded. A downpour of paper cups rained down from the stands. When we played Santa Paula a year later, they threw rocks at us and attempted to roll our bus over when we arrived. Supposedly a posse of Santa Paula players came looking for me in Newhall to take some revenge. They never found me.

Despite the Santa Paula posse, my life in Newhall was stable. I had a second home with the Atlers. I played on the varsity football, basketball, baseball, and track teams. The school offered me the opportunity to take the AP classes required by Cal. As I was striving to get to college, my mom and siblings were striving to keep up with R. D. They moved around California, to Tehachapi, to Greenfield, and up north to Stockton. I did my best to spend time with them during the summers as they migrated north. Their living situations in those times were particularly bad. Eventually, they ended up in Stockton, California, on East Eighth Street. While I was in Newhall, I missed my family and old friends from Salinas. Besides my family, I got letters from three people from the old days in Salinas: Bob Sartwell, Everett Alvarez, and Jim Langley. Their loyalty left a big impression on me. I've always appreciated loyalty and attempted to offer it in return.

Nobody was more loyal to me than Coach Lewis. He would pave the way to my future. Coach Lewis knew Pappy Waldorf, who was the Head Coach of Cal's football team. He recommended to Pappy that he give me a scholarship. I thought Cal was a better fit for me than UCLA, who showed some interest too. They were interested because UCLA ran the single wing, but I did not think I was a good enough runner for that offense. However, many people still think I was a better runner than a passer. Based on Coach Lewis's recommendation, I was sent up to Cal on a recruiting trip. It was a thrill to be taken to the airport by 1950 Cal All-Pacific Coast Conference fullback Pete Schabarum.

Later, Coach Lewis told me that Cal was going to give me a scholarship. I was ecstatic! As it turned out, Cal football didn't have any more scholarships to offer, but the basketball team did. I could have one of those, but I would have to attend summer school. I was happy to do so. I was heading to the center of the universe.

CHAPTER FOUR

THE CENTER OF THE UNIVERSE

A Golden Opportunity with the Golden Bears

In 1954, I was very proud of my 1948 Chevy. I had saved money from my various jobs and bought the car for $95. I would drive myself to Cal. I looked forward to enjoying the open road toward my future. I blinked and was past the outskirts of Newhall. Then my good old Chevy threw a rod, and she had to be left behind. I collected my cardboard box full of belongings and boarded a Greyhound Bus bound for Oakland. When I arrived at the Oakland bus station, I called Pappy Waldorf and asked how I should get to Berkeley. Pappy told me to take a cab. I hesitated—Pappy must have sensed that I did not have the fare. He instructed me come up to the office when I got to Cal. He would come down and pay the fare, which he did. Today, the NCAA would sanction the program for that kind of help.

At that time, a wonderful woman named Gale Reddon charted the course for California athletes. She registered us for classes, found us places to live, and generally gave us direction in the ways of the University of California. The first thing she had me do was complete a summer language course. Because I already spoke Spanish, I was encouraged to take Italian.

I took the class with basketball star Clarence Grider from Lowell High School in San Francisco. Our Italian instructor was a young man named Juan Valencia. In addition to his fluency in multiple languages, Juan was an accomplished opera singer and chef. Clarence and I were good friends, but average Italian students. He never quite got his vowels right, and my Italian sounded a lot more like Spanish, but I did make a lifelong friend in Juan. In 1970, Juan opened our restaurant and bar in Vancouver—Joe Kapp's Time Out Lounge & Peanut Gallery. He was the talk of the town, strolling through the dining room singing an opera with his chef's hat on.

Gale Reddon also directed me to the office of Tony Scallo, the campus landscaper, in order to get a job. Because I was studying Italian, I figured we would hit it off, and we did. My first day of work, I was dropped off at Tightwad Hill and told to hoe the weeds. This hill was part of the democratic system at Cal; if you did not have money for a ticket to the game, you could always watch it for free from the majestic Tightwad Hill. It was a million-dollar view overlooking Memorial Stadium and the Golden Gate Bridge. Tony did not know that I was a master with the hoe from all of my experience at Hart High School. When he picked me up at the end of the day, Tony became animated and shouted: "Joe, what the hell are you doing? That hill was supposed to take you all summer!" Tony was so pleased with my work ethic that the next morning, after the other guys were dropped off, he took me out for coffee, which turned into breakfast. We enjoyed a great talk about landscaping and playing football for the Golden Bears. This regimen went on most of the summer. Tony was a great boss.

It was in Gale Reddon's office that I met Big Kim Elliot from Vancouver, British Columbia, and Earl Robinson from Berkeley. Kim was a pitcher on the baseball team. Earl was an outfielder and point guard. They became my first two roommates. We lived in a beautiful old redwood home occupied by a Cal professor and his family. One floor was for us. We each had our own room. Earl, who went on to play for the Dodgers and Orioles, actually had two rooms—one to sleep in and another for his clothes. Earl was the best athlete on campus, and the best dresser.

Eventually, we had to move because the old redwood house lost its life to campus expansion. Kim and I moved in with Bob "Speedy" Gonzales, a halfback on the football team, at 2708 Channing Way in Berkeley. The new place had a kitchen, and we were excited about cooking our own meals; we designated Bob, a gourmet cook, as our house chef. That arrangement lasted only one week after Bob found Kim eating directly from a cold can of spaghetti. I think he was too cultured to waste his time cooking for someone just as happy to eat out of a can. Bob went on to enjoy a successful legal career that included serving on the San Francisco Board of Supervisors.

In addition to his love of cold canned spaghetti, Kim loved cars, driving, the ladies, and dancing. He was not a drinker, so he was always our driver. He even washed and took care of our cars. After a night of dancing, we returned to my "new" 1948 Chevy only to find a young man trying to remove the hubcaps. I asked him what he thought he was doing, and he jumped up with a hubcap and took off running. We chased him, and chased him, and chased him. When we finally tackled him, he was still clutching that hubcap like it was a football. His name was Jesse Kent. He was so young and scared that we did not have the heart to turn him in. Instead, we took him to the Nations Hamburger stand with us. We all sat around eating burgers and drinking milkshakes, talking about "the Great Chase." Jesse became a sidekick of ours through the rest of our time at Cal. Kim was a great pitcher and won two games in the College World Series, helping Cal secure a National Championship in 1957.

Another roommate and teammate of mine was Curtis Iaukea from Honolulu, Hawaii. Curtis claimed to be a direct descendant of King Kamehameha. He was a physical specimen and a free spirit, but a man of few words. Academics were not his top priority; he would sit in his room completely naked doing curls with a barbell for hours. When we would enter Sprowel Plaza, academics became a priority for Curtis. He would say, "Gimme a book!" He wanted to look the part of student for the young ladies he was trying to impress.

Another large and powerful man I met in football was Proverb Jacobs. Curtis referred to Proverb as "the Bull." Proverb was one of the only African American players on our team, and was easily the most imposing at six foot five and 250 pounds.

At one of the first practices of the 1956 season, Curtis and Proverb were lined up in a one-on-one drill. Actually, Curtis cut his way up to the front of the line so he could face off against Proverb. This matchup caused a great deal of anticipation and excitement among the rest of the squad. This would be a great showdown. The coaches barked out their commands. Curtis and Proverb got into their stances ready to pounce on the whistle blast. Proverb waited. Not Curtis— he exploded offsides and pancaked Proverb onto his backside. The coaches went crazy, blowing their whistles. Nobody had ever dared to do that to Proverb. They lined up again and dropped to the set position. This time, Curtis played it straight. Proverb jumped the whistle and knocked Curtis straight on his tail. From that point on they got along like brothers. Curtis would call upon Proverb to loan him a book or clean shirt, and Proverb patiently tolerated Curtis. Proverb went on to play in the NFL for the Philadelphia Eagles and the New York Giants, and in the AFL for the Oakland Raiders and New York Titans. His book, *The Autobiography of an Unknown Football Player*, is a meticulously researched account of social change in Oakland and Proverb's journey through it and sports. It must be the most complete and detailed autobiography ever written.

In my sophomore year, I got more and more playing time. With that, I was given the responsibility of calling plays. Coach Pappy was a smart coach. In fact, he was the father of the renowned West Coast Offense, a system that allowed us to run all the plays of a modern passing offense. One day at practice I was bothered, questioning my own playcalling. Coach Pappy responded in his big grandfatherly voice, "Just have a reason." From that point on, I never looked back. I called virtually every play during my career at Cal and for twelve years of professional football.

The highlight of our 1956 season was the Big Game against Stanford at home. I was a sophomore. It would be only my second start at quarterback. The first was the week prior against University of Washington. At that time, you had to play both ways by rule, so I played safety on defense. John Brodie was the All-American quarterback for Stanford. We didn't know it at the time, but it was to be Pappy's last game as our coach. We won 20–18. It was a huge upset. I can still remember Pappy waving to the hometown crowd from the balcony of his office in Memorial Stadium. I will always appreciate Coach Pappy for his help with my playcalling, for following Coach Lewis's recommendation, and for helping me to get that extra basketball scholarship to Cal.

1957 was our first season under Head Coach Pete Elliott. I was a junior weaned on Pappy's beautiful West Coast offense, but Coach Elliott shelved it in favor of the highly successful option offense he learned as an assistant to Bud Wilkinson at the University of Oklahoma. Coach Elliott was well organized and professional. He was a good and fair man, even if his offense only had four pass plays. Our first year running the option offense, we only won three games.

In 1958, during our senior year, we lost our first game at home, 20–24, to College of the Pacific, where future Los Angeles Rams star running back Dick Bass dominated. Dick deserved so much more recognition than he ever received. The only possible explanation for this has to be that he was African American.

We then lost on the road to Michigan State, 32–12, and we had a team meeting afterward. Jack and I told everybody that time had run out on the Cal team; either we start improving right away, or we forget it. The next day in practice, Jack spotted a linebacker who was dogging it. "Goddamn it," Jack shouted, "if you don't want to play, get out of here!" Jack grabbed that big guy by the seat of the pants and ran him across the field into a concrete abutment. Jack got everybody's attention. Sometimes you need a dramatic thing like that to shake a team up. We call that "internal enforcement."

One game in the 1958 season, against the University of Southern California Trojans, stood out because of an infamous member of the school's coaching staff, Al Davis. Yes, that Al Davis, the deceased owner of the Oakland Raiders beloved by Raider Nation. Davis reveled in his reputation as a bully. His mantra—"Just win, baby"—and the fact that the Raiders have often led the league in penalties showed his true colors. You can't have a win-at-all-costs approach and then pretend that you respect sportsmanship and fair play.

In 1958, Davis was on Don Clark's USC coaching staff. He coached a player named Mike McKeever, who, like his twin brother Marlin, was an All-American at USC. However, while coached by Davis, Mike became infamous for the late hit and using his elbows to injure opposing players. When we played the Trojans, Mike dropped the bully's calling card on me, a late hit two yards out of bounds. We got a fifteen-yard penalty, which led to the winning score for the Cal Bears. We defeated the Trojans, 14–12, before their home crowd in the LA Coliseum. Sometimes the officials are the enforcers. Good officiating helps ensure bullying does not prevail.

The next year, with Davis still coaching at USC, Mike McKeever did it again, this time to Cal Bear running back Steve Bates. He fractured Steve's face, and he never played football again. Good coaching assures that talented players like Mike McKeever are taught the right way to play, and they don't allow bullying; Vikings Head Coach Bud Grant was this way. Ironically, Mike's twin brother Marlin went on to be my teammate on the 1967 Vikings. He was a great teammate, a tight end—and tight ends were always favorite targets of mine.

We did turn it around in 1958, beating all our Pacific Coast Conference rivals, including Stanford in our final game at home, a 16–15 trouncing, to punch our ticket to the Rose Bowl. Going into the game, our backfield had toughness in Jack Hart and Billy Patton. It had speed in Hank Olguin. Hank and I probably created the first Latino backfield tandem in PCC history. (In fact, Hank has just written a book called *Who Let the Mexicans into the Rose Bowl: Navigating the Racial Landscape of America*.) But we were no match for the Iowa Hawkeyes and got whipped 38–12.

Football wasn't my only sport in college. I had the privilege of playing on the Cal basketball team. Our basketball coach was Pete Newell. He was the best pure coach that I ever had because he was the best teacher, counselor, and strategist. He and Assistant Coach Rene Herrerias created and nurtured an environment for success that was unmatched. Coach Newell treated us like men. His basketball system maximized the skill of his players. It was a system based on intelligence—out-thinking the opposition—and it was a learning experience for everyone in the gym. He taught us to be ready for the moment and trust each other. Coach Pete didn't want us to think; he wanted us to react. That doesn't mean he wanted robots. He wanted the system to be second nature so that on the court we were playing by our instincts but within the structure of the system.

Despite Coach Pete's great instruction, I reacted badly at a bad time. Coach Pete put me in with six seconds left against University of San Francisco (USF) in the '57–58 NCAA Tournament to throw the inbound pass. USF was up by two. This was the Western Regional, with a Final Four spot on the line. We had a play on for Larry Friend, our All-American leading scorer, to shake loose and tie it up. He was defended by USF's star player, Mike Farmer. Larry did break loose, but somehow my pass was a curveball that went straight up and straight down. Mike Farmer intercepted it. I ran down the court and stuck Farmer, trying to knock the ball loose. The refs blew the whistle on me. After Farmer got up, he hit two free throws that iced the game for USF. Everybody knew enough to leave me alone, even the press. Sometimes when you're trying too hard, interceptions result. It was one of the worst and most costly plays of my career. But you have to move on; you can't be afraid. If you compete, you will lose sometimes.

But Coach Newell liked my game. He had confidence in me and thought I could do almost anything I wanted to do. He was most appreciative when I sunk a buzzer-beater against Stanford. Most of all he saw me as a team player, a guy who would do whatever it took to support the team. If I was on the bench, and I was often, I was a cheerleader. Off the bench, I was usually in the role of Cal's enforcer. Coach Newell would tell me it was time to get physical. I knew what that meant. I've always tried to have the back and front of any teammate I played with, whether during a game or afterward.

My basketball career did feature a brush with a true legend. During the 1956–57 season we played the University of Kansas, a team that featured Wilt Chamberlain. He was seven foot one and weighed 275 pounds. Wilt was pushing our guys around, and Coach Pete called out, "Kapp!" I was enjoying the game from my usual spot, at the end of the bench. I jumped up and brought Coach Pete a towel. He was famous for chewing on towels. He said, "No, Kapp! I need you to get in there and be physical with Chamberlain." That was what I wanted to hear, so I got in there. In less than a minute, I was in a wrestling match with Chamberlain over a loose ball. Wilt must not have liked how I was grabbing for the ball, so he took a swing at me and I swung back and hit him in the ankles.

At another point in the game, Coach Newell said to me, "Joe, whatever you do, don't shoot." I was on the baseline, wide open with the ball. Chamberlain was a mile away under the basket. I was sure it would go in. I shot. Chamberlain jumped up and spiked that ball back at me so hard that I had to protect myself. The ball hit me and started to roll out of bounds. I dived for it and slid into Coach Newell's wingtips—he just looked down at me and shook his head. Although we were ahead at one point in the game, Chamberlain's Jayhawks were too much for us. We lost 66–56.

The basketball court was not a place immune from racism. We were playing USC at Cal's Harmon Gym. The home and visitor's locker rooms at the gym emptied into a tunnel. As we came off the court, USC's big center was calling Earl Robinson a racial slur. Earl was not only a teammate—he was my friend and my roommate. I got in the center's face and told him to shut up or I'd kick his ass. He shut up and went toward the USC locker room. As he was going in, he threw me the bird, so I went after him. But he got into the locker room, which was guarded by about four or five guys. When Coach Pete asked where I was, Denny Fitzpatrick spoke up and said I was "taking care of some business." When somebody insults my teammate like that, I'm in the enforcement business.

The saltier memories that I have described should not take away from how great our basketball team was, including the 1958–59 National Championship team. Members of our championship team were affectionately nicknamed the 59ers. I played on the 1955 undefeated freshman and 1956 and 1957 varsity teams, but was unable to play on the 1958 team due to the Rose Bowl. Coach Newell again showed me his generous team spirit when he insisted I be included when mentioning the 59ers. But the credit goes to everybody else on the team: Denny Fitzpatrick, who was our leading scorer, as well as our big men, Darrel Imhoff and Bill McClintock, who combined for nearly twenty rebounds per game. I wish Bill McClintock had played football! Bill went on to become a career school administrator. My old Salinas grade school teammate Jim Langley was also a member of the team.

Ned Averbuck was also a forward on the 59ers, and we have had a unique relationship ever since. I say unique because Ned himself is so unique. Ned grew up in East Los Angeles, and his parents were communists. His perspective on the world is totally unconventional. The thousands of students he taught at Laney College in Oakland over a thirty-year career received the gift of Ned. He is the most literate person I know, and he was never afraid to speak his mind with tremendous passion and force for extended periods of time. I guess that is why he was a professor of speech. We wrote a script and a book together that have never been published—we're still arguing about it!

Like all Coach Newell's teams, it was fundamentally sound, very close, and full of characters that went all out, and then later went on to do great things in their communities. Earl Robinson went on to be inducted into Cal's Athletic Hall of Fame. Both Earl and Ned Averbuck received the Pete Newell Career Achievement Award for upholding Coach Newell's and Cal's highest ideals.

During my years at Cal, I had two summers in Lake Tahoe. Roughly a two-hour drive northeast of Sacramento, Lake Tahoe is a crystal-clear lake surrounded by beautiful mountains and casinos on the state lines of California and Nevada. My first job those summers was in construction, working on the 1960 Olympic site at Squaw Valley. The foreman was a creep. While I was digging ditches, he would sit there, stare down at me, and make derogatory comments. Then, one day, he fired me. I don't think it was the quality of my work. It turned out that he was a USC fan.

My other job in Lake Tahoe was unloading slot machines at Harrah's Casino. Aside from the monotony of transferring coins from the machines to the coin room, it was a good job. I got to see Louis Prima, Keeley Smith, and Sam Butera on a regular basis in their Show of Shows at Harrah's Lounge. I made friends with some great people, including Jack Fourcade and Honk Williams, who were high school coaches and in Tahoe for the summer. I met Max Baer Jr., who was the son of Heavyweight Champ Max Baer. He played Jethro on the popular sitcom *The Beverly Hillbillies.* Max wanted to cut in front of

Honk for a drink in a bar. When I questioned the lapse of decorum, he turned out to be a fun guy and we hit it off.

Jack and Honk turned out to be great pass catchers. I spent a lot of time throwing footballs to them on the beach at South Lake. It was on that beach that I first saw Marcia Day. She was a student at San Jose State University studying fine art and was a talented painter. She worked summers at Harrah's as a change girl. Then she moved to the stage to work as a dancer in the variety shows in the South Shore Room, including the Dinah Shore and Teresa Brewer Reviews. We started dating that summer and were married on June 16, 1962.

The clock ultimately ran out on my playing time at Cal. My years in Berkeley had a profound influence on me on the football field, the basketball court, the classroom, and in life. Cal gave me an education and memories to last a lifetime, and better yet, friends to last a lifetime. I am, and always will be, a Cal Golden Bear. Decades later, I would return to Berkeley, but right after college, this Golden Bear was heading to polar bear country!

CHAPTER FIVE

THE NFL'S COLD SHOULDER AND CANADA'S WARM WELCOME

Heading into the 1959 NFL draft, I was an All-American and received the fifth most votes for the Heisman trophy. Former Stanford and Denver Bronco Head Coach John Ralston, who was an assistant coach at Cal during my time there, said I was the only player he ever coached that could start at all twenty-two positions. Despite that, I wasn't selected until the 209th pick in the eighteenth round by the Washington Redskins. But I never received a phone call from them, or any other NFL team. This was a serious blow to my ego, one that angered me. It gave me additional motivation to prove myself in pro football. I have come to believe that the player draft is unnecessary, un-American, and grossly overproduced, but at the time I was insulted.

However, I did receive a call from the Calgary Stampeders of the Canadian Football League. I signed a one-year contract for $7,500 to play for the Stampeders. For many years, I believed that the NFL was not interested in me because Cal ran an option offense in my last two years there. We barely passed the ball. However, forty years later, I was told that Calgary's general manager Jim Finks let it be known that I had committed to the Calgary Stampeders before the NFL draft. If in fact it was "known" that I had "signed" with Calgary, it would explain why I was drafted so late and why Washington never called. My arrival in Calgary would be the start of a twisted education in the business of sports with Jim Finks. As I would soon learn, "Gentleman

Jim" was the air traffic controller behind most of my migratory football life. The Calgary contract did at least enable me to make a down payment on a house in Stockton for my mother and siblings.

Many think of the NFL as the only real professional football league. However, the CFL is an older league than the NFL and truly is a unique source of pride for the country. Bud Grant, who coached in both the CFL and the NFL, was right when he said that the CFL game seemed to mean more to the Canadian fans. At that time, I think the CFL had more of a college sports atmosphere than the NFL. The CFL game is more wide open. It emphasizes passing on first down because you only have three downs to make ten yards. Having only three downs also means that each team has more offensive possessions, which makes lead changes and last-minute comebacks much more common. The field is longer (110 vs. 100 yards) and wider (65 vs. 50 yards). The end zones are twice as deep (20 vs. 10 yards). The wider field and deeper end zones pressure defenses to cover more territory. However, in Canada each team fields twelve men at a time, not just eleven. Any kick must be returned from the end zone or the kicking team receives a single point. There are no fair catches. All players in the backfield can be in motion at the same time and in any direction. The Canadian game of football is exciting and enjoys a deep tradition. Most importantly, the quality of players in Canada was comparable to the NFL at the time.

After signing with the Stampeders, I arranged a ride up to Calgary with Donny Stone, a running back from the University of Arkansas. He had a brand-new Cadillac, so we were riding in high style. Donny was so proud of the car that he barely let me drive; he said I drove too fast.

Somewhere in the middle of the Nevada desert on Highway 80, we stopped for gas. Donny went in the service station to pay while I was napping in the passenger seat, with the seat reclined all the way back. I woke up to the sounds of two guys shoving and picking a fight with Donny. They were making fun of the car and Donny's southern accent, but they were not aware I was in the car. I jumped out of the seat in a full surprise attack. Donny and I proceeded to pound the two guys into surrender. At one point in the encounter I tried to kick one of the guys and my huarache, a Mexican sandal, flew off my foot about twenty-five feet up in the air. After I retrieved it, an old-timer sitting out front in a rocking chair clapped and thanked us profusely for educating those guys. Apparently, they were local thugs. The old man said, "Those boys been needin' ass whippin' for a long time." With the excitement behind us, we rolled into one of Canada's largest western cities, but the sparse skyline reminded me of Modesto, California.

Soon after our arrival, I found myself at the Calgary Stampede Parade with my new teammate Ron Morris. Like Donny, Ron is originally from the state of Arkansas. Ron was a standout two-way player and punter from the University of Tulsa who was drafted by the New York Giants, but Calgary won his services for an extra $500. Ron, a.k.a. the Creeper, is a very interesting guy who has many talents off the field, including musicianship, flying model planes, riding motorcycles, and photography. At the parade, Ron played network news correspondent. He designated me as his film crew. I was responsible for carrying all of his photography equipment to hell and back, twice!

Mewata Stadium was our home field, headquarters, and training facility in Calgary. This twenty-five-thousand-seat relic was without a doubt the worst football stadium and locker room setup of all time. Your locker was a nail in the wall. There were two showerheads but only one of them had a spray nozzle. The other one drizzled like a faucet. The cold wind howled through the plank walls. At least they had a pot-bellied stove in Saskatchewan. My Vikings teammate, the great Jim Marshall, played a year for the Saskatchewan Roughriders before his twenty-year NFL career. He was shocked that there was a pot-bellied stove in their locker room. He said the facilities at his alma mater Ohio State made the Roughriders camp look primitive. What does that say about Calgary? Ron Morris remembers when one of the benches in the locker room crashed through the floor under the weight of his and another teammate's shoulder pads. All meetings, film study, ankle taping, dressing, and every other thing a football team now does in a sprawling training facility we did in one cramped locker room at Mewata Stadium. When the lights went off to watch film on our sixteen-millimeter projector, cigars lit up, making the small locker room even more special—although the smoke plumes made it hard to see the film.

Otis Douglas was our head coach. Otis was a no-nonsense Virginian and a very unique individual. He remains the oldest rookie in NFL history at age thirty-five. He won two NFL Championships in his four years as an offensive tackle for the Philadelphia Eagles. He was also the Eagles trainer. He went on to become the head coach at Arkansas before he came to Calgary in 1955. He was a tough guy. He had a stump where his right index finger was supposed to be because of an accident, but it was no big deal to Coach Douglas. His mind was sharp; he knew football as well as any coach I have ever played for.

I purposely got to town well before training camp to prepare. I got to know Coach Douglas. We spent countless hours watching film and scheming game plans for our first season. This was a real learning experience for me. I remember watching film of the BC Lions, and a giant figure playing defensive tackle caught my eye. No way I could have missed him; he was truly a lion on a field of alley cats. I wondered where they found a football suit big enough to fit him. I was worried about this guy and looked to Coach Douglas for some reassurance. He said, "Big Mike Cacic? No, Joe, you don't have to worry about Big Mike as long as you don't hold him, don't go for his knees, don't call his mother names, and most importantly, don't do anything to make him mad. I instruct our lineman to carefully follow those rules. Otherwise bad things happen, really bad things." That reassurance was cold comfort to this rookie quarterback.

As my first pro training camp drew closer, a brand-new 1959 Chevy pulled up in front of the dormitory. The driver was Jack Kemp. Yes, that Jack Kemp. I would be competing against him to be the Stamps' starting quarterback. His Chevy was full of books and weights, which I helped unload. In those days, it was very unusual for players to lift weights. He had clearly made use of them because he had a very strong arm. The number of books was impressive because most football players were not known to read much. We did not know then, but Jack Kemp aspired to be a member of the United States Congress and beyond. I wanted to be the quarterback for the Calgary Stampeders, and he wanted to be the President of the United States. In his race against me in Calgary, I was elected starting quarterback. Kemp was cut. He caught on in the AFL with the Buffalo Bills and had a successful career, including an AFL Championship. His momma got to watch him on American television while mine would have to wait another eight years before she could see me play on TV.

Finally, it was time to start working out on the practice field. My position coach was Frankie Philchok. He later became the first head coach of the Denver Broncos. I asked what I thought was a simple question. "Should I pass the ball on a five-step or seven-step dropback?" The coach let loose with expletives: "Three-step, five-step, seven-step—how the fuck should I know? You throw the ball when the receiver is open, and then you put the nail in the coffin!" It sounds simplistic, if not rude, but I learned what it meant, and it is still good advice. I learned to pass when receivers were open no matter where I was in the backfield, and when to throw the pass hard. My habit of throwing the ball without worrying about gripping the laces helped me play for Coach Philchok.

Early in the season we were in Montreal to play the Alouettes. The night before the game we were under curfew, so we set up a bar in one of our hotel rooms. Most of us were drinking quart bottles of Molson Ale, one of Canada's favorite brews. I was enjoying my beer and some laughs with my teammates. Out of nowhere, a reserve player named Doug Brown broke a Molson bottle and slashed me across the neck and chin. Blood was shooting all over the place. Everyone in the room was stunned. Nobody knew what to do. The sight of blood caused our trainer to nearly faint. Somebody snapped out of it and got Coach Douglas. When he arrived, he took his stump of a right index finger and jammed it into my neck to stop the bleeding. I was taken to St. Mary's Hospital, where my neck and chin were sewn up with over a hundred stitches. I played in the next game. According to the doctors, had the bottle slashed me an inch lower, I could have easily been killed. I was asked by Jim Finks if I wanted to press charges. As a twenty-one-year-old rookie, I only wanted to know why he did it. Doug Brown apologized and cried like a baby. When asked why he did it, all he could say over and over again was, "I don't know."

As a rookie, I had plenty of teammates older than me. There were times when certain veterans were not taking my direction and complaining about the plays I called in the huddle. Making it worse, some of the older Canadian players resented American "imports," as we were called. One of the Canadian veterans was Tony Pajekowski, an outstanding lineman. One day at practice, there was some grumbling about the snap count. I called the play to go on three, but several players wanted to go on one. Tony was fed up and shouted, "If the Big Mex wants to go on three, then we go on three!" Tony got their attention, and from that point on there was no more grumbling. It would have been easy for Tony join the other vets and haze the rookie, but his leadership helped our team to unite. We went on to go 8–8 for the season. We were disappointed but knew we were on the rise.

Three games into the 1960 season, "Gentleman" Jim Finks fired Coach Douglas. It was a terrible shock to me. I felt that he was a great teacher and really cared about our players. Stout Steve Owen was hired as his replacement. Stout Steve had been the head coach of the

New York Giants for twenty-three years and was a legendary figure. He looked like Santa Claus, but he was gruff and profane. He dipped snuff and spit into Coke bottles. His mandate from the top was to stop this rookie from throwing so many interceptions. "Quit trying to throw all these home runs," he would admonish me in a kind of lisp made worse by the plug of snuff between his cheek and gum.

Although we were having a good season, I was still trying too hard. My long bombs often yielded a pick, not points on the board for us. Once after I threw an interception, Coach Owen gently put his arm around my shoulder like a concerned grandfather as Stampeder fans looked on, probably thinking that I was receiving gentle advice. He stared me in the eye and cussed me out while spraying tobacco spittle in my face! Coach Owen had a million colorful quotes, and once said to a receiver who dropped a perfectly thrown pass, "If I shot you between the eyes with a 30–30 rifle, there is not a jury in the country that would convict me."

Under Stout Steve we were 6–6–1. In spite of the record, he made us a more disciplined team. Then, out of nowhere, Jim Finks fired Stout Steve. All of us were stunned. One of the saddest things I ever witnessed was Coach Owen telling us he was fired with tears welling up in his eyes. He must have sensed that his coaching career was coming to an end. Stout Steve Owen died in 1964 and was inducted into the Hall of Fame in 1966.

In 1961 my career was in Canada, but the Golden Bears needed my help. Cal wanted to sign Craig Morton, the star quarterback at Campbell High School located near San Jose, California. It was looking bleak for my alma mater; Stanford had offered Craig a scholarship. I wouldn't stand for it, so I made regular recruiting visits to Craig's house—so many that Craig's mother would say, "There's that man again." It worked. Craig enrolled at Cal. The rest is history. After a great career at Cal, he had an outstanding career in the NFL with the Dallas Cowboys, the New York Giants, and the Denver Broncos. He led the Cowboys and Broncos to their first Super Bowl appearances. He was as good a passer as anybody who has ever played. He may also be the most spirited Golden Bear! With Stanford having the edge in recruiting and resources over the years, I probably cost Craig the Heisman Trophy, but his enthusiasm for Cal and our friendship has never wavered.

Now it was my turn to deal with Gentleman Jim. I had to negotiate the third year of my contract with the Stampeders. I'd had a good season, and the team was coming together even though he was changing coaches like most guys change their socks. I asked for a raise to $10,000. Finks countered with $9,500 and would not budge. He was just as stingy with Ron Morris. Ron told Finks that his offer was fine for his offensive work, but what about his defense and his punting? Finks was unmoved. He would not budge on Ron. He would not budge on me—but neither would I. It meant I would soon be on the road again.

After the impasse, I was traded to the BC Lions for four starting players on August 24, 1961. That's the business of pro sports. When I arrived in Vancouver, the team was already in the hole, with a record of 0–3–1. I was formally introduced to my BC Lion teammates at a team dinner in Saskatchewan before our game the next day against the Roughriders. I was mingling with my new teammates when I was swallowed by a dark shadow. I thought they'd signed Frankenstein. It was worse; standing before me was defensive tackle Big Mike Cacic, the same Big Mike who Coach Douglas told me must never be offended, ruffled, or even mildly annoyed, even if unintentionally. In Calgary, I had played against Big Mike and survived. He stood six foot seven, but his weight was unknown. The story was that whenever a coach or trainer told him to get on the scale, Big Mike said, "No." Everybody said okay. I sat next to Big Mike. He gave me a few grunts as he devoured his prime rib dinner.

After dinner, I took a wild guess and asked Big Mike if he was still hungry. I got another grunt. We went down the street to a late-night diner. I asked Big Mike if he wanted a hamburger. He said yes, so I ordered a half dozen. I asked if he liked French fries. He said yes, so I ordered a half-dozen fries. I asked if he wanted a milkshake. He said yes, and I ordered two chocolate, two strawberry, and two vanilla. I had one hamburger and one milkshake and Big Mike ate the rest.

Bobby Ackles, the equipment manager, was showing me around the locker room. He's an amazing story. He started as the Lions' water boy at age fifteen and ultimately climbed the ladder all the way to the Lions' president, after stints with the Dallas Cowboys and the XFL. Bobby and I were getting to know each other. Then Big Mike arrived as Bobby was about to assign me a locker in the corner. Big Mike wasn't happy. He started dumping the contents out of the locker next to his, which belonged to Bob Belac. He ordered Bobby Ackles to put my gear next to his. I balked at bumping somebody; I wanted to maintain a low profile with my new teammates. But Big Mike would have none of it. He shushed me as Bobby obediently put my gear next to Big Mike, and noted, "What the Big Boy wants, the Big Boy gets." Later, Bob Belac told me being evicted from Big Mike's neighborhood was the best thing that ever happened to him. As for me, becoming teammate and lifelong friend of Mike Cacic was one of the best things that ever happened to me. I enjoyed many great friendships with my teammates on the BC Lions, but Big Mike was one of a kind.

I had only been in Vancouver a few months when I was told Doug Brown was looking for me at the Lions' football offices. He was the Stampeder who had slashed my face with a Molson bottle before the Montreal game when I was with Calgary. Brown had shown up at the office and was asking for me while wearing an overcoat and appearing to walk as if he had a peg leg. After leaving the Lions' offices, he went down the street and walked into a Catholic Church. He pulled out a shotgun and murdered the priest. My heart still breaks heavy for the priest and his loved ones. It was bone chilling at the time. Later, I learned Doug Brown had been diagnosed with schizophrenia and was committed to a mental hospital in Vancouver. Even understanding that he was very sick, I don't know why he was focused on me.

We did not win in our first two seasons, but good things were happening on and off the field. On May 2, 1963, my wife Marcia was about to give birth to our first child in Vancouver General Hospital. My mother was born on May 2, so all of us were hoping the baby would share her birthday. I did what most expectant fathers did—I waited all day. Fortunately, the obstetrician kept me company during the wait. Even more fortunately, the hospital was only a short pass from one of our favorite BC Lion hangouts, Primo's Mexican Restaurant. The owner, Primo Villanueva, was a famed running back from UCLA nicknamed the Calexico Kid. I spent the day attempting to persuade the doctor to allow me to watch the delivery. At that time, fathers witnessing deliveries was unheard of. I think my dad would have been impressed with my salesmanship.

But as the day turned to night, it looked like the clock would hit midnight before the baby arrived. Then, at 11:30 p.m., the doctor suited me up in a mask and gown and ushered me into the delivery room. I witnessed my son J. J.'s birth on May 2, before midnight, on my mother's birthday. It was a miracle, and a well-timed one! Later when we were observing all the babies in the nursery, we noticed that J. J. was the only baby with a shock of black hair. I overheard a lady who said, "Oh, look at the cute little Eskimo baby!"

No doubt, Big Mike was one of the toughest football players I ever played with. Off the field, he was a sought-after carpenter. Getting an appointment with him was harder than catching our star running back Willie Fleming from behind. Finally, I got Big Mike out to our house in West Vancouver to fix a table. He pulled up in his '60 T-Bird, the nose up and the rear end sagging. The trunk was loaded with tools. I came out on the driveway to give him a warm welcome, and my son J. J. followed me out. Big Mike got out of his car, pulled out a toolbox from the trunk, took one look at J. J., and pointed at his red-speckled face. Big Mike said, "What's this?"

"Oh, he just got over the chicken pox," I replied.

"Chicken pox?" asked Big Mike. Without saying another word, he did an about-face, put his toolbox in the trunk, got into his nose-up '60 T-Bird, and burned out of the driveway. He didn't get chicken pox, and I didn't get my table fixed.

In 1961, my first year with the Lions, we finished with a record of 1–13–2. That was good enough for last place in the Western Conference. Coach Wayne Robinson was fired in the middle of the season and replaced by Head Coach Dave Skrien. Despite a disappointing record, our team was getting better. In 1962, we made great strides and finished 7–9. During this time, we also had the short but memorable impact of my old Cal teammate Curtis Iaukea. Curtis arrived to try out for the Lions and at some point was told to hold a blocking dummy. So disgusted was Curtis with this command that he tossed the dummy to the ground and pronounced: "I hold a dummy for no man!" He proceeded to walk directly to his convertible, leaving a trail of sweaty pads and Lions practice clothes. By the time he got to his car and drove away he was down to his jock.

Our defense was becoming stingier and our offense was coming alive. We led the league in passing yards and touchdowns. We had a great trainer, Roy "Rocky" Cavilan. He was a former professional soccer player and really knew what an athlete needed. He gave all of us the best care. He had a special way of taping my knee that held me together for six years with the Lions. When I went to the Vikings, I made sure to pass on Rocky's special taping technique to their trainer, Fred Zamberletti. Like Rocky, Fred was a pro. Likewise, the Lions had a great equipment man in Bobby Ackles, and the Minnesota Vikings had a great one in Stubby Eason. Every team needs great people on and off the field to succeed.

Anybody who knew Big Mike knew he was proud of his family and Croatian heritage. Seeing that it was a great source of inspiration for Big Mike on the field, I concocted a plan to make him mad before a game against the Toronto Argonauts. I yelled across the room to Dick Fouts, our resident gigolo defensive end who was also opposing quarterback Tobin Rote's former teammate at Toronto. "Hey, Dick, did you hear what Tobin said about Croatians?" Willie Fleming, who was from Hamtramck, Michigan, and knew the spirit of the Croatian community, picked right up on it and encouraged Dick to answer. Big Mike was right next to me. He gave me a big nudge and grunted to Fouts, "What's this?" Dick played hard to get on the answer like he wanted to protect Big Mike's feelings. When Big Mike was burning hot with curiosity, Dick blurted out, "Yeah, Tobin said all them Croatians ought to go back to Croatia!"

Incredulous, Big Mike said, "He said that?" We all confirmed it with grim faces; this might have been my first acting job. Needless to say, Big Mike had a big game. He sacked Tobin so many times in the first half that Tobin refused to play in the second half! Ron heard later that Tobin said he wasn't going back in there if that big Croat was in the game. Tobin was truly a great quarterback but very underrated in spite of his NFL, CFL, and AFL accomplishments. Big Mike may have been a little naïve and gullible, but he summed up the game of football as accurately and succinctly as I have ever heard anyone do it. He said, "Football is a mug's game."

The 1963 season was our drive to the top. By then we had a lineup of great and unselfish players. Here are but a few: Willie Fleming, Mike Cacic, Tom Hinton, Dick Fouts, Norm Fieldgate, Tom Brown, Neal Beaumont, Jim Charpin, and Ron Morris. We also had Bill Munsey, a defensive back and fullback. He was the older brother of Chuck Muncie, renowned NFL running back for the New Orleans Saints and the San Diego Chargers. More than that, we had become a group of men who cared more about the team than we cared about ourselves. At that time a CFL team consisted of thirty-eight players, so many players still played both ways. Norm Fieldgate was a tremendous and thoughtful captain. He took that position seriously without being officious or obnoxious. I remember after practice one day during a beer strike in Vancouver he had a bus chartered to drive us down to Blaine, Washington, so we could have our customary post-practice ration of beer. Bonded and well rationed, we tore through the league in '63 with a 12–4 record.

But I got torn up physically that season. I was getting suited up one game, being careful to slide my uniform around my injuries—a dislocated finger taped to another one, a taped knee and two taped ankles along with my taped bruised ribs, and my taped, partially separated shoulder. Norm Fieldgate saw me and said, "Hey, it's El Cid!" I took that as a compliment. *El Cid* was a movie starring Charlton Heston as a Spanish hero who died but was strapped into his saddle by his men to lead the charge and scare the hell out of the enemy. I prided myself on finishing games I started.

Besides toughness, all team sports require more than discipline and skill. You have to become one cohesive unit; every player knows they are a vital organ that must perform their best to help the body succeed. A player on a team with a "we-first" attitude is inspired to add their spirit and talents to the collective effort. Likewise, each player derives strength and confidence from being surrounded by players who have his back. I've always strived to have my teammates' backs, and their fronts! This approach increases success, which increases confidence and builds momentum. It also makes preparation and game day fun. Teams with a strong work ethic that have fun along the way are the most effective.

Riding this approach, we met the Saskatchewan Roughriders in the playoffs. Back then the playoff format was a two-out-of-three within the space of eight days. It took us all three games to knock them out. Their quarterback Ron Lancaster was only five foot ten but played big and was a CFL all-time great. We beat the Roughriders on the road, 19–7, then lost at home, 13–8, before we beat them decisively at home, 36–1, to take the series.

After nineteen football games (not including three preseason games), we took on the Hamilton Tiger-Cats for the CFL championship in the fifty-first Grey Cup. The game was played at home in Vancouver. Needless to say, my biggest memory of that game is Angelo Mosca's late hit on Willie Fleming that knocked him out of the game, and ultimately knocked an unsteady Angelo Mosca off a riser at our banquet in 2011. We lost that game, 21–10. But we knew we would be back—and we were right.

In 1964, we tore through the league again with an 11–2–3 record. We beat the Calgary Stampeders in the same three-games-over-eight-days format. We earned the right to a rematch against the Hamilton Tiger-Cats in Toronto for the fifty-second Grey Cup. The night before the game, our team went out to the movies together and saw the James Bond classic *Goldfinger*, featuring the iconic villain Odd Job, played by Harold Sakata. His character was a martial artist who threw his steel-brimmed bowler hat with lethal accuracy. After the movie, I knew that things were looking up for the BC Lions when I saw our defensive lineman Tom Brown throwing room-service plate covers around the hotel like Oddjob threw his bowler hat. Tom was quite a character. On another occasion, we saw him scaling the exterior of one of the hotels we stayed in up to the tenth floor. Tom's Oddjob impersonation showed me we were loose and confident heading into the Grey Cup game.

We had a great game plan. We knew Ron Morris was going to draw their best defensive back, Garney Henley. This opened up the passing game for our other receivers. We used extra-wide line splits to spread out the Hamilton defense. (Line splits are the distances between linemen when they become set in the initial formation. This was a strategy actually schemed up by the players.) This opened up extra space for Willie to run. We dominated in every phase of the game in spite of the final score sounding close, 34–24. We were the fifty-second Grey Cup champs, and BC's first national champion football team. British Columbia and the Lions had arrived. It was a victory for all of us.

Playing on a team like our BC Lions was a dream come true, but Vancouver offered us unexpected kinship. I got to reunite with my old roommate from Cal, Kim Elliot, and meet his family. His mother Sue, father Ray, and sister Joy took us in as part of their family. Their generosity and love were incredible. My son J. J. thought Sue Elliot was actually his grandmother until he was seven years old!

Vancouver also offered us unexpected business opportunities. In my career, I have seen too many professional athletes blow through their dough. It's easy to do because there are plenty of people who are ready to take advantage of athletes, and as Ron Morris says, "A lot of football players aren't too smart, Joseph." I was fortunate enough to partner with Bob Lee. He was a first-generation Chinese Canadian who grew up in Vancouver's Chinatown to become a real estate mogul. He and his wonderful wife Lillie have raised a dynasty with their kids growing the family business. The apartments that we built were investments that sustained our family for over fifty years.

But in sports and in life, great things never last forever. After the 1964 season, Coach Dave Skrien and the front office started dismantling our championship team. Key players were traded. The truth is that any coach needs good players to win. Consequently, the 1965 and 1966 seasons were disappointing. After the 1966 season, I knew it was time to make a run at the NFL. I had made good on my promise to the Lions Chairman Al McEchearn to bring a Grey Cup to BC. In return, he had promised me that he would help me return to the US. More importantly, I had promised my mom that someday she would have the opportunity to watch me play on TV. It was time to fulfill that promise too.

Leaving Vancouver wasn't easy. Our time there was special for my family and me. Parting with the Elliots, the Lees, and Ron and Val Ann Morris in particular was difficult. The fans were knowledgeable and treated us with great respect. Our BC Lions not only accomplished our team mission, but also established lifelong bonds with each other. Everything was top shelf, including the level of competition. I believed then, and believe now, that our BC Lions teams could have competed against the AFL and NFL teams at that time. My Lion teammates were as good as the NFL players that I played with in Minnesota and Boston. Looking at all the professional football leagues of the time, there were fewer total teams to absorb all the available talent. There were nine teams in Canada, twelve in the NFL, and ten in the AFL. The talent was deep enough in the CFL that high-caliber players like Jack Kemp were cut.

The CFL attracted great American players like Willie Fleming, Ron Morris, Tom Hinton, Tobin Rote, Tom Brown, Jim Marshall, Bud Grant, and Wayne Harris. Tom Brown, our middle linebacker, won the Outland trophy at the University of Minnesota in 1960. Tom was a gifted athlete and a very agile big man. I played against many great linebackers in the NFL—Nitschke, Butkus, Lucci, Walker, Wilcox, Nobis, and all the great Vikings linebackers that were teammates—and Tom Brown was as good as any of them. But as good as Tom Brown was, he never beat Tom Hinton, our offensive guard, in one-on-one drills.

Tom wasn't the only top-tier talent we had. Willie Fleming was the fastest and most elusive back I have ever played with. He averaged an unheard-of 7.1 yards per carry for his career. Our fullback and cornerback Bill Munsey was outstanding on offense and defense. And of course, the Creeper excelled in all three phases of the game without anyone noticing.

I believed our BC Lions could compete against anyone. When I met with Mr. McEchearn and Lions advisor Clayton "Slim" Delbridge after the 1966 season, I suggested that they have the Lions join the new AFL. They seemed a bit surprised. Mr. Delbridge said very seriously, "We can't do that to Canada, Joe." At the time, I did not consider the international aspect of my suggestion. It was more a comment about the high quality of BC Lions football. Rightly so, the team would remain in Canada, but I would be heading south—just a little bit south.

CHAPTER SIX

THE VIKING PASSAGE

Fun and Games in the NFL

In 1967, this migratory football player headed south to play football in America at a time of great change. By that year, the American Football League, which started in 1960, was firmly established in the United States. Aiding the AFL's rise was a television contract from day one. In fact, by 1967, the AFL and NFL had already negotiated a merger that would be implemented in 1970. The new NFL would have an American Conference (AFC) and the National Conference (NFC). To balance out the new conferences, the NFL's Pittsburgh Steelers, Cleveland Browns, and Baltimore Colts would be moved to the AFC.

While visiting my mother in San Jose, I went to watch the East–West Shrine Game practice. The meat market was in full swing. I had a conversation with Al Davis in the parking lot. He slicked his hair back as he was recruiting me to become an Oakland Raider—but I was remembering getting hit out of bounds against USC by Mike McKeever.

Besides Davis, I met up with an old Cal trainer who had gone to work for the San Diego Chargers. He connected me with Sid Gilman, the legendary Chargers Head Coach and General Manager. I was excited because I wanted to return to California. The Chargers were excited about me too. So were the Houston Oilers. Their general manager, Don Klosterman, wanted to offer me a contract. The Oilers flew me out to Houston. I met with team owner Bud Adams and Klosterman in Adams's downtown Houston office, which was complete with an indoor waterfall. This was a far cry from the broken shower faucet at the Stampeders' facility.

I did not have an agent, so I was negotiating for myself as I always did. After some back and forth, Klosterman offered me a contract for $100,000 with a $10,000 signing bonus, but there was a catch. Klosterman said, "Don't tell anybody."

"Don't tell anybody?" I replied. "Is this legal?"

Klosterman assured me that it was perfectly legal; he just did not want to be accused of "tampering." I did not tell anyone and flew back to Vancouver with a $10,000 check in my pocket. But when I arrived back in Vancouver, there were headlines in the paper that I had signed with the AFL's Houston Oilers!

The following day, I had a meeting with Al McEchearn and Slim Delbridge. They said the Lions had to suspend me from the CFL because I had signed with Houston. I was confused because they already knew what I was doing; we had talked previously about me heading to the NFL. The next day things got even worse. The NFL Commissioner, Pete Rozelle, voided the Houston Oilers contract because the team did not own my rights. I thought I owned Joe Kapp's rights! In fact, the commissioner announced that the Washington Redskins, who'd drafted me in 1959, still owned my rights. In the space of a week I was signed, suspended, and voided. I had no team or country to play in.

I needed help. I needed a good lawyer. I contacted John Elliot Cook. "Doc" Cook was an elderly, highly respected San Francisco lawyer who had negotiated a very lucrative contract for John Brodie from the San Francisco 49ers. He was semi-retired by the time I needed his services. I tracked down Doc Cook in Glenbrook, Nevada, where he had a summer house on the shore of Lake Tahoe. When he said that he would talk to me, I jumped in my 1959 Ford Thunderbird in Vancouver and drove nonstop for more than a thousand miles to his home.

When I arrived in Glenbrook, I found Mr. Cook sitting on a lawn chair pointing out toward the lake. He greeted me cheerfully and introduced me to his wife. He sat me down with a glass of iced tea and said, "Start from the beginning." I started talking about signing with the Oilers. He said, "No, start from the beginning." I started explaining how I was suspended by the CFL. He said, "No, the beginning." I started describing how I was drafted by Washington, but they didn't call and Calgary did. He said, "No, the beginning; where were you born?" Finally, I got the drift and realized he wanted to hear my life story, so I told him everything over the next couple of days. I emphasized that I just wanted to play football—somewhere. After the last question was asked and answered, he said he'd give me a call in a few days. Everything about Mr. Cook impressed me. We got along very well. He was not only a persuasive and influential lawyer; he was also a caring and wise person. He not only took my case, he also became a lifelong mentor and absorbed much of the cost for litigation that was to come. That is a most uncommon attorney-client relationship. I was lucky to have him. But I still had to wait to see if he could work his magic.

After a few days, Mr. Cook called me. He asked if I would be interested in playing for the Minnesota Vikings. What a surprise. The team's general manager was none other than "Gentleman" Jim Finks, my old boss in Calgary. I thought Finks thought I was damaged goods with a twisted and torn knee when he traded me from Calgary to the BC Lions, but after six years at BC he must have realized I was healthy enough to lead his Vikings. Mr. Cook explained that they had acquired my rights from the Washington Redskins.

The NFL commissioner was willing to allow me to sign with the Vikings based on a complex transaction between the two leagues. The BC Lions traded Dick Fouts and Bill Symons to Toronto in exchange for Jim Young's rights. Young was playing for the Vikings (his Canadian "rights" were held by Toronto), who waived him out of the NFL, allowing him to sign with BC. I was waived out of the CFL by the BC Lions, enabling me to sign with the Vikings. Jim Young went on to become a BC Lion and a CFL all-time great. Mr. Cook negotiated a two-year contract for which I would be paid $100,000 per year with a club option for the third year at the same amount. The club option was standard at that time. Also, there was a rule that if a player completed the option year and signed with another team, the signing team was required to return a player as compensation for the loss of the player who "played out his option." If no agreement could be reached on the compensation, then the commissioner would decide. This rule was also known as the "Rozelle Rule." These arrangements prevented players from signing with other teams after meeting all their contract terms and amounted to an elaborate cover for owners who would not allow free agency under any circumstances.

If I accepted, I would be making a lot more money than I had ever made before, but I was somewhat confused about why Gentleman Jim wanted me to join the Vikings. I thought about it, then told Mr. Cook I would accept, that I was happy with the contract. I was a Minnesota Viking. I went from playing football in the North Pole to playing football in the North Pole. Once again, I would be going to a team that needed building, but I was ready for the challenge.

The Vikings' new head coach was Bud Grant, who had also come down from Canada. We had faced off many times; he'd been the very successful coach of the Winnipeg Blue Bombers. He was a straight shooter who believed in playing hard and fair, values that Coach Lewis and others instilled in me. By the time all the signing, suspending, voiding, and reinstating were worked out by Mr. Cook, I had missed the Vikings' training camp, the exhibition season, and the first game. On September 22, 1967, I joined the team in Los Angeles at the LA Coliseum.

The Los Angeles Rams were known and feared for their defensive line, nicknamed "the Fearsome Foursome." The Rams were crushing the Vikings, and especially our Vikings quarterbacks Bob Berry and Ron Vander Kelen. The Rams front four were quite imposing. As I faced them, the left end was Lamar Lundy, who was six foot seven and 245 pounds, and had to have been eighteen pounds at birth. The left tackle was Merlin Olsen, six foot five and 270 pounds, an FTD flower salesman and the kindly Father Murphy on TV's *Little House on the Prairie*. The right tackle was Roosevelt Grier, who they called Rosey. He was actually known for his expert needlepoint. Do you really think Merlin and Rosey cared more about flowers, arts, and crafts than about killing quarterbacks? Last but not least was the right end Deacon Jones, their infamous "Secretary of Defense." Watching him play, my guess was that Deacon had never been to a church in his life, or at least didn't see quarterbacks as worthy recipients of brotherly love. In the offseason, he should have sold tombstones to the families of quarterbacks he sacked. He would have made a fortune.

The Vikings had no choice but to put me in the game. Bob and Ron left by airmail, tossed and injured courtesy of the Rams' defense. In my first NFL huddle, I did not know any of the Vikings terminology except that most teams went on two. During a time-out, I ran out and joined the huddle for my big debut on American soil with the Minnesota Vikings. I looked my new teammates in the eyes and stressed the snap count was "On three. On three! Not two! On three!"

I walked up to the line of scrimmage and took a quick look up at heaven and the nosebleed seats, where there were at least a dozen Chicanos praying for my survival. At the line I barked, "Hut one! Hut two! FUCK YOU, DEACON!" The laughing Rams were beside themselves. I barked, "Hut three!" Our running back Bill Brown went down the field. A thirty-yard run. Later, the Rams stopped laughing. I survived. The Rams beat us that day, 39–3, but I had my teammates' attention. And they had mine, especially Mick Tingelhoff. He was the best center I ever saw, a true center. He did all the snaps for extra points, field goals, and punts, and never missed a game (240 straight in seventeen years). They have finally put him in the Hall of Fame. If they didn't put Mick in it, they should not even have one.

———

I would soon learn that the NFL was full of larger-than-life figures that I'd have to find a way to beat—or at least survive. Bears linebacker Dick Butkus was more ferocious than even his devastating reputation would indicate. We faced off against him and the Bears in Chicago at Wrigley Field. We took advantage of his hyperaggressiveness. The Bears would overshift their line so Butkus could blitz. When they shifted, I was supposed to audible for a dive to our halfback Dave Osborn. Basically, we'd let Butkus in the left-side gap, right as Dave ran out the right-side gap. But the Bears were not only aggressive— they were smart and adapted to my audible. Rather than letting Dick get caught in the revolving door, they adjusted their shift to the right-side gap when they heard the audible and crushed Dave. We had to adapt too. Whenever I had a hunch their shift was on, I called the dive in the huddle so that there was no audible called at the line, so Butkus would not be tipped off. I also told Ozzie very enthusiastically he was going to the posts (as in "Ozzie, you are going to break off a great run and score touchdown"). I took the snap, handed the ball to Ozzie, and watched him go the posts for six points, as did Butkus. Dick was so mad he was frothing at the mouth.

Years later, I did my best to break Dick's ribs. Detroit Lions quarterback Bill Munson and I were sitting together at a charity event in Monterey, California. There were several other old-timers there, including Dick, who was in the buffet line in front of me grabbing chicken wings and popping them into his mouth. Like most linebackers, he must have been eating them bones and all. He started choking, for real. Dick Butkus was in trouble. I did my best to do the Heimlich maneuver, but I could not get my arms around his ribs and gut. I was about to yell for help from Cowboys defensive end Ed "Too Tall" Jones when a tiny waitress charged at Butkus in a dead run. She dropped her shoulder and slammed into Dick. Out popped the wing. The waitress would have been right at home in the Vikings secondary. The wing soared out of Butkus's mouth like a Roman Gabriel bomb. I sat back down with Munson feeling good about my attempted good deed, only to find Munson in disbelief: "What the hell did you do that for? If anyone deserved to die it was Butkus!"

The Green Bay Packers' defense was anchored by Hall of Fame linebacker Ray Nitschke, whose missing front teeth were an iconic symbol of his rugged play. At that time the Vikings, like practically every other NFL team, ran some form of the Green Bay Packers offense. We even used the same numbering system as the Packers. Once against the Packers, I audibled out of a pass and into a run. Nitschke's eyes lit up and he gave me that huge, toothless grin. He called out to Willie Davis, their left end. "Hey, Willie! It's comin' to you!" Of course, he was right.

Despite the transparency of our offense, once they drew up our plays, offensive coordinator Jerry Burns and Grant usually did not meddle with my playcalling. There were two times I can recall them sending in advice or a play, both with negative results. Once against the New Orleans Saints during a torrential rainstorm, Burns sent in a play calling for a pass when we were inside the ten-yard line. I threw a pass that slipped out of my hand. The Saints defensive back Bo Burris picked it off and ran it back ninety-four yards for a touchdown. We lost, 20–17.

The second time came in 1967. Despite a losing record, we were showing signs of life, including a 10–7 road win on October 15 over Vince Lombardi's defending-world-champion Green Bay Packers. Both defenses played well. They came to Minnesota on December 3 for a rematch. Offense was the story this time. We were tied, 27–27, late in the game. Bud instructed me to keep the ball on the ground and play for the tie. I did just that, but I bumped into Bill Brown and fumbled. We lost the game, 30–27, on a last-minute Don Chandler field goal.

After the loss, I was upset. I blamed myself for the fumble that cost us the game. My consolation of choice was to get home to be alone with my old friend Jose Cuervo. However, our team had been invited to an annual preplanned team party for the players in a nice suburb of Minneapolis. I was also getting phone calls reminding me to come.

Captain Jim Marshall and his cohort Carl Eller came to my apartment. I didn't want to go, but as defensive ends, they had an easy fix. They lifted me and my chair to take me out to their car. With that I relented and attended the party. A captured and hostile QB clutching my amigo Jose Cuervo, I could still see it was a beautiful night. But I was in no mood to party.

We arrived at this beautiful home. When our party walked through the front door, I noticed there was a side yard walkway. I headed over there to be alone. But lo and behold, who was sitting and sipping on some Jack Daniels? Señor Lonnie Warwick, a.k.a. Big Sam, my favorite middle linebacker.

Lonnie and I had a history. He invited me to sit down and enjoy the evening. I apologized for losing the game with my fumble. Lonnie wouldn't have it. He declared that the defense had given up thirty points and was to blame for the loss. I wouldn't have it. I'd fumbled at a critical point in the game. Case closed! Not by a long shot, not to Lonnie, who was enraged that I would take the blame for the defensive collapse. We should have known that Mr. Jack Daniels and Mr. Jose Cuervo were presenting our cases.

We slowed down a bit to enjoy the warm Minnesota night, but then I made my fatal mistake. I murmured, "You know, Lonnie, you could kick my ass, but I might get a shot in." Music to his ears. We were up, and I was running. There was no place to go in the yard. I was trapped. He was coming at me like Rocky Marciano and I was doing my best impersonation of Fred Astaire to escape. We were dancing in the dark. Just as the party crowd came out to see the show, Big Sam cornered me. We traded blows. Despite my courage, dexterity, and agility, he had both hands around my throat. Lonnie was preparing to waste all that Jose Cuervo on a dead body. Gasping for air, this old quarterback found something to grab—Lonnie's balls! It was a total victory for the Vikings offense. Big Sam might have been the first middle linebacker "sacked" by a quarterback!

The next morning, Lonnie called me to say he had a headache. He asked if I had some beer for it. I told him my left eye was closed and he said so was his. I said to pick me up—we'd go to the doctor together. We put on some sunglasses and called Fred Zamberletti, the Vikings trainer. We made an appointment with Coach Grant. Lonnie thought we should let Bud know there was no dissension, just a bit of discussion. We met with Bud, who asked what was with the Hollywood sunglasses routine. I let Lonnie do the talking, since my provocative words to Lonnie had gotten us in this trouble in the first place. I knew I should have stayed home. Our captain, Jim Marshall, fully admitted his guilt. He was the instigator. He brought me to the party. My postmortem: never argue with a middle linebacker.

If you were a Minnesotan who loved fun and games, you would likely find yourself at Duff's Tavern in downtown Minneapolis. If you did, you would keep coming back. It was a beautiful place, and one of the first bars I can remember that always had sports on TV. It was a watering hole for the Twins, the North Stars, and of course, the Vikings. We had a lot of team meetings there. We loved Duff's because it was a fun place to meet other athletes in town, as well as the fans. Vikings fans were in a class by themselves. They embodied the Vikings spirit. They were loyal to us rain or shine, blizzard or polar vortex. You had to have that toughness to come watch us at the Met in December. We were fueled off their intensity to get through the rough ones, especially the wars of winter. But at Duff's, everybody could just talk about playing arctic football in a warm, welcoming environment.

Even Lonnie Warrick could relax at Duff's, unless the Cleveland Indians were in town. At one of our Vikings team meetings, we were sitting around a table with some of the Indians, including their pitcher Sam McDowell. He was a big guy with a devastating fastball. Unfortunately, he also had the nickname Big Sam. Lonnie showed up and was introduced to the group. Sam McDowell was introduced as Big Sam. Lonnie did not like that, at all. In fact, he hated it, and things got tense. Lonnie announced in a very loud voice: "There is only one Big Sam!" He added that Sam McDowell should move on. He did.

Another regular at Duff's was Yankee legend Billy Martin, who was a Twins coach and then manager in that time period. We hit it off. He was from Berkeley. I followed him as a player with the Oakland Oaks through his days as the Yankee second baseman. Everyone knows how competitive he was. That's a polite way of saying he could have a temper. And like Big Sam, Billy liked to control his turf. One night we were sitting at the bar enjoying a conversation over a drink. A guy came up and interrupted us to talk to Billy, who shushed the guy politely. The guy ignored Billy's suggestion, and interrupted again. Billy didn't say a word—he just punched the guy in the face. There were no more interruptions.

Outside of Duff's Tavern, far bigger conflicts were raging. In 1967, the Vietnam War was raging. While I was playing the game I loved with teammates I loved for a great city, the real American heroes were being asked to kill, and risk being killed, across the Pacific. My younger brother Larry was one of them. It seemed as though as soon as he graduated from San Francisco State, he was drafted in 1967. Larry was and is a force of nature. At five foot seven and 170 pounds, he was an All-City guard for the St. Mary's High School football team in Stockton, California. In his senior year, their quarterback was a great athlete but not much of a strategist. Unbeknownst beyond the huddle,

Larry often called the plays for the offense. His football chops were that good. He went on to play at San Joaquin Delta Junior College. Larry was a great boxer too. I will never forget his performance in a Golden Gloves tournament. He beat the hell out of a guy who was five inches taller than him with body blows. He was just the type of guy the Army would like.

He served a nine-month combat tour of duty in Vietnam until he was almost killed after stepping on what is now known as an IED—an improvised explosive device. He still has shrapnel in his leg to this day. In fact, he is fortunate to have the leg at all. He was a squad leader in combat. He left the army as a sergeant awarded with the Purple Heart. Larry is a man amongst boys.

Meanwhile on the field, the 1967 season was a struggle, and we finished at 3–8–3. There were signs of life heading into our 1968 season. It was clear that we had a nucleus of good players who cared. It was only a matter of time, and a lot of hard work. After my first season, I started working out with the guys before training camp in the Twin Cities area. I spent a lot of time with team captain Jim Marshall. Like Norm Fieldgate of the BC Lions, Jim was a natural leader and a great team captain. He cared more about the team than he cared about himself. He could build up a teammate's self-confidence with glowing, irreverent rants about the particular player's skills, strengths, good looks, pedigree, you name it. As a football player, there was no one more tenacious. His records speak for themselves: 270 starts, 282 straight games, most fumbles recovered (thirty), 125 sacks, a twenty-one-year professional career, and four championship teams. His conspicuous absence from the Hall of Fame is just plain unbelievable.

I took notice of Jim's workout routine too. He was a physical specimen, at six foot four and 245 pounds and not an ounce of fat on him. Jim may have been light for a defensive end, but he was so quick and fast it seemed like he was involved in every tackle on defense, or at least near the ball. I never saw him touch a barbell. It was a different world then; athletes didn't train the way they do today. Weightlifting wasn't a given. Neither was running for miles and miles. The most I saw Jim run was one lap around the track. I would join him for a gentleman's lap. Jim and I were veterans, a nice way of saying we were getting old in football years. Even then, teams knew enough to preserve the bodies of older players for the long season. We'd take it.

To his credit, Bud Grant was a very well-organized coach who always put together a solid coaching staff. 1968 was no exception. Even so, as a Mexican American, our training camp was missing one of my favorite ingredients: salsa. Bringing the salsa made any activity a party. To spice up practice, defensive back Ed Sharockman and I started betting on plays with each other. Quietly, all the other defensive backs joined the action; one buck for me for every touchdown pass caught over the defensive backs and one buck to them for every interception. Big Sam saw the action and didn't want to miss out on the fun. He declared, "I'm in!"

Halfway through the drill, he got a pick off me and hammered it up while running it back for a touchdown. I chased him down, gave him an All-American tackle, and knocked him on his *como se llama*. Lonnie was stunned that a quarterback would do that to him. I hoped my teammates would see that I was willing to do anything they were asked to do. I hoped they would see that if I was not intimidated by Lonnie, I would not be intimidated by Butkus, Nitschke, or any other notorious Vikings foes. And, yes, I threw the pick, so I paid my buck. But I made my point. Leadership is action, not just talk. With these friendly bets, Lonnie and I wanted to do our part on the long road to the Super Bowl. Another Viking who wanted to do his part was defensive back Dale "Hack" Hackbart, but we would soon find out that his methods were unconventional, especially for Bud Grant's team.

The excitement around the Vikings was building. One day at practice, I lined up over center. Across the line of scrimmage, I noticed that Hack was making faces at me; really odd, contorted faces. Then

I noticed he was waving something at me—his weenie. Everybody laughed. Whistles blared! The coaches didn't laugh. But the damage was done. Dale was now "Rubber Face" and a vital part of Vikings team culture.

There are few things more beautiful than seeing the moon hovering over the deeply forested Minnesota landscape. There are few things less attractive than seeing two. One night, I was driving my 1939 La-Salle home from practice. A blue Ford Falcon was weaving recklessly in the lane ahead of me. I went into defensive-driving mode; I didn't want this knucklehead causing an accident, especially with my vintage LaSalle. Probably a drunk driver, I thought. Then, out the driver's side window popped a moon, the hairy kind. It looked familiar. Yup, the owner was Hack. Aesthetics aside, I was impressed that Dale could get his butt out the window and keep the car on the road. He was an even better athlete than I realized. It was only years later that I learned Dale had an accomplice who was ready, willing, and able to keep the car on the road while Dale climbed over him to line up the moon shot. The wheelman was Dale's pal Dave Goff.

Hack was a Wisconsin native. Grateful to his home state's great brewing tradition, he could drink more beer than any teammate I ever had. And believe me, he had stiff competition. Hack's thirst fueled his other special talent: he could piss over a bus or up to a second story! We won more than a few rounds making bets on his "special" talents. While Hack was a great football player, he would have been an MVP in the MFP (Minneapolis Fire Department).

When Hack wasn't making us laugh, he was protecting us. He was the Vikings' team enforcer, one of the best I ever played with. Dale was well known for his hard, well-timed hits.

Near the end of his career, Dale was assaulted after the whistle by Cincinnati Bengals running back Boobie Clark. The hit left Dale with permanent damage to his neck. Dale sued, and his case was the first to establish a civil cause of action for on-field misconduct. That is justice.

In 1968, with the Vietnam War raging, riots and protests flooding the streets, and the shock of the assassinations of Robert Kennedy and Martin Luther King still fresh in our minds, the Vikings were getting our act together. We finished the year 8–6, marking our first season as NFL Central champs, supplanting Vince Lombardi's mighty Packers, who had won the Super Bowl against the Oakland Raiders the previous year. The Vikings were going to the playoffs for the first time.

Our matchup was against the Baltimore Colts. It was a rainy, muddy game, and we lost 24–14. Mike Curtis picked up a fumble that got knocked out of my hands as I was trying to pass and ran it back sixty yards for a touchdown. It was a really tough loss.

Adding insult to injury was the fact that we would have to play in what was called the Playoff Bowl, a.k.a. the Runner-Up Bowl, which consisted of a game against the other playoff loser. This year it was against Dallas, and it would be played in Miami. That was the great Don Meredith's last game. We lost that one too. I have no recollection of the game at all—it's better to just forget some games and move on. I do remember talking with Bud Grant in the bar after the game, though. I am sure I was mad that we lost, but Bud was impassive and said, "Dallas has better players than we do." I took it as an insult. I did not agree with him. We had great players and got more. We drafted an All-American defensive lineman from Cal, Ed White. In 1969, the Vikings moved him to offensive guard. Ed rose to the challenge.

In 1989, my lifelong friend and Cal Golden Bears basketball teammate Ned Averbuck took an in-depth look at the 1969 Vikings, our best season while I was a Viking and a turning point in my life and the lives of many others. We wanted to break down the season, understand the team, and see how we got as far as we did. We hoped readers would enjoy the trek to the Super Bowl and learn something from it. That book never got published. That is, until now. What follows is Ned's and my original book. We'll pick up with the rest of the story on the other side.

CHAPTER SEVEN

FORTY FOR SIXTY

The Beginning of a Tradition

It wasn't premeditated, but as I walked up to the podium, I realized something wasn't right. In a season dedicated to working and playing as a team, it seemed out of place to single out one player as most valuable. Our credo was "forty for sixty," an expression of our values and philosophy. It meant that in order for us to be successful, we had to be a team willing to do what it took to be winners. The forty symbolized that everyone on the forty-man roster was a team player with an important role to fulfill. The sixty represented playing all out, 100-percent effort, every minute of every game. We flourished because we realized that group accomplishment is preferable to individual achievement.

The concept crystallized for me during a heartbreaking defeat at the hands of the New York Giants in the first game of the 1969 season. I didn't play that day. It was the first time I wasn't starting the regular season at quarterback in my professional career. I stood next to defensive tackle Paul Dickson, a huge man with the soul of a poet, who had also been beaten out for his position. We accepted our roles and became the team's biggest cheerleaders. We cheered enthusiastically, almost to the point of being obnoxious. Sometimes it's good to be reminded that if you really care about your team, there are many ways to contribute. Everybody should know what it's like to play second string sometime during his life.

But our cheering came to an end as we watched the game slip away in the last minute of play. I could see the season start to fade. All our hard work, our building, our dedication!

On the plane ride home, I was talking to myself. The loss festered in my stomach and brain. I became so angry and frustrated that I screamed, "*Basta! No mas!* This can't happen again." If we were going to win, we would have to do it as a team—every player finding a way to contribute and playing every play as if it might be the last.

As a team, the 1969 Minnesota Vikings became the start of one of the greatest organizations in the National Football League and one of the NFL's all-time greatest teams:

- Western Conference Champions
- NFL Champions
- First Vikings Super Bowl team
- The league's longest winning streak (twelve games) in thirty-five years
- The league's highest-scoring team; 379 points in fourteen games
- Fewest points allowed in a fourteen-game season in history, less than one touchdown per game
- Entire defensive front four went to the Pro Bowl
- Bud Grant named Coach of the Year
- Two Players named NFL All-Pro

However, it's not the team's record or any individual accomplishment that makes this story worth telling. It's also not a soap opera or a trip down memory lane. After all, over fifty years have passed, all the skeletons are out of the closet, and there have been forty-eight Super Bowl champions since. What does make this story worth telling is that it effectively and dramatically illustrates how a team forms and develops around a core set of values and principles.

The year 1969 was not only a turning point for the Minnesota Vikings, but also for the nation. It was a time when traditional values were being questioned. The concept of winning at all costs, or even winning at all, was being challenged. At the movies, we were watching *Oliver* and *Chitty Chitty Bang Bang* playing across the street from *Easy Rider* and *Alice's Restaurant*. College campuses were beginning to become restless, and some turned into battlegrounds over the Vietnam War and would explode the next spring with strikes and the confrontation at Kent State.

In the summer of that year, a generation flocked to Woodstock. It had been only five years since the Civil Rights Act of 1964, and growing racial tensions, black pride, and a cry for minority rights permeated through this volatile atmosphere. We had landed on the moon and now saw our world as small, finite, floating in endless space.

In the NFL, Broadway Joe Namath and the New York Jets had taken on the Baltimore Colts and defeated them soundly in Super Bowl III as a statement of a growing parity between the recently merged NFL and AFL. The Jets accepted all the personal accolades and became celebrities, and that team was never the same again. Football became a spectacle and big business. It wasn't a kids' game anymore!

Through the sixties, Coach Vince Lombardi and his Green Bay Packers were looked upon as legends. They had won three consecutive NFL Championships and the first two Super Bowls. Lombardi was a classic authoritarian, famous for torturous training camps and total control of his team. To him, "winning [wasn't] everything, [it was] the only thing."

Within this backdrop, the Minnesota Vikings needed to find their own sense of identity and values if we were to become champions and establish a winning tradition. The transformation really began in 1967 with a changing of the guard. Norm Van Brocklin, the original Vikings coach who was cast in the Lombardi mold, left to coach the Atlanta Falcons. He was a fiery coach, and the team reflected that spirit with high highs and low lows.

Bud Grant, the new coach, couldn't have been more different in personality and approach to the game. He believed in discipline, maintaining an even keel, and keeping things simple, consistent, and objective. He installed a system that allowed each coach and each player the opportunity to do what he did best. This gave the coaches and the players an important role in forging a team. The team was now responsible for its own success.

From 1967 through 1969, new players were added to a solid core of veterans. The team developed a personality that was ideal for playing on a frozen, snowy field in sub-zero weather. We were tough and unrelenting. We weren't a stylish team. We took our opponents head on rather than trying to go around them. We weren't going to beat ourselves, and we weren't going to fold in the fourth quarter.

I think you can recognize the character of a team by looking at its running backs. We weren't a finesse team with backs who would prance and dance and go down with a shoestring tackle. Our starting running backs Bill Brown and Dave Osborn were really throwbacks to another era. I'm sure they would have been just as happy playing in the days when you could fold up your leather helmet and put it in your back pocket. In the violent game of football, the play isn't over until the ball carrier is knocked down. Time and again our backs refused to let the play end. The attitude of the team was evident every time a Minnesota Viking carried the ball.

We didn't believe quarterbacks should receive any special treatment. Our quarterbacks didn't wear the special red jerseys in practice that tell the other players, "Don't hit me, I'm a quarterback." We were all Vikings, and our color was purple, not red. We didn't hook slide to end a play. And the only time we ever ran out of bounds was to stop the clock, not to avoid being hit. As a kid growing up in Salinas, California, you couldn't go back to the neighborhood if you ran out of bounds. Football is a game of inches, so we all tried for every possible inch on every play.

Our defense became known around the league as the Purple

People Eaters. It was a swarming, hard-hitting defense that would line up head to head and beat you with speed, strength, determination, and experience. It was a defense that made our opponents earn every yard. It created opportunities, scored points, and intimidated the opponents. Our defense was a solid unit in 1967 and 1968 and had to shoulder much of the burden until the offense began to take on its fair share.

The Minnesota fans shared the same tough, hardy spirit. I still remember the roar of a Minnesota crowd and the muffled sounds of 47,900 pairs of gloves and mittens ringing through the cold December air.

What you couldn't see from the stands or the press box, though, were some of the quieter, less obvious things that knit this team together. At some point in the season, each player stepped up to lead in different ways. They led by example, sometimes quietly but always effectively.

I remember the Western Conference Championship Game with the Rams. We were close to scoring the go-ahead touchdown after coming back from a 17-7 halftime deficit. You could see our frozen breath as we huffed and puffed for air. Trying to catch my own breath, I asked, "How are we doing?" No answer. I was losing concentration and needed some help. I looked down at the end of the huddle at guard Jim Vellone. He had that ugly lineman's nose that was bloody across the bridge. At that moment, he gave me the biggest wink. It meant, *Call the play. We'll get the job done. You can count on us.* That small gesture was a sign of real leadership. I called the play, the spark rekindled, and we swept around end for the score.

Vellone, like a lot of our players, found a way to perform to his fullest potential. I think if there were any "most valuable" Vikings, it would be those unsung and unknown soldiers who deserve the awards. Awards should come at the end of a career, and all of us thought our best games were yet to come. Leaders know that no matter how well we perform, we can always do better. Everyone on the team contributed. If you look at the record, week by week, different players came to the forefront in big games and in crucial situations. It seemed as if each week a different player made the big play. We were constantly improving.

Finally, 1969 wasn't just a year or a team to remember because we won our first NFL Championship. It should be evaluated and studied as the start or foundation of a tradition of winning teams that continued to share the values of "forty for sixty." We should examine the lessons about team dynamics learned by the 1969 team and how these concepts can be applied outside of sports.

Sports fans are constantly arguing about what makes the difference between a team that consistently wins and one that consistently loses. Every Monday-morning quarterback has pondered the question of why one team is always a contender while another team is mired at the bottom of the standings. Some say it's the coaching, others say it's the players, and some say it's a good front office.

When you examine teams with long-standing winning traditions, you find that there is no single formula for running a successful team. The Green Bay Packers, the Dallas Cowboys, the Pittsburgh Steelers, the Oakland Raiders, the San Francisco 49ers, and the New England Patriots all were able to make the transition from losing to winning traditions. They had different personalities, different systems, and different philosophies. However, common to all these teams and to the Minnesota Vikings is that they developed a solid foundation, a foundation built upon seven interdependent and integrated pillars.

PILLAR ONE: SYSTEM

A system is a rationalized process of how a team operates both on and off the field. In other words, it's clear to everyone in the organization that "this is how we do things on the Minnesota Vikings." A good system creates consistency by establishing guidelines and processes both on and off the field.

In football, a system includes a philosophy and approach to preparing for and playing the game. In 1967, Bud Grant's first year as coach, he began to change the Vikings into winners. The system changed from an authoritarian approach with all the direction and control flowing from the coach to a system built around allowing players and coaches to do what they did best, keeping it concrete, objective, flexible, and understandable, while rewarding positive execution.

Bud had a set of rules that reflected his own experience as a player. While these rules weren't always popular, they made sense. We followed them and they were enforced in a consistent manner. One unwritten rule: Bud didn't like to get to the games too early. When we were on the road, the team bus never left for the stadium until the appointed hour. Although flexible, Bud really didn't understand Los Angeles traffic. We got to the Coliseum but ended up running off the bus onto the field, tucking in our jerseys after the game had started. We were penalized five yards for being late to the game. We were late, but we were late as a team.

Bud was a stickler for no smoking except in the restrooms. That meant the air was clear in the locker room, but practically needed a second-stage smog alert if you had to use the facility. We all left training camp at precisely the same time every year. We even lined up and practiced how we would stand for the national anthem. Bud's rules made us consistent and unified.

As a quarterback in Canada, I played against Bud Grant–coached teams for eight years. His Winnipeg teams were known for their discipline and execution. In a league with twelve men on the field and more than one back going into motion at once, discipline and order were a rare sight. In fact, his teams were so disciplined that you could sometimes use it to your advantage—you could count on where the defensive players would be. Yet, his teams were always tough to beat. The Vikings became the same type of team in the NFL through Bud's way.

Almost every new coach tries to bring in a new system that reflects his philosophy. Some have more success than others. The keys to establishing an effective system are:

Make Sure Roles and Responsibilities Are Clear

Each player and each coach needs to know what's expected of him and how his role fits into the overall team approach. This also holds true for having clearly defined policies and procedures. For example, in our system, the coaching staff created a game plan, and within that framework the quarterback called the plays.

Make Sure Lines of Communication Are Clearly Defined and Open

A system is really all about how information flows through a team. Effective leaders and coaches are able to identify barriers to communication and overcome them.

Reinforce Shared Values

Whenever a system is modified or changed, there is usually an initial resistance. "That's not the way we do things around here," someone will usually say. To be successful, it's important to recognize and confront this resistance and work on building positive shared values.

We played Cleveland early in the 1967 season. Toward the end of the first half, Dale Hackbart enthusiastically and blatantly made a late hit on the Browns' Gary Collins in the end zone. Later in the locker room, it was the only time I ever heard Bud really raise his voice. He said, "This has to stop! We're not going to be the most penalized team in the league anymore, and we're not going to beat ourselves with stupid mental mistakes!" Together we shared this important new aspect of winning.

Have a Reason for Making Changes

Making changes for change's sake only breeds resentment and resistance, especially if the team is already successful. This only makes management look capricious or egotistical. Good coaches have a reason for making changes, and they sell their teams on the change. The next time we played in Los Angeles, we left for the game a little earlier—but not much.

PILLAR TWO: RECRUITMENT

A football team starts to come together by finding and recruiting players, coaches, and front-office personnel with the skills, experience, and shared values that will blend together well. It's not enough just to find a quarterback who has a strong, accurate arm if he's also supposed to be a team leader. A big, strong running back with blazing speed can find himself on the bench if he lacks good work habits in practice or can't learn the plays. A coach who is a great strategist but who can't instill team loyalty can soon find himself out of work.

Winning teams have an overall philosophy of recruiting and understanding the role they need each player to play. George Allen and his Washington Redskins and Los Angeles Rams teams were noted for trading away draft picks for experienced veterans who wouldn't make mistakes. Dallas was famous for its systematic, computerized search for talent in the draft and through free agents. They always seemed to find the players other teams would overlook. Washington under Joe Gibbs built a Super Bowl championship team on free agents and so-called retreads from other teams.

The Vikings had the philosophy of finding or drafting the best players available and then giving them the time and training to develop. Jerry Reichow and Frank Gilliam were with the Vikings in a variety of personnel roles for the greater part of the team's fifty-plus years and were instrumental in the years of playoffs success, through their recruitment of outstanding personnel. In addition to having great physical skills, the Vikings looked for players with the following winning traits:

Toughness

The ability to bend and twist without breaking and to remain firm and aggressive in the face of difficulty. Fullback Bill Brown was the embodiment of toughness. We were ahead of the Bears 31–0 late in the game on a freezing day. In the huddle, Bill Brown was arguing with Dave Osborn about who was going to carry the ball. They both wanted one more shot at Dick Butkus. That's tough!

Initiative

The ability to make an impactful first move that puts the opposition on the defensive. The secondary is always the last line of defense. Players need to know when to play it safe and when to go for the interception. Safety Karl Kassulke was able to show great initiative and change the tone of a game when he was finally turned loose on a safety blitz.

Determination

The ability to work unrelentingly toward a goal or purpose. No one was more determined than center Mick Tingelhoff. Playing the Bears, Mick was assigned to block Butkus, who was bigger and stronger than he was. On the game film, you could see Butkus trying to shoo Mick away like a fly—but he wouldn't shoo. He kept coming at him.

Resourcefulness

The ability to go beyond personal limits and be creative on the playing field. Alan Page embodied this trait. Within the confines of a very structured defensive-line scheme, Alan was able to attack the offense and find ways to make the tackle even after he was blocked.

Uniqueness

The ability to bring unique skills, experience, and values to the team. Every team needs someone who can be a catalyst. In that role no one was more unique than Jim Marshall. Marshall loosened up practice by playing the part of the modern-day Viking. He informed us that his great-great-grandfather discovered Minnesota with the original Vikings. He personally knew the god Odin and was designated to brave the cold and the treacherous seas. He lined us up and made us pledge to carry ourselves like brave warriors to sail our Viking ship down the Mississippi and to fight brave new wars. The work and toil of practice became fun. We were happy in our work with Jim's special leadership.

PILLAR THREE: DEVELOPMENT

Recruitment only gives a team the raw material for success. A team can be stocked with superstars and never win a game. Football is a game that requires eleven men to work together as a team on every play. It's easy to be a quarterback when the line does its job and blocks well, and the receivers get open, make the catches, and run for the scores. No one man makes it happen—Ray Kroc, founder of McDonald's, was right.

Development is really a two-part process. First, it's the process of developing the skills and providing the experience that will allow each player to reach his full potential. One of the primary qualities of a good assistant coach is to be able teach both the basics and the fine points of the game. Bus Mertes was our backfield coach who taught the fundamentals, but the man on the field must ultimately take responsibility.

Dave Osborn came to Minnesota as the man from Cando, North Dakota. He was a low-round draft pick. He didn't have blinding speed, and he had hands of stone. But he worked harder and stayed longer at practice than anyone. He made himself a complete player. During the

1969 season, each one of his receptions was a circus catch, even the easy ones. But he never dropped a ball. He was also our leading rusher and a great example of perseverance in expanding his own skills.

Second, development is also the process of molding a group of individuals into a team. The elements that meld a team together are:

A Common Goal

Our goal was to become world champions. In order for that goal to become a reality, actions needed to speak louder than words. We became a team of doers.

Doing It

Commitment is the doing.

Doing without favorites or prejudice.

Doing for people first and foremost.

Doing for all not swayed by titles and positions.

Doing right because it is your judgment.

Doing while not denying disagreement.

Doing through testing to build trust. Doing through openness and disclosure. Doing with character to the best of talent.

Doing what is called for, not just the passing or popular.

Doing actions based on strong ideas.

Doing knowledgeable action is a noble goal.

Doing is commitment to correct practice.

A commitment to actions based on great motives.

—Ned Averbuck

A Team Philosophy

Ours was simple: forty for sixty. Forty players working as hard as they could in a game for all sixty minutes. Setting aside personal gain and differences for the good of the team. Individual achievement develops within team accomplishment. The mantra became a work ethic for practice as well as a credo for game day.

A Common Experience

Winning and losing together as a team established what it would take to be winners. Each game provided a lesson for the team. Talking about and analyzing each game together created a common bond. Sometimes there is more to learn from losing than winning.

Strong Leadership

Leadership has to come from more than just the coaches, so-called stars, or vocal players. The best leadership is often quiet and comes from those who lead by example. On the 1969 Vikings team, we had an abundance of leaders from unexpected places. Leadership is a process and a result. Real leadership is when players care more about team success than individual success.

Continuous Improvement

Every practice and every game is an ongoing process of improvement. Football is a game of constantly looking toward next week. Even when you win a Super Bowl, you go back to work again trying to improve to win another one. Every day you're either getting better or getting worse. There's no status quo.

PILLAR FOUR: DELEGATION

Football is too complex and physical a game for one player or one coach to do it all. A head coach needs to be able to give up enough control in order for his assistants to do their job properly. Each position has a responsibility. Players need to be able to trust their teammates to do their own assignments. Without this trust, players start to question each other's contribution to the team, which eats away at the team's foundation.

Delegation as a management style and practice starts at the top of the organization and works its way eventually to the playing field. In the Vikings' organization, the front office gave Bud Grant the authority and responsibility to run the team on the field. Jim Finks didn't send down plays on third and short. Wise delegation creates balance and harmony within an organization.

Bud chose to be in charge of the big picture and direction of the team. He delegated the day-to-day coaching to his assistants. For example, the game plan was put together each week by the assistant coaches. The head coach was as eager to see the game plan for the first time on Wednesday as all the players were. In turn the players were responsible for executing the game plan on the field. But Bud was also a great gameday coach. He brought his overall experience and leadership to the team effort. He delegated, but he was still there when it counted.

Bud allowed us to take risks as long as we were prepared to be responsible for the consequences. We had studied the Bears' game films and we noticed that cornerback Bennie McRae was coming right up on the line and playing head-to-head with the wide receiver. This was the first time we'd seen the bump-and-run. Fellow QB Gary Cuozzo and I came up with the strategy that the best way to beat this defense was to call a "fade" pattern—the wide receiver runs straight down the field and fades to the corner.

On the first series of the game, we were on our own twenty. There was Bennie McRae right up in Gene Washington's face. I recognized this opportunity and audibled for the fade. Gene flew right by him, but I sailed the ball over his head. On second down, there he was again right back on Gene's nose. I audibled again, and this time I threw a perfect spiral. The ball was knocked out of his hands and at the last second fell to the ground on the fifty-yard line right at Bud's feet.

Now it was third down. There McRae was again; I couldn't believe it. I called the audible, passed the ball perfectly, and Gene caught it perfectly, one foot out of bounds. As I came off the field, Bud looked me straight in the eye and said, "I think you've got 'em loosened up now."

In a successful organization, everyone has a clear assignment and role to play, and then is given both the authority and responsibility to carry it out. Delegation of duties fortifies the system by complementing positive recruitment and strong development of players.

PILLAR FIVE: ENVIRONMENT

By environment, I'm not talking about Met Stadium on a freezing day in December. Instead, environment refers to a feeling, mood, or atmosphere within which a team operates. Environment is sometimes referred to as a team or corporate culture. Creating and maintaining a motivating and winning environment is a process of communicating consistent leadership, continuity of tradition or shared values, and a practice of encouraging "we" instead of "me." Some of the things teams can do to promote a positive team environment include:

Enabling Individual Achievement through Team Accomplishment
It's always nice to receive individual awards and accolades, but this tends to lead to a star system rather than a team system. Tracking team successes and finding a way to reward those successes encourages individuals to pull together. Hall of Famers Gale Sayers and Dick Butkus were among many great players whose teams never played in the Super Bowl; individual ability didn't translate into team accomplishment.

Working and Playing Together as a Team
Teams work best when individuals get to know each other beyond just working on a task together. Teammates need to freely communi-

cate with each other, which is often developed in a social setting. In a dangerous, competitive game, where every play could be your last, players need to share solitude, sanity, and safety—something more than football.

Bud always insisted that during training camp we all eat meals together. He didn't care if we ate, but he wanted us there. It may have seemed old fashioned to eat family style, but it created an environment that encouraged players to interact on a personal level. It was always comforting and encouraging for us, the Root Beer Gang, to see the Wall Street Club over at one table, the Sunday Prayer Group at another, and the Overeaters Anonymous at a third. We all felt more secure. Everything was in its place together. It might have looked like cliques, but there was a feeling of togetherness.

Our team's closeness was unmistakable; we were a fraternity, a gang. We even had our own team car, and what a car it was!

In my time with the Vikings, we spent our practice time at Midway Stadium in St. Paul. Most of the players lived in Bloomington because it was where we played our games (at Metropolitan Stadium). On the road to work we passed through neighborhoods, and for me, a California boy, it was interesting to see and feel who our fans were.

On our normal travel path, when the sun was shining and before Odin came in with the cold, we would pass a home with this beautiful, shining black automobile parked outside in the driveway. One day we stopped to take a closer look, and this fine old gentleman came out and let us have an up-close look at the car, which he informed us was a 1939 four-door LaSalle. She was a beauty! The car was his pride and joy.

We became friends, and along with a few teammates I would stop and visit when we were not in a hurry to get to work. One day I found the courage to ask if the car might be for sale, and the owner responded that he would think about it. So, one fine day when we stopped, he offered to give us the car, which I thought was unacceptable. I made several higher offers, which the owner rejected, and we finally agreed on $100.

The Vikings now had a first-class chariot to get to the arena—and maybe to a few watering holes even as far north as Hennepin Avenue. For those who were in need of a ride home, the chariot was always available to pick up those with driving impediments. The LaSalle quickly became identified as our team car, and too often it bedded down in locations all over town. More than once I had to reassure the police that the car was not stolen from its parking place at the Met.

Eventually, I was sent away to another city in my travels as a migratory quarterback. Captain Jim Marshall offered to keep the lady in the Twin Cities, but I could not bear to leave her behind. To this day, if you ask any of my former Vikings teammates about the LaSalle, you will likely be met with a devilish, cake-eating grin. It was yet another way in which we bonded as teammates and as brothers, and it set the stage for what was to come in the 1969 season.

Reinforcing Common Goals and Values

As corny as war cries and slogans may sound, they are an important tool in reinforcing common goals and shared values. When we said "Forty for sixty," it reminded us of why we were here and what we had to do to win. Also, over time these goals and values become institutionalized to keep the spirit alive.

Laughter can reinforce team unity and spirit. The dog days of training camp were made more bearable by our high prince of humor, Dale Hackbart. He could contort his own face into a clown mask. We spent the camp copying him and calling each other "rubber face." We weren't forty Vikings; we were forty rubber faces laughing at ourselves and each other. We all became part of the everyday ongoing drama we dubbed "In Search of the Super Bowl."

PILLAR SIX: CONTINUITY

The mark of a successful team is the ability to maintain a high level of performance over a long period of time. Teams such as the Vikings that have been winners for decades understand the principles of continuity. Continuity is the process of retaining values, players, system, and environment, year in and year out. On a winning football team, it's the veterans and the coaching staff who bring the core values and goals of the team back the next year to pass on to the new players. Keys to continuity include:

Building a Stable Organization

It's almost impossible to build and maintain a unified sense of purpose and shared values with a revolving-door policy. Changing coaches every year, replacing veterans too quickly with unproven talent or engaging in too much front-office turmoil disrupts the development process. Bud Grant stated it well when he said that if you've got a brick that fits into a wall, you should be reluctant to replace it if it's solid.

Keeping an Even Keel

Great players, like great teams, try to maintain a high level of consistent performance. Teams that are on a high one week and on a low the next are seldom around at the end of the season. Vikings teams have a long-standing reputation for being professional and businesslike. In 1969, we had a realistic chance of winning every game we played.

Practicing the Way You Intend to Play

You can't expect to do anything in a game that you don't in practice. Good teams practice hard and practice all the situations they expect in a game. The next time you watch a game, notice how the good teams never seem to be confused in crucial situations because they have prepared for them.

Promote Working with Successors

Even though every player is always competing for his position, on good teams incumbents work with and train their successors. I remember when I first came to the Vikings, veteran quarterbacks Ron Vander Kelen, Bob Berry, and later King Hill spent a lot of time working with me on recognizing and attacking NFL defenses. Despite being competitors for a position, they were teammates, and they showed me what sharing was all about. It's our duty to pass the game on.

Vikings veterans had enough confidence and self-respect to share their knowledge with the younger players so that they would be ready to step in when their number was called. Promoting working with successors and providing rites of passage is vital to the continuation and duration of an organization. Bud's way became the Vikings' way, and the Vikings' way became the winning way.

PILLAR SEVEN: CELEBRATION

When I came to the Vikings in 1967, I was told by the players that I was expected to be at the team's Halloween party and I was expected to wear a legitimate costume (not to be taken lightly, especially when it's Carl Eller telling you). Frivolously, at the last minute, I decided to use my four-year-old son J. J.'s Batman outfit with the miniature mask and tiny cape. It looked like the last-minute effort it was.

When I arrived at the Radisson Hotel, home of the Golden Strings, it looked like a high-society masquerade ball. Everyone had an expensive, elaborate costume. Alan Page had a caveman outfit with the furs and club. Earsell Mackbee, an African American, was dressed in full Ku Klux Klan regalia with a white sheet, hood, and all. I was insulted until I recognized Earsell's perverse sense of humor. Lonnie Warwick played himself and came as a West Virginia hillbilly, and Dale Hackbart came as a prima ballerina in ballet slippers, tights, and a pink tutu. I could see I would fit in with this group of creative crazies even though my costume wasn't up to the splendor of the moment. These guys took their celebrating seriously.

Win or lose, a team needs to celebrate together. Football is a game and it should be fun, but it's no laughing matter. Celebration doesn't just mean parties and partying, but rather a way of sharing successes and failures. We learned to accept each other with all our foibles. A team also needs to celebrate small successes along with the big ones. Only one team wins the Super Bowl, but every team needs to celebrate in order to grow and prosper. Cheering the defense after a good series, telling stories after a practice session, playing pranks during training camp, or just going fishing together are all important ceremonies of celebration. Every individual and every team has their own way to celebrate, and it's important that they find it and that it's encouraged. Performance is improved through a greater understanding and knowledge of each other.

Forty for Sixty Is a Team Celebration

We gain from those who came before us. From this experience we develop beliefs and values to live by. This is the reason for personal credos. Our slogan incorporated all the pain, frustration, and agony of working so hard yet still losing games by close scores. The margin of error was so small: a yard, a foot, an inch, one play here, one play there, one player out of step, one player out of sync. It was the bridge. We finally began to believe that if only we could focus and endure as a complete team for sixty minutes, we would win.

You, Me, We, Us, Together!

We all work and play in the arena of life. Life is a competition for the basics of food, shelter, clothing, and reproduction, yet there is much more. We are now beyond bare existence. The issue and challenge is not only what *is*, but also what *can be*. An ongoing challenge to the human spirit is to examine, discover, and act on our inner depth, quality of character, and potential in our lives. We have the alternatives and options available to explore and maximize our ethos, the group, and universal elements that form our individual characters.

So many different groups and relationships in our lives could be seen as a team: family, mates, sisters, brothers, job, church, neighborhood, city, state, country, world. A commonality of categorization and definition links us together at various levels and during many moments. Team is everywhere, all the time; the consciousness of this fact and how we relate to it requires close attention and study.

By being part of a team, we are part of a group that will develop shared values and identify shared goals. Consequently, an implicit and individual responsibility exists for each member of the group to bring the best version of themselves to the arena, or to their particular job or role. This necessity requires understanding, time, honesty, effort, respect, momentum, and knowledge. The result will be a participatory and satisfactory role, balancing consistent exertion and generous giving for the ultimate good.

Individual achievement can be commensurate to and proportioned by team accomplishment. Teams create synergy that can build great bridges and produce championship results. The power or dynamic of a team is achieved through a concentrated and active force, a collective and sustained motion built on cooperative essential principles.

Teamwork ultimately requires an execution of fundamentals, the acquisition of learning methods and system to change, an understanding of time and of truth, an internalization of quintessential values, and the mastery of communication processes and leadership skills. This striving is both the means and the end. Winning is participation. Winning is the process itself, reflecting the Cervantes statement that "the road is better than the inn." The path is calling. Let us travel it together.

We must take time, have a plan, form correct habits, embrace honesty, and work genuinely with others if we are to keep our goals alive.

Now is the time to begin. Human solidarity shows how to maintain cooperative balance atop shared values. Winning teams cannot be upset or shaken. Championship teams are resilient to hard knocks. They face fear and adversity together, and work with surety and strength. Units may suffer deeply, but they do not sour. Frustration does not become failure; fruition does not become fluff. Team dynamics rise up from an inner core. Great teams do not have the time to die, and that is the truth. These enduring elements of team play led us to live our mantra for the 1969 season: forty for sixty.

CHAPTER EIGHT

FORTY PLAYERS

The Power of Shared Values

Bob Berry and I met as competitors for the quarterback position with the Vikings in 1967. Our friendship has endured for the past forty-five years. We each bring something to the relationship—his great expertise in sailing and the sailing life, and my hot salsa recipe and humble knowledge of Mexican cooking. Together this has led to spicy and exciting times at sea and a growing closeness between us.

In an effort to examine our experience in football and its meaning to our lives, we meet from time to time for breakfast down near the beach at Santa Cruz. We like to sit outside at Aldo's, which overlooks the small harbor filled with sailboats. In my time as a migratory football worker and the places football has taken me, there has been no more beautiful breakfast spot than Aldo's at the harbor in Santa Cruz, California.

Bob was one of the Vikings' quarterbacks during the Van Brocklin years. He was signed by Atlanta before the 1968 season, then came back to the Vikings during their three Super Bowl drives in the 1970s. He had played for Van Brocklin, so I was interested in finding out what the Vikings team was like before Bud Grant became head coach. He told me that like most expansion teams, the Vikings had struggled in the early years to become competitive. By 1966, the Vikings had assembled a core of solid veterans and a number of really talented players.

Norm Van Brocklin became the team's first coach in 1961 after leading the Philadelphia Eagles to an NFL Championship in 1960 as their quarterback. Van Brocklin was a hot-tempered, volatile, fiery coach who would try to control everything—the players, the officials, and even the weather if he could. This was really evident on game days. Back at old Metropolitan Stadium where the Vikings played before they moved indoors, both teams used to have their benches on the same side of the field. By gentlemen's agreement, an imaginary barrier drawn at the fifty-yard line was supposed to divide the teams. But no line could control Coach Van Brocklin. Bob can still recall his coach running halfway down the opposing team's bench arguing with the opposing coach, then chasing officials all over the field. This led to wonderful drama, but of course had nothing to do with the important goal—winning a football game.

While I don't think a team totally reflects the personality of a coach, they do imitate some of their coach's beliefs, values, and attitude. This is how teams develop identities and performance traits. Under Van Brocklin's leadership, the Vikings learned how to be aggressive, scrappy, and even intimidating. It was a team that would look for a fight rather than run away from one.

It's not all bad to have a team of fighters. Some teams don't have many players that will stand up for their teammates or assert themselves, and it quickly gets known around the league that these teams can be intimidated. (By fighters, I don't mean brawlers but rather individuals who represent themselves and their team in an aggressive manner under the rules.) However, in search of a fight, the Van Brocklin–era Vikings often lost sight of winning the game. In 1966, the Vikings were the most penalized team in the NFL. The Vikings were winning the battles but losing the wars. Van Brocklin's teams were tough, boisterous, volatile, and exciting, but they were searching for unity and a positive direction. The early Vikings were a team of talented individuals who lacked cohesion and coordination to compete consistently.

The Vikings leadership went from fire to ice with the change of coaches in 1967. To the outside world, Bud Grant was cool, stoic, and expressionless, a glacier. But the players knew that he was an intense competitor who had strong feelings and values about the way the game should be played. As a result, he didn't put out the fire; instead, he gave it discipline. Good leaders realize there is a substance from the past that can be built upon in a positive way. Bud built on the positive aspects of his predecessor while molding and teaching his values to the team.

Slowly and steadily, the Vikings began to evolve into a well-disciplined team that played on an even emotional pitch. Bud wouldn't allow us to spike the ball after a touchdown or taunt the opposition after a big defensive play. We even lined up in military-parade fashion for the playing of the national anthem, quite a change for our scrappy bunch.

On some teams, if you got fined for a cheap shot by the league, the team or the coach might pick up the fine, which only encourages breaking the rules. With the Vikings, you not only got a league fine but a team fine as well. Through these rules a team gains integrity and respect for the game and each other, which is necessary for it to function as a unit. In a well-functioning organization, values become standards. Then each individual must make a choice to live up to these standards.

While the team's public image changed, Bud's rules weren't designed to sublimate the personal character and values of the players or the other coaches. We weren't robots or automatons. We still had our rah-rah guys, tough guys, loners, pranksters, and clowns. We could be who we were as long as we played by the rules. If we beat you, we beat you fair and square. In the arena, there's a certain dignity and self-satisfaction to honest competition.

By the start of the 1969 season, the forty consisted of nineteen holdovers from the Van Brocklin regime and twenty-one new "rubber faces." The nineteen holdovers, which included Grady Alderman, Jim Marshall,

and Mick Tingelhoff, still controlled fourteen of the twenty-two starting positions. The new young recruits—Alan Page, Ron Yary, and Gene
Washington—would become the foundation for the Super Bowl teams
of the 1970s. The Vikings now had a very talented group of individuals,
which created fierce competition for each position.

The new Vikings players were coachable and receptive to the concept of team. They shared four fundamental values necessary in all
human endeavors. These forty players exemplified a respect for self
and others. They played with a common integrity that was complete
and sound. There was a commitment to achieving our worthwhile
goal with all our energy. That energy was a sustained effort by each of
us to be the best that we could be for the team.

All players bring three things with them when they become part of
a team. First, they bring their skills: blocking, tackling, passing, and
catching the ball. No one makes a team like the Vikings without com-
petency in the basic skills. Second, players bring their knowledge and
experience: how to beat the blitz, how to play a zone defense, and
how to adjust a pattern. Veterans play an important role on a team
because of their depth of experience and their willingness to pass on
their knowledge to younger players—little things learned over time.
Finally, every player brings to the team a set of values. Values are
traits built on beliefs, creating attitudes that shape the character of
the individual and ultimately shape the substance of the team.

Winning teams find a way to bring out or heighten the positive
values of the players and control the negative qualities. This happens
formally and informally in a number of ways. At a coaching level,
coaches set and enforce rules that reflect certain values. Bud's rules
about being on time were an important way of communicating that
the organization valued discipline and respect for others. Work rules,
policies and procedures, and mission statements all are methods by
which organizations communicate values.

Coaches display organizational values in the way they decide who will play and how players are rewarded. When a team says it values team play, but contracts are based on individual achievements like rushing for a thousand yards or number of touchdown passes, it sends the wrong message. When a team says it wants to be a first-class team and then travels by bus and stays in third-rate hotels, the inconsistency can be destructive. In 1969, Bud did a good job of not creating quarterback factions by shuffling Gary Cuozzo and me in and out whimsically or making it a controversy in the press. An organization with fuzzy values will be a disorganized and confused team.

At a player level, values are often communicated and reinforced by player example. Actions are values in motion and always speak louder than words. When Brown and Osborn are fighting over who gets one more shot at Butkus, it sends a message that competitiveness and toughness are part of the team. When players don't air their problems in the press, it's clear that respect and loyalty are shared values. Players use peer pressure to set boundaries. When I was reprimanded for my Halloween costume, it was a clear signal that celebrating is serious business.

By the end of 1968, we were really starting to come together as a team. In only the second year under Bud Grant, we had won our first Central Division championship. Our defense and our running game were solid. We weren't beating ourselves with mistakes and we were competitive in every game. Our skill and experience levels had improved. Both physically and mentally, we were ready to be champions, and now we were playing as a team.

THE FORTY FORMED

The following chart shows the development of a team, bringing together the physical talents, experience, and values of each player. I've listed next to each player the quintessential value that player contributed.

THE DEVELOPMENT OF THE 1969 VIKINGS

	PLAYER	#	POS.	HT.	WT.	EXP.	COL.	VALUE
1961	Grady Alderman	67	T	6-2	245	10	Detroit	Control
	Paul Dickson	76	DT	6-5	250	11	Baylor	Loyalty
	Jim Marshall	70	DE	6-4	247	10	Ohio State	Spirit
	Ed Sharockman	45	DB	6-0	200	8	Pittsburgh	Commitment
RECORD: 3–11								
1962	Fred Cox	14	K	5-10	200	7	Pittsburgh	Responsibility
	Mike Tingelhoff	53	C	6-2	237	8	Nebraska	Determination
	Roy Winston	60	LB	5-11	226	8	LSU	Wisdom
RECORD: 2–11–1								
1963	Bill Brown	30	FB	5-11	230	9	Illinois	Toughness
	Karl Kassulke	29	S	6-0	195	7	Drake	Enthusiasm
1964	Carl Eller	81	DE	6-6	250	6	Minnesota	Confidence
	Milt Sunde	64	G	6-2	250	6	Minnesota	Dedication
RECORD: 8–5–1								
1965	Dale Hackbart	49	DB	6-3	205	9	Wisconsin	Humor
	Gary Larsen	77	DT	6-5	255	6	Concordia	Effort
	Earsell Mackbee	46	CB	6-0	195	5	Utah State	Concentration
	Dave Osborn	41	RB	6-0	205	5	No. Dakota	Perseverance
	Lonnie Warwick	59	LB	6-3	235	5	Tenn. Tech	Intensity
RECORD: 7–7								
1966	Doug Davis	71	T	6-4	255	4	Kentucky	Awareness
	Jim Lindsey	21	RB	6-2	210	4	Arkansas	Reliability
	Jim Vellone	63	G	6-3	255	4	USC	Empathy
RECORD: 4–9–1								

	PLAYER	#	POS.	HT.	WT.	EXP.	COL.	VALUE
1967	John Beasley	87	TE	6-3	228	3	California	Faith
	Bobby Bryant	20	DB	6-1	180	3	S. Carolina	Courage
	Bob Grim	27	WR	6-0	195	3	Oregon State	Poise
	Jim Hargrove	50	LB	6-2	233	2	Howard Payne	Steadiness
	Clint Jones	26	RB	6-0	200	3	MSU	Attitude
	Joe Kapp	11	QB	6-3	215	10	California	Hunger
	Alan Page	88	DT	6-4	245	3	Notre Dame	Resourcefulness
	Gene Washington	84	WR	6-3	208	3	MSU	Respect
	RECORD: 3-8-3							
1968	Bookie Bolin	66	G	6-2	235	8	Mississippi	Cooperation
	Gary Cuozzo	15	QB	6-1	195	7	Virginia	Pride
	John Henderson	80	WR	6-3	190	5	Michigan	Courtesy
	Paul Krause	22	S	6-3	188	6	Iowa	Patience
	Bob Lee	10	QB	6-2	195	1	Pacific	Ambition
	Mike McGill	55	LB	6-2	235	2	Notre Dame	Judgment
	Oscar Reed	32	RB	6-0	220	2	Colorado St.	Desire
	Steve Smith	74	DT	6-5	250	3	Michigan	Harmony
	Charlie West	40	DB	6-1	190	2	Tex. El Paso	Integrity
	Ron Yary	73	T	6-5	255	2	USC	Trust
	RECORD: 8-6							
1969	Kent Kramer	89	TE	6-4	235	3	Minnesota	Balance
	Bill Harris	35	RB	6-0	204	2	Colorado	Initiative
	Wally Hilgenberg	58	LB	6-3	231	6	Iowa	Aggresion
	Mike Riley	56	LB	6-1	230	2	Iowa	Alertness
	Ed White	62	G	6-2	260	1	California	Madness
	RECORD: 12-2							

THE GAME OF LIFE

People who seem to give and get the most out of life have two things in common. First, they do whatever they are doing all out. Whether work or play, dull or exciting, little or big, they give the matter their focused attention and try to do their level best. Without being stuffy about it, they have made a creed or habit of being satisfied only with their utmost effort.

The second thing these people have in common is the sufficiency and deep-down joy they get out of a very simple thing: being helpful to other people. Just to be able, in the course of their everyday lives, to do something a little extra for a friend, a client, a patient, a customer, or perhaps a complete stranger is a most rewarding experience.

These people are all around us. They are truly happy people who make this life gloriously worth living. These two qualities challenge me every day, pushing me to do a little better than I know how and make a point of giving a hand to others. Every moment we do this makes us more fortunate people.

Finding the right game, playing that game to its fullest, reaching for your best, and enjoying other people makes life a continual learning celebration.

By employing the proper skills, experience, and values, we specialize teams by positions and unit. The game of football is a microcosm of life in a magnified arena, which is why we can identify these units easily. Specialization is taught and accepted in our society and often creates amazing progress and keen results. But like any system, it departmentalizes and can distance, separate, and alienate people from each other.

Good teams learn how to accept and appreciate each other's skills and values, generating a powerful team. The worth of each component is valued and valuable to all. The connection between specialized units and the common goal is accomplished through the process of shared values. In other words: if you give, you get!

CHAPTER NINE

THE DEFENSIVE UNIT

"Defensive ballplayers take pride in knowing that they're rough and tough and mean and that they just have to hit and sock and smack and tear and whatever happens it's going to be all for one and one for all."

—Carl Eller

The press was starting to look for names to describe the way our defense played. Whether they were called the Purple Gang or the Purple People Eaters, it was a sign of a growing respect and fear of our defense. Nicknames are a useful tool for creating a team identity and a rallying point. As a team, we gave a lot of players new names as a sign of admiration, affection, and respect. However, once you have a nickname, you've got to live up to it.

THE DEFENSIVE LINE

The Vikings played a 4–3 defense, which makes the front four the first line of defense. Jim Marshall, Carl Eller, Gary Larsen, and Alan Page became the dominant front four in the NFL, taking the title away from the Rams' Fearsome Foursome. They won the title in combat, and each of the four starters went to the Pro Bowl in 1969.

Defensive linemen are big-hearted, happy giants—but can also be moody. They usually have thick ankles and hairy legs—but are still cuddly. They are late weaners, and truly love their mothers. They are very consistent and open admirers of John Wayne. They are great pals; get one for a friend if you can. Above all, you can count on them. They are big, fast men who can squeeze you to death or maul you with their melancholy madness.

Jim Marshall was the captain of the defense and the spiritual leader of the team. Jim was an iron man. He played in a record 282 consecutive games, which is amazing for someone who played in the pits. He relied on his speed and experience to create terror and wreak havoc on offenses. "Fast Jim" has always been full of life, living every day as if it were his last or as if he would live forever. He is like a cat with nine lives. He almost died twice—once getting stranded while mountain climbing and again when his parachute refused to open while skydiving, landing in the middle of a hayfield. I don't know if Jim's still alive today, because I haven't talked to him since yesterday. Jim's ebullient spirit became the vital force that was essential to our team quality. He was the catalyst for our becoming more animated and buoyant.

At the end of training camp each year, Bud had a rule that no one left camp until noon. At noon sharp the parking lot looked like a Le Mans road race with everyone revving their engines in anticipation of being the first one back to Minneapolis. Against my better judgment, I got talked into riding with Jim. There was no way anyone was going to beat him. We piled into his new Lincoln, and the wheels were screeching before I could close the door. We cut across cornfields and hubcaps flew off as we rounded corners. I thought I'd bought the farm several times on that ride back—and unlike Jim, I only have one life to live. Jim was also twenty years ahead of his time. He used to run around with a mobile phone in his briefcase.

Carl "Moose" Eller was a giant of a man who had the speed to chase down running backs from behind. He was the archetype for great defensive lineman in the future. Some guys look good in the uniform and don't play well. Eller looked great in the uniform and was awesome on the field. He walked and played with confidence. He's the kind of guy that makes you glad he's playing on your side. Eller played with the University of Minnesota on their championship teams and, as a result, was a longtime favorite of the local fans. He made you believe that you and those around you were equal to any task, and his presence ensured every team project would turn out for the best. We leaned on him.

Alan Page was one of the few players who could dominate the game from a defensive-line position. He was just starting to reach his potential in 1969 and later would be only the second defensive player ever to be named the league's most valuable player. (Defensive end Andy Robustelli of the Giants was MVP in 1962, winning the Bert Bell Trophy.) I called him "the hoot owl" because there were times during the dog days of training camp and practice when he would stop and hoot and howl to the wind just to relieve the monotony. He was extremely intelligent. He was the start of a growing trend among players who were concerned about ethics in society and how football affected the lives of players. Even with all this concern and internal turmoil, Alan was able to switch gears on game day and play an intense, aggressive football game. We all respected him for that. Alan, through his ingenuity, brought us together to draw upon all our talents and diversities in dealing with difficulties. He was decisive and unrelenting in the way he played football. He was a resource and resourceful, and truly lived advice from Descartes: "It is not enough to have a good mind. The main thing is to use it well."

Gary Larsen was our team's only true Norseman by ancestry. Gary was the anchor of the front four. His job was to stay at home and control the line while Marshall, Eller, and Page put on an all-out rush. The other players could take a little more risk because Gary was solid in the middle. Gary and I loved to watch the movie *The Vikings.* Our favorite part was when Ernest Borgnine would raise his sword and call to the Viking god Odin as he went into the pit of wolves. So, before each game, we too would call to Odin as we went into the pit with the Bears, Lions, and Packers of the Central Division. Gary worked hard to achieve his goals. His relentless work ethic challenged others to work, sweat, and strive to reach their full potential. Odin surely would appreciate the words of Tibbon: "Skill is nil without will."

Paul Dickson was an original member of the Vikings' front four. He was known as "the Growler" because he was always making bear-like sounds. He was a Baylor Bear, but the word that best describes Paul is *loyalty*. He gracefully assumed his position as the fifth defensive lineman and rooted for the others while patiently waiting his turn. His eleven years of experience in the NFL made him the elder statesman to the Vikings.

Paul always worked for the good of the team rather than his own immediate desires. Loyalty must be nurtured, and those who practice loyalty know its reward. Paul's devotion and fidelity to his teammates could be counted on. In spite of the outside appearance and demeanor of a hostile growling bear, Paul wrote beautiful, sensitive poetry.

Steve Smith, in his third NFL year from Michigan, was emblematic of those values that made up this unit. Although he did not have the opportunity to play much, his effort, spirit, confidence, and resourcefulness as a defensive lineman were carried out daily in practice. His value to the team in the everyday rigors of preparation for the opponent is not measured in cheers or accolades, but in the appreciation of his teammates.

THE LINEBACKERS

Linebackers have to have two personalities. They have to be tough and ferocious to stop the run, and sly and analytical in passing situations. Linebackers have to play with aggressiveness, intensity, and wisdom. Our starting linebackers Lonnie Warwick, Roy Winston, and Wally Hilgenberg were like the Three Musketeers, or maybe it was more like Larry, Daryl, and Daryl from the 1980s TV show *Newhart*. Where you saw one, you saw all three.

Linebackers are united in their hostility to all others, so they have to stick together for any type of human companionship. To be a linebacker you must hate your own mother, your grandmother's pet dog, and little kids. They are the mean little boys you used to know. They break toys for the fun of it. They have bad breath and are hard of hearing when they want to be. They love rules so they can break them, but they are leaders whether they want to be or not. Their position demands it. They have great pride in territory and protect it with ferocity. Thank God for football to keep these contrary souls off the streets.

Middle Linebacker Lonnie "Big Sam" Warwick needs no introduction. We called him "Big Sam" because he told us to. Suffice it to say that the madness and ferocity required of the middle linebacker position are exposed in the stories about Lonnie in the preceding chapters.

Roy "Moonie" Winston was the quiet mentor and leader of the linebacking core. He utilized his football skills and knowledge of the game and his ability to process information like a computer to become a homing missile. Before each play he would communicate to his side of the line where the play was going to go and the snap count, and he was almost always right.

His short stature meant he missed out on some interceptions that a taller linebacker would have hauled in. But it was his wisdom, experience, and ESP that put him in position to make the interception in the first place. Moonie brought his nickname with him from the "Chinese Bandits" of the collegiate national champion LSU Tigers. He played to his full potential and maximized his contribution to the team more than any Viking. Moonie was a bright light in the Vikings' sky.

Wally Hilgenberg played outside linebacker. He was the newest member of this trio and didn't want to be left out of anything. After the Lions game he characterized the camaraderie between the three of them well: "Lonnie and Roy have more knowledge of football than any linebackers I've ever known. I've learned more football in the last one and a half seasons than in the four or five previous seasons. It's not just the experience, although that's very important, it's what I've learned from my associations with players and the coaching staff."

Wally was an aggressive, consummate, and assured learner. By studying his teammates, he improved and brought his game to another level. The linebacking core was the Three Musketeers, learning, laughing, and playing together.

Jim Hargrove, Mike McGill, and Mike Riley didn't play a lot in games. They were second-year players who were still learning our system and waiting for an opportunity to play. Mike Riley capitalized on his chance to play in the first Bears game when he blocked a kick and ran it back for a touchdown. It was a good example of how we had forty men ready to play and contribute. A good system brings young players along. They are not rushed into action without preparation. That preparation takes place primarily in practice with the daily process of correct execution. These men contributed through their work ethic and intensity in making our practices feel like games.

THE DEFENSIVE BACKS

The defensive backfield didn't have great speed, but it had quickness, experience, and toughness. This suited playing a zone defense for most of the 1969 season. With the big rush up front, the Vikings could win a lot of games if the secondary could limit the number of big plays by the opposition. Not only were they able to prevent the big play, but our defensive backs also made big plays themselves. Together with the linebackers, we led the league with thirty interceptions.

Most defensive backs are weird, but not as much as wide receivers. Defensive backs are wide receivers who couldn't make it on offense. They do play a position where they can catch a ball—sometimes. Every defensive back has heard his coach say, "When the ball is in the air, it's yours." This adds to their natural schizoid mentality. They are fearless, lonely, studious, and reflective. They have been known to streak a crowd, and if you absolutely need something delivered, they are great couriers. They stand naked and are always in great jeopardy to be exposed when a ball is thrown over their heads, but their thick skin protects their egos and makes them even more dangerous.

It gets lonely out there on the corners. The only time I ever thought about quitting football was back in my first year of college ball versus UCLA. In those days, you had to be a two-way player, and our system called for the quarterback to play one of the corners. I lined up against Craig Chudy, the state low-hurdle champion, and he flew right by me for a touchdown. As the game progressed, I played five yards off him, then ten, fifteen, and finally twenty. He still caught three touchdown passes. Fortunately, they changed the system, and the next week I was playing linebacker. I have an undying respect for cornerbacks.

Ed "Bozo" Sharockman and Earsell "Evil" Mackbee manned the corners with help from second-year man Bobby Bryant. I used to call Sharockman "Stiletto" because he had a knife-like way of coming in and making key tackles. It might have been lonely out there, but he didn't make many mistakes. He was a veteran and knew how to play the sideline, and he knew where and when he could receive help from his safeties. This alert ability prevented our opponents from making big plays on us. Ed always moved with timeliness. He was watchful, ready, and vigilant.

In 1969, we were on the road for our first league game in New York, playing in New York but staying in New Jersey. Bud left us just enough time between eating, meetings, and curfews to visit the Big Apple. Groups of us would taxicab it into Manhattan. As we were departing the hotel looking for a taxi, one of us was mistaken for the doorman. Earsell Mackbee always was a colorful dresser, and his ensemble that day was a houndstooth hat, a purple blazer, and orange slacks. A tourist coming out of the hotel mistook this *GQ* cornerback for the proud doorman of the establishment. "Could you please get me a cab?" he inquired.

Earsell retorted, "Yes, of course, sir, in about two hours when I get back here." Earsell personified the streetwise aplomb necessary for survival both in New York and as a defensive back in the pros. It's lonely on those corners. You can look great for forty-five plays. Then up pops the devil and seventy-five thousand people know you made a mistake. Evil Mackbee added fixed focus and big-play capability to our defense. He stopped a lot of drives with key interceptions.

Cornerbacks such as Earsell can ignore disaster. They have an ability to concentrate on the job at hand. They have no room or time to dwell on past mistakes. Otherwise the mistake compounds itself and becomes fatal. Earsell could stare disaster down with his glowing Evil smile.

Bobby Bryant was too small to tackle big running backs and too slow to cover fleet receivers. All he was able to do was make one big tackle after another, make the key interception, and give us the added dimension of a kick and punt blocker. The Vikings' reputation for being a team that blocked kicks started with Bobby Bryant. The program had Bobby listed at 180 pounds, but that weigh-in had to include a sack full of South Carolina gamecocks on his back. It didn't matter what Bobby weighed; he played with an oversized heart and the soul of a gamecock.

Any test in the arena requires courage. In the face of difficulty and adversity, Bobby's strength always was evident. He was fearless with valor and pluck. He saw danger and conquered it. A team is lost without the fortitude, daring, and mettle that Bobby brought to the team. He was crucial in helping our team cultivate a spirit of courage.

Paul Krause was our centerfielder. He'd play about twenty yards off the line of scrimmage, and with all the horses up front he didn't always get into the action. He often was teased by teammates for not coming up on running plays and sticking his head into the fray. Sometimes he was so far back he didn't show up in the game films, but in our system, that really wasn't his job; he was our final line of defense. In a season where the defense gave up less than one touchdown per game, almost nothing got past Paul, and he never let an interception slip out of his hands. By the end of his career, he was the NFL's all-time leading interceptor.

You wouldn't be far off if you called Paul the Ghost of Patience Past. He had the ability to wait and endure, a steadiness and self-control for the duration of a game. He knew in a sixty-minute game he would find his moment to excel for the team. Our coaches were patient in their leadership and our players responded with their own diligence, self-control, and persistence.

At the other safety position was Karl Kassulke. The team called him Hunky. He didn't know why, but he said it never bothered him. Karl was as full of spirit and enthusiasm as any man I've ever known. He loved to sing and dance. When we'd get near the end of game that we were leading by two or three touchdowns, he'd start the chant: "Are we going to sing tonight?" On the field he was a fierce hitter; off the field he was a thrill seeker. I remember that he had a great laugh like a Mexican burro—*hee haw, hee haw*. He was one of these people who was always called an overachiever because others only measured his stature and not his substance.

Karl exuded inspiration, warmth, zeal, passion, and excitement. He helped each of us to stretch our limits and push out our boundaries. Karl was always the first to volunteer, and always with a smile on his face. Whether it was a tackling drill, a chug-a-lug contest, or a canned-food drive, Karl did it with a fire and spirit that were infectious. Hunky paid the price more than once for his overzealousness, and he went through life without his front teeth. As a strong safety, his assignment was to cover big tight ends, and this little big man made them hurt.

I called Charlie West "El Gato" because he moved like a cat: graceful, flowing, sure, and quiet. As a rookie from west Texas, he brought a genuine innocence and naivete, but also the essence of integrity. I got to know and respect Charlie even more when he was one of our coaches at the University of California. He had a feel for the game and understanding of people that made him an outstanding coach. During the 1969 season, Charlie was a backup safety and was used as an extra defensive back in passing situations. Charlie has within him a completeness, candor, and rectitude that give fiber to an organization. Football teams are in constant search of toughness. But no team is tough without integrity—that's Charlie West.

Dale Hackbart, "the Hacker" or just "Hack," was an All–Big Ten Rose Bowl quarterback at the University of Wisconsin, an exceptional, versatile athlete in football and baseball. He was our heavy hitter on the kickoff team. In a game of hit-or-be-hit, he was a devastating tackler who liked to get the other team's attention early and often. Hack had more nicknames than Red Skelton had characters. With his long legs and rubber face, it was easy to call him Goofy Goose, Daffy Duck, or Crazy Crane.

He played both safety and linebacker, but his versatility was more than athletic. An accounting of his leadership would require a full-blown novel or textbook. Dale's vehicle for leadership was humor. His greatest talent was his ability to make us laugh at ourselves and our situations. It allowed us to maintain our balance and perspective.

His roommate at training camp was Karl Kassulke, who was the perfect partner for his comedy act. Their running gag was: "Who stole Karl's teeth and where did he hide them?" A typical Hack act was getting us all to gather wire coat hangers after lunch before a hot afternoon practice. He put a pair in each helmet and quickly coached us on robotics. We came on the field as a united group of Vikings robots, complete with antennas and beeping sounds. If Bud and the coaches wanted precision and timing, they would get it, Hackbart style!

He was very interested in astronomy and became a master "moon-shooter" before Paul Newman made it popular in *Slap Shot*. He was a legend before his time in the NFL. We called him "Rubber Face" because he had one uncontrollable face. At a training camp he could have everyone in camp making rubber faces, loosening us up. He had the ability to make us discover and appreciate our own vulnerability and self-oddities. If laughter is the best medicine, we should have called him Doctor Hack. Every team should have a Dale Hackbart!

CHAPTER TEN

THE OFFENSE

"We will have an improved team . . . We expect to be better than we were in 1968 . . . We must improve every phase of our passing game as a team to be within reach of the top."

—Bud Grant

In 1968, we won most of our games with a strong running game. The character of the Vikings' offense was a group of tough, experienced veterans who would rather run over you than around you. The 1969 season would see us endure, improve our passing attack, and become a more dynamic and dangerous unit. Bud was realistic in his assessment of our offense and team goals. I was confident we would improve our passing production, but I was dead certain we would be champions at the top.

THE RUNNING BACKS

It is worth repeating that a team's character can be measured by the toughness, determination, and perseverance of the running backs. The game of football consists of equal parts pleasure and pain. It is a certainty that running backs will experience the physical pain of direct body contact, but they also know that pleasure that every little boy who wants to be a football player dreams of: to carry the ball in the open field.

Running backs are the "stars" of the team but sometimes don't know it. The good ones want to carry the ball on every play. They have an easy, natural self-confidence because they know they are entrusted with carrying the king's sack of gold. They are very happy people—unless, of course, they are not carrying the ball. But being a running back is a rough life. They don't last long and they die young, but they are loved for all the pleasure they bring football fans when they break through a gaping hole and go all the way.

"Boom Boom" Bill Brown, with his bowlegs, flat-top haircut, and thick, muscular chest, was built like a fire hydrant, only a lot tougher to knock down. Bill was traded to the Vikings by Chicago for a third-round draft choice because the Bears were overstocked with fullbacks. This trade came back to haunt the Bears, as Bill Brown became one of the NFL's top fullbacks for almost ten years. He was not only a hard-nosed runner and blocker, but probably the best receiver coming out of the backfield in the league.

With Bill in the backfield, it was dangerous for the rest of us any-time there was a fumble. The ball belonged to him, and there was no way anyone else was going to get it. The word *tough* can have neg-ative connotations, but in the game of football it is safe to say that "tough" football players are what every coach is looking for and what every team needs. Bill was strong yet pliant. He had an unmistakable moral firmness.

Before the Metrodome, when football was played outdoors in the snow and cold—where Vikings football should be played—you could always see two guys wearing short-sleeved shirts and cutaway jerseys. One was Bill Brown, and the other was his running mate, Dave "Ozzie" Osborn. It was a good-spirited competition between the two to see who could be tougher and practice harder. As a pair, they were always the last to leave practice.

Dave had been our leading rusher in 1967 with a team record of 972 yards. Then he missed most of 1968 with a knee injury. In spite of all obstacles, Dave Osborn was going to be on the field for the Vikings in 1969. His tenacious running style had media announcers calling his runs great examples of second effort. What these people were seeing was not a second effort, but rather Dave's deeply embedded sense of getting it done, no matter what. His breaking of a tackle, or his diving catches, or the way he kept his feet alive, or the way he twisted over a pile of bodies for additional yards were part of Dave's first shot, not his second. When the coach said a play was designed to score a touchdown, Ozzie believed him without question. The opposing team were just eleven obstacles in his way, but most certainly weren't going to stop him from crossing the goal line. I truly believe that when Dave Osborn dies, his heart could be transplanted five or six times and five or six rejuvenated halfbacks could have great careers in the NFL.

In 1966, the two most acclaimed college running backs were Nick Eddy and Clint Jones. When Notre Dame challenged Michigan State for the national championship, it was billed as a duel between these great halfbacks. Clint was a slasher and a charger with a nice, easy gait. It would look as if the defense were about to capture him, and boom—he'd change directions and explode with speed upfield. Notre Dame discovered this, and so did the Vikings. That's why I called him Cadillac Jones. It was a beautiful thing to watch him run with the ball.

At our training camp in Mankato, the Cadillac took a lot of loud and sometimes constructive criticism from Jerry Burns, and Clinton was letting it upset him. I picked up some cotton from Stubby Eason, our superlative equipment manager. Then before each practice, just as Clint put on his helmet, we stuffed cotton in his ears. It was amazing how much his performance improved when he was wearing the proper equipment—even if he missed a few snap counts.

For a guy who could have been a prima donna coming out of college with All-American credentials, Clint was a real team player. His love of life helped us all in our daily work. The attitude he exuded made work more like play. We had a job to do, but Clint's joy and positive approach to the game helped the coaches in their effort to create a positive environment and mood, a place for teamwork and play to blossom.

A real testament to Bud's eye for talent was finding and utilizing Oscar Reed. As a relief back, Oscar often crossed up the defense because of his different style of running. He ran like a pumpkin seed squirting in and out of the tackler's arms. The crowd would roar: "Give the seed to Reed." The fans loved his ability to start and stop on a dime and give you nine cents in change. I called him Bonavena, which means "good life" and was a reference to Oscar Bonavena, a heavyweight contender who had that same eminent desire as our Oscar.

Jim Lindsey was one of the Vikings' best all-around players. He was called Captain Crunch and was captain of the special teams. He would play halfback, fullback, and sometimes receiver. His versatility made him reliable. He was known as somebody to be called on as a "finisher." He would follow through on all assignments and obligations. Jim's reliability and sense of duty were evident in the coaches' confidence in his ability to handle any situation.

With all this great talent at the running back positions, Bill Harris found it difficult to find playing time. But in the true spirit of forty for sixty, he became a star player on kick- and punt-coverage teams, pinning the opposition deep in their end and forcing fumbles. Alongside Hackbart and Kassulke, returners learned that the only safe way out was a fair catch. As a young player, his fresh eagerness to contribute to the team helped us all reach a higher level of motivation. The running backs as a unit gave us a concrete, firm aggressiveness that we all could be proud of.

THE RECEIVERS

Quarterbacks love receivers who can run precise patterns, burst past defensive backs with blinding speed, and make clutch catches. If there was one group of players who really improved in 1969, it was the receiving corps. The three years of working together finally paid off. John Beasley, Gene Washington, and Bob Grim had joined the Vikings as rookies in 1967. This time together allowed us to fine-tune our execution of patterns and timing, which rely on familiarity between quarterback and receiver. John Henderson joined the group in 1968, and Kent Kramer rounded out the "soft hands" corps in 1969.

Wide receivers are ballet dancers. They are called "wide outs," spending much of their time isolated and alone. Like gifted artists who are sensitive to sight, sound, and feeling, they hate contact. With all their aloofness they still are nice people, but on the football field they can be lethal weapons capable of striking from any place to put up a quick six points. They are every organization's super salesmen. Wide receivers are slick and have all the moves to get you on the scoreboard.

It seemed as if Gene Washington spent the entire season ten yards behind the defense scoring key touchdowns. Gene could catch anything, including my so-called knuckleballs, lame ducks, and end-over-end passes. I asked Gene if it bothered him if the ball didn't spiral. He said it didn't really matter, but that he actually preferred the tail fins in back.

Because of Gene's great speed and ability to get open, he was usually double- or triple-covered. This opened up the field for the rest of the receivers and helped us become a better passing team. I've met few people who are as warm and sincere as Gene, and he was a role model of decorum for the team. He had the self-assurance and composure to stay calm under pressure. His poise evened out our performance.

John Henderson and Bob Grim teamed to give us great punch at flanker on the other side of the field. Both were reliable receivers who accounted for a lot of clutch catches. No matter who we had in the game, we always could put a great deal of pressure on the defense with our passing game. John was the perfect complement to Gene's explosiveness. His efficiency was sometimes unnoticed, yet it brought balance to our attack. John, in knowing his own identity, had an assurance of steadiness and professionalism that made us more secure and solid.

Although Bob Grim was shorter and more compact than John, he brought the same meticulous and steady performance to the flanker position. Bob was one of the early students of weight training and used his sinew and muscle to complement his other attributes. Bob was also a neatnik in everything he did. He took pride in the exactness of his pass routes. His conscientiousness complemented John's steadiness, which led to a flanker position played with pride and precision. Our depth at flanker made us much stronger as a team.

In the Vikings' system, the tight end was required to block most of the time and yet have the ability to break free and make a key reception when needed. Tight ends need agility, sturdiness, tenacity, strength, coordination, and toughness. Although receivers are brothers at heart, tight ends have a different makeup. On one play they are running free downfield and on the next play they're blocking a huge defensive lineman—they don't know whether to be an M-1 tank or a jet plane, so they're always just a little off.

Tight ends have to be everything to everybody. They can have big necks and slender fingers. They can be slow, but quick. They are walking contradictions, antithetical to themselves. The way to really get them uptight is to tell them a lie—like you're going to throw them the ball and you don't. Tight ends sort out these contradictory elements by being reliable receivers, sustaining their blocks, and being diverse in their skills and capabilities. They tend to be true believers, thus becoming the team's crusaders.

John Beasley, a fellow Golden Bear from Berkeley, had sticky hands. The Beaser was a believer, in spite of being a college linebacker. This allowed him to trust the system, block like hell, and just possibly get one ball thrown to him a game. Some guys aren't greedy. His sense of purpose was straight and fast. If there was trouble lurking, we could count on his action. This cultivated faith and fidelity between teammates.

As a rookie in 1967, John took on the all-time-great linebackers, players such as Dick Butkus, Ray Nitschke, Dave Robinson, Tommy Nobis, and Mike Lucci. He drove, he blocked, he dug, and he fought to keep these players off his teammates. And he came back to the huddle like a kid that just sneaked into the movies. He was happy and delighted to be alive and playing in the NFL.

Kent Kramer joined us during the season, which can always be a difficult situation for the player and the team, but he fit in immediately with a professional, giving attitude. Good teams readily accept newcomers when they bring something to offer. He brought experience and knowledge of the league and a desire to be part of our quest.

THE OFFENSIVE LINE

In war, it's the artillery that conquers, but it's the infantry that occupies. The long bombs, the sweeps around the opponent's flank, or the quick hitter up the gut all are made possible by the men in the trenches. The job of the offensive lineman is simply to keep those big, ugly defensive linemen from knocking the tar out of the quarterback, and to open gaping holes for the running backs to run for daylight.

For the most part, the Vikings' line consisted of experienced veterans who were small in stature by today's standards. A 245-pound tackle or a 235-pound center would be considered light in today's game. Of all the positions on a team, it takes the most time to develop as an offensive lineman. Offensive linemen must focus on technique; they must maintain balance, timing, and coordination while working together. They are five men who must act as one. When they accomplish this precision and unity of effort, the center, the two guards, and the two tackles become one position: the offensive line.

Look at your hand with five open fingers. Now close it into a fist. It's obvious. The fist is tighter, compact, impregnable, stronger, and can deliver a blow. This is the formula all offensive lines strive for. Offensive linemen are wide bodies. Part of their job is to take up space. They are surprising in their ability to read the *Wall Street Journal* and understand it. They wear button-down shirts, power ties, and wing-tip shoes, and when they grow up, they're usually three-piece-suit accountants. Their necks are thick and they're always squinting, looking for someone to block. These big guys who always have their bloodied noses to the grindstone only get recognition when they screw up. Offensive linemen are the last of the rugged individualists who sublimate themselves to a singleness of purpose. And for those who know that feeling, they have the answer to what "teamwork" is all about.

Offensive captain Grady Alderman became a Viking in the expansion pool of 1961. By 1969 he was an experienced veteran who survived the changes of a developing organization. But Grady did more than survive; he prevailed through his intelligence and developed into a leader who brought a dignity to his position and the team. In those everyday little things that affect a team, Grady was always thoughtful and conscientious. If there was illness in a player's family, if a player was hospitalized, or if someone needed help for any reason, Grady always knew and would offer support. It's in these small matters that true leaders show character. That same concern for detail worked for him on the field. The difference between making a block or missing it is a matter of inches. He would make that precise maneuver necessary to achieve his goal.

Doug Davis was our starting right tackle until he injured his knee. Once your position is filled and the team is doing well with your replacement, it is very difficult to regain your spot. The chemistry of momentum is seen as a trust that can't be disturbed. Doug lost his job to an All-Pro but maintained his competitive attitude. He showed this positive approach through his diligence and fortitude without complaint. Doug was a team player with the awareness and ability to focus on the ultimate goal of team success.

Ron Yary came to the Vikings as a two-time All-American from USC, a number-one draft pick with tremendous physical qualities and great desire. What Ron added to our line was the ability to take on the opponent's best player and beat him in a physical matchup. He was literally a support pillar, making our line secure and cohesive. With Ron on our side, we knew we could block anybody. This type of trust leads to a belief and loyalty at every position. Once you trust yourselves, you have the courage to succeed.

Ron broke through two stereotypes for me. First, I didn't think any of the USC bullies could ever be good guys. He was! Second, he absolutely relished the opportunity to take on the best player the opponent had. He loved returning to play in Los Angeles for more reasons than one. He loved to visit his mom, but mostly he wanted to fire out on the great Deacon Jones one on one.

To love one Trojan is to love two, especially if the second is Jim Vellone. He came to the Vikings as unacclaimed as Ron was heralded. The 1969 season was his fourth year in the NFL, and through his aggressive play he looked at least twenty years older. That's the price you pay in the pits, and he was willing. No one loved people more. His warmth and zeal for his teammates were constant. This gregarious gladiator with a Jimmy Durante schnoz would stick it into everything—opponents, pizzas, conversations, and any huddle. He was a listener who showed empathy to everyone, including strangers. In bars, on the street corners, or the locker room, you could always see Jim listening and engaging with what was being said.

He possessed an openness to life that made for a winning environment. Maybe it was because he was prematurely bald and looked older than his years that players naturally gravitated to him for conversation and advice. I believe it was his genuineness and warmth. Every team needs a communication conduit. We all banged the drum slowly for Jim Vellone when he died in 1977 of Hodgkin's disease.

If anyone was a self-made man on the Vikings roster, it was guard Milt Sunde. He was the only one I ever knew who would rig up a blocking dummy in his garage so he could take his work home. I saw him going after that dummy once, but it looked as if the dummy were winning. Milt came to the Vikings as a low-round draft choice from the same University of Minnesota team as All-Americans Carl Eller and Bobby Bell. If the Vikings hadn't lost Bobby Bell to the Kansas City Chiefs during the AFL–NFL bidding wars, all three would have worn purple.

Milt was the only Bloomington boy to become a "hometown" player when he replaced the retired Larry Bowie as the starting left guard. The type of dedication Milt played with made him constantly intent on improving. By competing for and appreciating the earning of a starting position, he knew and proved that it is not enough just to make the starting lineup. The starter now has a responsibility to help achieve the team's goals. Milt's decisiveness and understanding of that responsibility made him bring that momentum to our practices every day.

Mick Tingelhoff had the determination and endurance to play seventeen seasons in the NFL. He was named All-Pro seven consecutive times (1964–1970) while playing in four Super Bowls. As center and anchor of the Vikings' line, Mick's ability to persevere while keeping the goal in sight and moving toward it was a beacon for the team. He was an iron man, not big, but his quickness, agility, and determination compensated for any lack of size.

At that time most teams were playing a 4-3 defense, which meant Mick would block middle linebackers or double up with the guards on defensive linemen. He controlled his position through mental discipline and lightning reflexes. Obstacles did not deter him through stern persistence. He did not change his mind. His rural Nebraska stubbornness led to his commitment to reach an ultimate performance. We all realize quarterbacks spend many hours throwing the football, perfecting their craft. Mick spent a lifetime perfecting the pass from center to quarterback. Without that short pass, no ball is put into play. The perfection of that timing must be absolute. He was master of his position. Trusting that the ball would be delivered on time, in the proper position, made me a more effective quarterback. There is a partnership between these positions that often goes unnoticed.

First-year man Ed White was built like a baby bull. The Vikings were converting him from an All-American defensive lineman to an offensive guard. This was not only the process of learning the position, but also learning to control his defensive lineman's disposition. Every now and then he'd lose his cool and toss his opponent to the ground. Coach Johnny Michaels would yell, "Hey, Ed, you're an offensive lineman now. You can't do those kinds of things anymore." Then Ed would get this chagrined look like he'd just been caught with his hand in the cookie jar.

Ed became the world wrist-wrestling champion, which you might expect from a wide body; but more than that, he was a graduate of the University of California, Berkeley, School of Architecture, and a professional artist in sculpture and painting in oils. Ed is an example of the depth and breadth of talent, skill, and values found in members of a good team. During the 1970s, Ed White and Ron Yary teamed up to be the best guard-tackle combination in the NFL. Ed played seventeen seasons in the NFL, concluding his career in San Diego, where he anchored the offensive lines that made Dan Fouts a Hall of Famer, yet mysteriously no call for Big Ed.

Bookie Bolin was an eight-year NFL veteran who joined us from the New York Giants. He played swingman behind starting guards Vellone and Sunde. To be a long-lasting professional in any career requires skill, style, and strategy beyond the norms. Bookie was a proven player who added his exceptional competence to our unified, cohesive offensive line.

THE QUARTERBACKS

A quarterback makes things happen by turning words and signals into results. The position is the coaches' concepts, thoughts, and ideology on the field. The quarterback must use tempered judgment dealing with others, and gives encouragement, praise, and direction when necessary. He must exhibit sound sense and uncompromising decisions. A quarterback's working partners are insight and foresight, requiring that he be a student of his game with the ability to project the results of his purpose. He must see around corners.

His evaluation of situations should be based on objectivity and experience, knowing always that his responsibility is to the team first, while maintaining an independent overview of what is correct on the field. He should always perform in the manner that he demands and expects from other players. Quarterbacks should cherish the challenge of choice and risk. They are the key to symmetry and balance by keeping events in perspective and controlling the tempo of play. The quarterback must accept final responsibility for winning and losing.

Although quarterbacks usually are the best-looking guys, they have bird legs, sunken chests, and bad bodies. They require much love and adulation, not unlike politicians and babies. Linebackers believe that quarterbacks wear dresses and sing falsetto. Quarterbacks, especially when being sacked or chased, get religion and pray a lot. "Oh, God, why me?" The position requires a most trusting person because they turn their physical well-being over to other team members who don't care if the quarterback lives or dies, mostly because of his oversized ego. The quarterback's main job as seen by teammates and fans is hook-sliding for safety. All parties, from coaches to spectators, expect quarterbacks to have eyes of eagles, the perception and judgment of Solomon, and the control to win every game. The team expects this position to be the catalyst to move the machine full throttle across the goal.

Every player in the NFL is a supertalented athlete. They have gone through a process of elimination physically, mentally, and emotionally to compete at the highest level of football. These are the chosen few of the tens of thousands of young people playing the game. Most of the NFL quarterbacks were either too small or too slow to play any other position, so they spent hours as a kid throwing a ball through a tire hanging from a tree. By the time a quarterback gets to the NFL, he has all the necessary mechanics wired into his brain.

The quarterback position is demanding in that it involves handling the ball on every play. But to master the position and play at a professional level, the quarterback must gain the experience and confidence to read sophisticated defenses. His primary physical specialty is to provide the pass. However, passing isn't just throwing the ball, but a complex act in coordination with ten other players. In attacking these varied defenses, quarterbacks must have the ability to throw long-, medium-, and short-range passes all over the field with correct velocity, accuracy, and touch.

The excitement and productivity of the forward pass can be achieved only through the concentrated and concerted effort of every element of the offense. Each unit is totally dependent on and entrusted to each other. This is no longer just the fist of five but the punch of eleven in complete orchestration.

The Baltimore Colts proved how a good team makes good quarterbacks. One year they won a championship as expected with Johnny Unitas at the helm, and the same team took backup quarterback Earl Morrall to a championship and made him the NFL's Most Valuable Player. Finally, with both Unitas and Morrall hurt, the same team won crucial games down the stretch with running back Tom Matte stepping in.

The business of professional football is precarious at best for the player. The risks of injury, age, and competition take their toll early and often. There is a constant changing of players on rosters in search of the right chemistry on the team. There is very little job security in a field that demands loyalty and continuity. Every player should keep at least one bag packed—even the so-called superstars, and even the franchise quarterbacks.

The Vikings had traded away their veteran quarterback Fran Tarkenton in 1967. When I arrived from Canada with eight seasons of experience, I joined Ron Vander Kelen, Bob Berry, John Hankinson, and later King Hill, a twelve-year NFL veteran. I came to the team without benefit of training camp. Bob Berry was an All-American at Oregon and an outstanding pro quarterback. At five foot ten, he had to overcome the size bias with skillful play and competitive fire. Bob was always willing to get into a scrap on or off the field. He also understood the value of celebration. This attitude and approach served him well when he got his opportunity with the Atlanta Falcons. Like Bob, King Hill was very generous with his knowledge of the league and shared it with me over many hours.

These men who—through attrition and trades—would be gone the following year shared and helped guide me in a crash course in NFL strategy. I had come from a free-wheeling, three-down offense based on passing and wide-open football. Even with football's tenuous tenure, knowledge and insights are passed on and incorporated. Every person contributes to the development and growth of their predecessors.

Gary Cuozzo joined us for training camp in 1968 with seven years of experience in the NFL and with the benefit of playing with John Unitas and Billy Kilmer. Besides being a Phi Beta Kappa and dental student, Gary was a walking encyclopedia of winning quarterbacking. At camp, he was expecting to room with an old friend, Fred Cox. I told him that plans had changed, and he was going to be my roommate in the royal suite at Mankato State. I felt that if we were going to be winners, both Gary and I had to work together.

We each brought our different styles and perspectives to the position. We proved that competitors can room together and learn together. The pages to Gary's knowledge were always available and helpful. I think it was reciprocal. The 1969 season demonstrated that we were on the same page in our commitment to our common goal. Gary brought us a cerebral and intellectual approach to the study and execution of football. He balanced theory with practice, and he taught me to step back and analyze.

We learned to pay closer attention to detail, in order to understand how every player on every play in practice and in games completed each assignment to its conclusion. If I threw an interception in practice, the easy thing to do was shrug it off and head back to the huddle for the next play. The correct response is to cover the interception with your teammates and make sure the interception is not returned for a touchdown.

It sounds like a small detail, but if it saves a touchdown a season it's worth it. This type of concern for the little things makes a statement to the team. Vikings quarterbacks will pay the price to execute exactly those things that add up to victories. Gary taught me to make the best use of knowledge, experience, and understanding from an objective viewpoint.

Bob Lee was a rookie in 1968 who gained a year of seasoning on the so-called Taxi Squad. Nowadays they call it the practice squad. He made the "forty" as a first-year quarterback, but his primary contribution was that of an accurate, reliable punter. It gave the forty-man roster more flexibility because any time a position player has another specialty, it makes the team stronger. There are some rookies who know it all, and there are some young players who learn and give in their learning.

Bob played in the NFL until 1981 on three Super Bowl teams, and he maintained that whatever success he enjoyed was a direct result of his 1969 experience. Bob had the most beautiful head of red hair, and I always wanted to call him "Red." Nobody deserved the nickname more, but we didn't call him Red. His son Zach would later play against my son Will in a Central Coast section (California) high school football playoff game. Zach and Will went on to play college football for Nebraska and Cal, respectively.

CHAPTER ELEVEN

THE SPECIAL TEAMS

"There are no special teams, only special situations."

—Bud Grant

The Vikings paid attention to special teams play. Most teams used their benches to stock their special teams. We expected our so-called stars to be special-teams players, and many in fact volunteered. As a result, when we needed to run a kickoff back a long way to get in position to win or to block an extra point, we knew what to do and had the players to do it. We spent a lot of time in practice working on special teams, and it paid off.

The coaches believed in the importance of special teams by allotting enough practice time to make them more than effective. These teams became a force, part of our arsenal of weapons to put points on our scoreboard and keep the opponents from gaining any advantage. Much like the transition game in basketball, the special situations in the kicking game create opportunities for quick turnarounds. A blocked field goal, a long kickoff return, or a well-placed punt can each control the tempo and direction of a game. The kicking aspects of the game most resemble the rugby origins of football.

This part of the game, often spoken of but little prepared for, requires the integration of specialized departments. When you come to the special forces from your offensive or defensive units, you become part of a new unit within the team. Special teams remind us we all have to apply our unique skills whenever it's necessary, no matter what. And if it becomes meaningful to enough players, it becomes a powerful force. It was an honor to be a part of the Vikings' special teams.

Those players who were not always in the starting lineups exercised this opportunity to get on the field to score points and put us in great field position. Jim Hargrove, a young, quiet Texan, brought stern discipline and determination to the kickoff team. Mike McGill, a second-year player from Notre Dame, was aggressive and hard hitting. Mike Riley, traded to us from the Bears, was an alert and intense player. These three linebackers put their active, mobile, nimble skills and zest for work to advantage on the kickoff team. These men fulfilled the duties of running full speed to the ball, staying in their lanes, taking on all blockers, and rooting out the ball carrier. These men joined Karl Kassulke, Dale Hackbart, and Charlie West in creating a dynamic unit.

Special teams don't always attack; they also must protect. It is no major change for the offensive linemen to protect the kicker as well as the quarterback. The most vulnerable part in protecting the kicker, the part most dependent on split-second timing, is at the flanks. Tight ends and fullbacks now are the focal point of this shield. John Beasley and Kent Kramer brought their tenacity and pride to this endeavor.

The immediate beneficiary of this protection was our exceptional kicker, Fred Cox, and his holder, Paul Krause. Paul, with his soft, sure hands and his poise, was the perfect holder. It was unusual for a safety to be the holder; that job usually fell to a quarterback. Paul's versatility allowed our quarterbacks to have more time to work on their specialties, become less vulnerable to injury, and allow more time for strategy on the sideline during the game. In an age of specialization Mick Tingelhoff had transformed the long snap into an art of accuracy and dependability, in spite of an automatic forearm in his face from his opponent.

That year Fred Cox was the league's leading scorer with 122 points. While he didn't make many fifty-yard field goals, he made almost all his attempts from forty yards in and was automatic on extra points. His uncanny reliability was highlighted by Fred's steadfastness on and off the field. He is a forthright, serious, purposeful individual. Fred understood and accepted the pressures of kicking and carried out his role at the highest level of achievement.

As "Chairman of the Board" of the Root Beer Gang, he was the epitome of concentration. He focused on the job and put his toe to the proper point on the ball, possessing the strength to ignore distractions and the courage to be ready at any moment. Fred was emblematic of our special teams, which is the difference between failure and success—doing a thing nearly right and doing a thing exactly right.

The easiest way to gain field position is through the punting game. But the possibility of this tactical maneuver blowing up in your face is always present. A poor snap from center, a muffed ball, leaky protection, a flubbed kick, poor coverage, or—worst of all—a blocked punt can turn a game instantly. All those men on punt teams have been grossly underpaid. Picture loading a slingshot and having it backfire. It was "Captain Crunch" Jim Lindsey's responsibility to keep order to this organized chaos.

Bob Lee was not a great punter for distance, but he fulfilled Bud's requirements for safe, consistent, controlled, pinpointed punting. Bob's hang time allowed our punt team to provide coverage, eliminating big plays against us. This is a great example of standard statistics not being the measure of effective play on the field.

I don't think the Vikings ever had a year where they had more long kickoff and punt returns, especially in key situations. Clint Jones and Charlie West split the duties running back kicks, and both hold Vikings records for their efforts. These two made up a dangerous team in any situation. El Gato and the Cadillac preceded Cheech and

Chong by ten years. They were cruising the Met and the Twin Cities before low riding was popularized.

As a forty-man squad, the Vikings were skilled at every position. We had a careful blend of experience and youth, which would keep the tradition alive in the next decade. Each man brought his own special talents and individual values to the team. We still could have been a group of individuals and prima donnas; what transformed this team were the values we shared that fueled the concept of forty for sixty.

We shared a commitment to team, and we believed that none of us individually was as good as all of us together. Our veterans shared their experience with the rookies because they believed in passing down the traditions of the game. Every player knew he had a role to play and needed to be ready to contribute. We were willing to pay the price for success.

CHAPTER TWELVE

TRAINING CAMP
A Lesson in Unity

Training camp is one of the rare times that grown men give up their liberty to pursue a career and a common goal. Training camp is a combination of the tough physical demands of Marine boot camp, the rigid routine and endless hours of waiting around for the next practice, and the hijinks of summer camp on the lake. Training camp has the potential to bond a team together or pull it apart. There is a certain unity that can develop when a team goes through hell together in such close quarters for eight weeks.

Training camp is a little bit like preparing for war. Players can learn how to kick, pass, punt, or catch a football on their own. They can go to the gym or down on the field every day and get in shape, lifting weights and running sprints. But the only way they can learn teamwork and team play is through an intensive and concentrated training session.

Learning how to pick up the blitz, working on returning punts, and perfecting a Green Bay sweep requires the instruction, coordination, and repetition of a training camp. It's also the time where we began to develop trust in the guy playing next to us. Quarterbacks start to trust that the center will deliver the ball properly. Guards learn to trust that the tackles will help out in certain situations, and defensive backs learn the trust it takes to play a zone. Practicing together starts the process of sharing values that blends the chemistry of a team.

We live in a world of constant challenge and continual change. Training camp prepares us for the work, ideas, attitudes, decisions, and essentials not always clearly defined or developed. We learn to use the basic tools necessary for future success. In training camp, individuals begin to share a common understanding of what team and teamwork really mean.

Going into training camp, we all realize that it is the last time until the end of January that we will be free of aches and pains, cuts and bruises. We've all had six months to prepare ourselves for the new season. The veterans know the routines and what to expect in the long days ahead. They are all aware of a common goal to become world champions. The rookies, I think, have to be a bit frightened. They look like first-year campers, not sure if they wouldn't rather be at home. This may be their first and last exposure to the National Football League. To make the team, they will not only have to prove their skill, but they also will have to become true professionals. This mixture of knowledge, fear, pain, and pleasure creates the environment of intense competition.

Bud Grant had his own unique style of running a training camp. The Vikings were always the last to come into camp each year, usually two weeks before the first preseason game. This still gave us eight full weeks before our league opener. A veteran team that comes to camp in shape needs less time in physical conditioning and can spend more time on skill development. It's also fewer weeks of wear and tear that might make us fresher at the end of the season.

Some teams really hype the conditioning aspect of their training camps. I can still visualize the films of Vince Lombardi grinding his troops into the ground. The Vikings, as well as all the other teams in the NFL, went through the same routines without the media blitz. Teams that beat other teams by conditioning do so by the year-round effort of the players. What shape are you in when you come to camp? Do you go all out during the workouts? This is why each player must take upon himself the task of being physically prepared. Each member's physical shape is a forward impetus for team play.

The Vikings came into camp in 1969 in the best physical condition of their lives. There was little body fat on anyone. Every player wanting to make the team knows that every extra pound means extra exertion and possible wilting in the sun. We were a lean and hungry group. As leaders and examples, Lonnie Warwick and Roy Winston had learned their lesson the year before when they found themselves wilting in the heat. This year they both came into camp at their fighting weight. Alan Page had slimmed down from 270 to 250 pounds, and he was faster and quicker than ever. The entire offensive line was lean and hungry for action.

Conditioning in those days was really different than it is today. We did push-ups, sit-ups, jumping jacks, and leg raisers. We called it calisthenics, not jazzercise. We ran laps and wind sprints instead of jogging, and there was very little talk about whether an exercise was aerobic or anaerobic. There was a weight room about the size of a closet with a set of free weights; no universal gym, no Nautilus, no rowing machine, and no computerized stationary bicycle. You weren't supposed to have fun getting into shape. It was supposed to be grinding, painful, and monotonous. Recent technology and training methods have made today's players bigger, stronger, and faster, but there still is no shortcut—it still takes hard work.

In training camp as well as throughout the season, the training room has its own mystique and can reveal a lot about the character of a team. Some guys would avoid the training room like the plague, while others could spend all day there. Bill Brown's idea of treatment would be to get an aspirin and tape it where it hurts. We had a saying that you can't make the club in the tub.

Football players have to know the difference between pain and injury. You can play with pain—in fact, most players have aches, pains, bumps, and bruises all the time. On the other hand, you can quickly

TRAINING CAMP | 135

end your career trying to play with fractures, tears, pulls, and dislocations. Trainer Fred Zamberletti and his assistant Larry "Cowboy" Nelson patched us up and kept us moving.

At camp, we also were reintroduced to Stubby Eason's equipment room. An equipment manager needs great patience to deal with all the requests made by the players. Some were very particular and wanted their equipment just so. They wanted their socks a certain length and a tailored look to their uniforms. Other players treated their equipment like old friends. They demanded certain pads and pants that were broken in, like old shoes. Players have a lot of superstitions about their equipment. Some have to put their pants on left leg first and then right leg. Others put their socks on first, and so on. It's all part of a rhythm or groove that players try to get in. When you're winning, you try to change as little as possible. As a team, the Vikings were one of the last teams to get rid of the black shoes. It was sad to see them go in later years because they really fit the character of our team.

Most teams started their seasons with a rookie camp a few weeks before the veterans reported. For us there was only one camp, and we all reported together. Again, it was Bud's way of trying to build one Vikings team, not two. Separation often creates disparity. To win together, we must work together. And that meant starting together.

THE DAILY GRIND

Our training camps were extremely disciplined with the same routine day in and day out. We rose at 6:30 a.m. The day started at seven o'clock, and everyone was expected to eat breakfast together whether you felt like eating or not. Then it was back to the rooms to study the playbook and get ready for the team meetings. Practice went from nine to eleven. We took half an hour to freshen up after practice and then met for lunch from 11:30 a.m. to 1:00 p.m. The afternoon meetings, which typically lasted about three and a half hours, were spent viewing films of our performance and the competition's. Professionalism in any endeavor is based on a timed routine with the integration of the mind and body. Football demands the daily grind of training camp!

We were expected to be taped and dressed in time for practice on the field at 4:30 p.m. Just like the military, we were told the uniform of the day for each practice, depending on the level of contact: helmets only for no contact, helmets and shoulder pads for light contact, and full dress for all-out contact. Whatever the practice, aptitude and desire to play were tested moment to moment.

During practice, we'd go through a series of drills on a position, unit, and team level. Positional drills break down the components of a football game into the necessary skills and techniques. Receivers practice running precise pass routes and the footwork they need to keep their feet in bounds. Over and over again, they practice patting both feet inside the boundary as they catch a ball. Defensive backs practice grabbing interceptions from tipped balls. Linemen practice their blocking techniques on dummies and sleds.

On a unit level, the offensive line practices working together on blocking a sweep and assignments on pass blocking. Quarterbacks work with running backs on the timing of handoffs and with receivers on timing pass plays. Then the offense comes together to practice running plays and the defense comes together to run through coverages.

Finally, the team plays a mock game, or scrimmage. This can range from a walkthrough, to half speed, to all-out full contact. Full-contact scrimmages need to be carefully controlled. While a team needs to practice playing full speed, it's important not to cannibalize your own team. In team practice sessions, I think we had an advantage over other teams. We had the opportunity to practice against the best defense in the league, which means we were constantly being pushed to our limits. A form of teaching is moving from specific individual drills to general team execution. This develops a welded, conscious chain of understanding, each part to the whole. Each member needs to understand why and how they fit into the puzzle.

Toward the end of practice, it was time for conditioning drills. It's important that all the learning happens when you're alert and rested, so conditioning is always the last thing. You do your conditioning when everyone is dragging because it forces you to stretch yourself to the limit.

Early in training camp, we'd go through two-a-day practices, which meant we spent extra time on the physical aspects of the game, especially conditioning. To signal the end of this phase, a truck pulled up in the end zone, and the driver set up two long tables and spread out five hundred pounds of sliced watermelon—Bud's way of rewarding us for hard work in the hot Mankato sun.

We were all expected to roll in for dinner at seven o'clock, more food for the hungry horde. In 1969, no one really knew or cared much about cholesterol, fat, and sodium.

The training table was set to make sure no one went hungry, but being in Mankato, Minnesota, there's a real shortage of good chilies, enchiladas, and burritos—the kind of food a real quarterback needs. An institutional dining hall can be as bland as the food if everyone goes about their business and there is no interaction. It's the spirit of singing, joking, and interaction between players at mealtimes that brings spice and spirit to a team.

After a brief rest, we had team meetings from 8:30 to 9:30 p.m.: more film, more talk, more study. From 10:00 to 11:00 p.m., we could do anything we wanted as long as we were in bed by 11:00. Day in and day out we ate, slept, studied, and practiced football. Most importantly, we practiced being a football team.

Bud had his own philosophy about practicing. He felt that a team gets better through repetition, but he also felt that if things weren't working out just right, or if a player was having an off day, it was better just to take some time off and let your head clear. Practicing too hard when things are going wrong sometimes ingrains those mistakes. A kicker who tries to get out of a slump by kicking hundreds of balls can permanently change for the worse if he's not careful. Sports, as in any of life's activities, need repetition of correct habits.

At the start of camp, Bud set out three things that he wanted to improve in the upcoming season, so we spent hours and days on all three. First, he wanted to increase the number of interceptions by our defense. Bud had a knack for throwing the ball perfectly for the tip drill. The ball is thrown, a player tips the ball, and the defensive players scramble for the interception. This gives the defense practice in reacting to the ball in the air and catching it properly. All the work paid off. We increased our interceptions from seventeen to thirty, leading the league with more than two per game. That really put our opponents in a hole.

The second goal was to work on our defense against the run. With the coming of age of our defensive line, linebackers, and secondary, this was an easy task to accomplish. During the season, we were able to shut down running teams like the Bears, Browns, Colts, and Packers as well as great running backs like Leroy Kelly and Gale Sayers.

The final goal was to become a more potent passing team. The elements of our passing game were just starting to mature. All our receivers had only one or two years of NFL experience, and Gary Cuozzo and I had only been with the team for a short time. My first full Vikings training camp was 1968. With the addition of my second trip to the Vikings' camp we were able to get down the plays and timing needed for a more explosive passing attack and offensive unit.

The value of training camp goes beyond Xs and Os. It's the consummation of the battle to make the team and to bring the individuals together as one. It's the reaffirmation of fundamentals, the season for camaraderie, the implementation of a system to fit the individuals, and the development of a cohesive strategy to face the oncoming foes. Ultimately, the pain of training camp says to the individual, "You have earned the pleasure to be selected as one of the chosen few to work at the game you love, to earn a living doing what you have trained your whole life for, to compete with others for a championship, and to know the satisfaction of being recognized and accepted as a professional football player."

MAKING THE SQUAD

Being a rookie in 1969 was a tough job. Seventeen rookies came to camp but only one made the squad, offensive guard Ed White. The attrition started early. Two rookie running backs didn't pass the physical. Then Ed Duren, a middle guard from the University of Minnesota, called it quits after thirty-seven minutes of practice. He told the coaches it was just too tough, and that he'd had enough.

Flanker Volly Murphy, the Vikings' second-round draft choice, had his own troubles. Midway through training camp, he was involved in a different sort of draft and had to report for active duty and two years of military service. We were fortunate that tight end John Beasley and tackle Ron Yary were in the reserves—we lost them for only short periods of time when they got called up for reserve duty.

There also were four players who hadn't made it the year before who were back for a second try. This time around Bob Lee, who was a seventeenth-round draft choice in 1968, survived. Even the veterans could sense the fierce competition that was about to start. Players such as quarterback King Hill, receiver Tom Hall, and tight end Billy Martin knew that they were on the bubble. Dale Hackbart started to relearn how to punt, thinking if he could help the team as a punter, it would help him keep his job. I volunteered to be on the kickoff team, but Bud said I was too slow.

We started training camp with seventy-five veterans and rookies all trying to become one of the forty. The players usually know who's not going to make the first cut when the team is pared down to sixty. There are seldom any surprises. It's the final cut, when the team goes from forty-four to forty, where the truly hard choices are made, and it feels the most devastating.

I don't know if there's really a good way to tell a player he's been cut, but I've seen a lot of cruel and heartless ways of doing it. Players find their lockers cleaned out, or notes to go see the coaches, or a list of players who had been cut. Other teams will have an assistant designated to do the dirty work. In Calgary, our team's lockers were in a big, barn-like structure. On cut-down days, you'd see the rookies hanging around outside the building afraid to go in to see if they'd been cut.

Once a player is cut or retires, he's old news. It's a lot like being fired without notice or severance pay. Only the players keep some type of emotional tie with each other. It's really one of the sad and unfortunate parts of football: teams continue to prosper from the spirit of a Jim Marshall or the determination of a Bill Brown, but the players come and go.

Sometimes when a cut is made, as a veteran you feel that you should stand up. This is how I felt about Art Powell. In 1954, we were both All-California Interscholastic Federation (CIF) basketball players, although we did not know each other then. Art was an outstanding player who had played mostly for the Raiders, and is one of the all-time greats of the AFL. For reasons I still don't know, he was considered to be a troublemaker and a black militant. Art was aware of his undeserved and unearned reputation. He did everything he could to dispel the perception. After the team inevitably cut him, I went to the coaches, asking them to reconsider. I said, "I know I'm not a coach, but we need Art." The response was: "You're right, Joe, you are not a coach." To me, his presence in camp was pure tokenism.

Not all players who don't make the team are immediately cut or released. Every day at 4:00 p.m. Eastern time, the waiver wire would go out. The Vikings had a teletype in Mankato and at the home office in Bloomington. (In 1969, teletypes were much more fashionable than fax machines or email, and there was no such thing as the Internet either.) Teams put players on waivers for two reasons. First, it gave a team a chance to test the waters to see who might be interested in a given player for a trade. A player put on waivers could be withdrawn within twenty-four hours, and then the teams could talk trade. Second, in order for a player to become part of the Taxi Squad, he had to clear waivers and then be resigned. Players on the Taxi Squad were allowed to practice with the team and could be called up to replace an injured player.

On an average day there were about twenty-five players put on waivers, and about seventy or more on cut-down days. The cost of claiming a player was $100. Teams did find good players on the waiver wire; in 1968, Atlanta picked up Paul Flatley from the Vikings, and we picked up Wally Hilgenberg from Detroit.

CHAPTER THIRTEEN

COACHING

Training camp really belongs to the coaches. It's the only time they have all season to work with the players on their individual techniques and team play. The coaches have eight to ten weeks to install and refine their system, bring the team together, and select a roster for the season.

Coaches need to have an in-depth knowledge of the game, its techniques, and its strategies, but the skills and values of a good coach are different in many ways from those of a good player. Players must have great physical talents. They need to know how to play their position and how they fit into the offensive or defensive scheme. Players practice these skills over and over until they become automatic or subconscious. A great player often can't tell you how he did something, only that it happened.

Coaches, on the other hand, can be slow, overweight, and have bad hands. They aren't the ones who are going on the field on Sunday. A good coach needs to have the skills that will allow him to fulfill three distinct roles. The primary role is that of a teacher. Coaches share the secrets and subtleties of the game through hands-on instruction and constant feedback. The best coaches constantly tell players what they did right and what they need to improve. They work with players on making small, constant improvements throughout the season. Often times, players for whom nothing came naturally, those who really had to work at the game, make the best teachers. They've had to break down every part of the game and analyze it over and over.

The second role of a coach is that of a strategist. Coaches spend hours, days, and months poring over game films, looking at the strengths and weaknesses of each opponent. In these sessions, the head coach is the general and the assistants are his lieutenants. To be a good strategist, a coach needs to have an overall understanding and knowledge of the game, a view of the big picture. He needs to understand the ebbs and flows of a game and how each of the parts acts as a whole. Then the coach must be able to translate this strategy to each player at each position. He's the one who has to make sure that every player is on the same page of the playbook.

The third role, and probably least understood, is that of a counselor. An effective coach must know how to relate to others, how to build trust and loyalty to the team and to each other. Coaches need to be able to communicate openly and freely with players and create an environment in which players want to learn and excel.

Many teams have won because of their coaches, and some teams have won in spite of their coaches. Teams that have a long-standing winning tradition continue to win because of the system, continuity, and environment established and maintained by the coaches.

Over the years while playing, coaching, and sharing with other coaches and players, I've tried to learn about leadership and the role of coaches. Out of this study has grown an A-B-C Leadership model.

Attitude is all-important. Our biggest job as leaders is the development of proper attitude among coaches and players. We must exhibit a positive attitude ourselves, or we can't ask others to follow us.

Back down when wrong. It takes a big person to admit mistakes, but this honesty and willingness to take responsibility create loyalty and respect.

Crystallize responsibility. Players can't be held responsible for foul-ups that result from the coach's failure to fix responsibilities clearly.

Delegate decision making to others. Trust builds by giving others the responsibility and authority to succeed or fail. Trying to do everything yourself creates a star system, which defeats willing cooperation.

Enthusiasm is contagious, and if we generate it within ourselves, we will see it spread to others.

Follow the rules. We need to set a good example by making very sure that whatever rules we set, we lead by example.

Give credit where credit is due. One of the most overlooked jobs of a coach is to give meaningful praise and recognition. It's almost impossible to get things done right if you only criticize what others do wrong. Try catching others doing good things instead. It works a lot better.

Hard work is integral to a successful result. You get out of an endeavor or activity only as much as you put into it.

Interest ourselves in people. People want to feel the concern and care of being part of a family or the feeling of belonging to the group. By showing genuine interest in others and their problems, we create a team atmosphere.

Join the work group. If we are aloof and unapproachable, we can't get the best efforts from our people. A lot can be learned by walking, talking, and listening while participating with the group.

Kill rumors. Straight, plain facts kill rumors. If we have the confidence of our people and open lines of communication, they will believe the truth.

Listen. Listening means more than hearing. It means remembering and understanding what others say.

Make the best use of players' ability. Players need to experience a sense of growth and accomplishment in order to feel they are an important part of the team.

Nagging gets nowhere. Constant fault finding can be destructive. Pick the spot, timing, and words carefully, so that what you say has real meaning.

Organize the work environment. One of the clearest marks of a successful leader is the ability to organize work, see positive ends, and complete tasks on time.

Plan for tomorrow. Every leader needs to have and share a vision of the team's goal and future. Everything the leader does should follow from this vision.

Quiz ourselves occasionally. Critical self-analysis is a positive tool in our own development as leaders. Those who can't stand to look in the mirror are usually the ones who need it the most.

Recognize the concerns and needs of others. Understand that every player has different needs, wants, and concerns. The best way to understand others and show empathy is to listen.

Secure the environment for those who need it. Security means giving others the freedom to risk and challenge themselves without ridicule or fear of unwarranted consequences.

Tell the full story. Misinformation or lack of information leads directly to team failure. It breaks down trust and pulls at the fabric of a team.

Understand the players. Understanding is the key to unlocking all human relations and people problems.

Violation of rules can't be tolerated. We can't expect others to do what we won't do ourselves. We must set examples by keeping the rules. If rules have to be changed, we change them together for a reason.

Walk and talk. Get out among the players and experience their environment. Listen to what they have to say.

X-cellent effort pays off. It's the time, effort, and thought that separate good leadership from great leadership. If you emphasize excellence, the team will also strive for that standard of excellence.

You versus we. The little word "we" works wonders. "We" becomes meaningful and real. "We can do it" creates productive teamwork.

Zealously lead others. A true leader must be possessed by the mission and common vision. Challenge yourself and others around you.

THE COACHING STAFF

Good coaching staffs need to be managed and led at the same high level that players do. The seven pillars of a team—system, recruitment, delegation, development, environment, continuity, and celebration—hold true for creating a coaching staff as well. Coaches indoctrinate players into a system that features the imbedded values that shape the team. Coaches project a strategy toward every aspect of the game, a blueprint or design of how every player and every play should work. Coaches set a tone through their mannerisms and their way of doing things. Their methods must fit the system and the credos they espouse. Most of all, they must be real to themselves. False personalities with power sooner or later destroy powerful action. Good coaching instructs the team in where it's going, what its objectives are, and what adjustments must be made to win.

Bud Grant was our head coach, and it was his responsibility to ensure the performance of his coaching staff. Bud was a natural athlete who was an outstanding performer at everything he did. In college at the University of Minnesota, he was an All–Big Ten end in both his junior and senior years. He also lettered in basketball and baseball.

After college, he played basketball with the professional Minneapolis Lakers for two years before going on to play offensive and defensive end with the Philadelphia Eagles. Bud left the United States to become an all-star end with Winnipeg of the CFL. At age twenty-nine, he became Canada's youngest coach as head of the Winnipeg Blue Bombers. In Canada, his teams won the Western Conference Championship five times and the Grey Cup four times. He had the best winning percentage (.635) of any coach in the CFL's history.

Jerry Burns was the offensive coordinator. In those days our offense was very conservative, but we found we could strive under those constraints. As Coach Burns gained more experience, he was able to open the offense up a lot more in later years. Burnsie joined the Vikings in 1968 after two seasons as defensive backfield coach for the Green Bay Packers. Prior to coaching for the Packers, he was head coach at the University of Iowa from 1950–1956. During those same summers he worked as a part-time coach for Bud Grant at Winnipeg.

He was known as the little man with the big bark and always seemed cranky, but the players had a deep respect for the man and the honest effort he put into preparation for every game. He not only had good technical skills, but also knew how to deal with people in the way that a coach should.

The defensive coordinator was Bob Hollway, who later went to be a head coach at St. Louis and then returned to Minnesota as an assistant general manager. (Good organizations always seem to develop head coaches for other teams.) Bob was a twelve-year veteran of the coaching staff at the University of Michigan. He first was hired to be the Vikings defensive-line coach before being promoted to defensive coordinator. Being a former college coach, he brought a lot of the college enthusiasm to the Vikings locker room. On some teams, the veterans snicker at this type of approach. They feel that, as professionals, they already know the importance of every game and how to be self-motivated. However, with the Vikings, Coach Hollway's personality added just one more dimension to the team. His enthusiasm was contagious.

The next level of coaches features the first-line supervisors. These are the coaches that do most of the hands-on teaching with the players.

Bus Mertes was the offensive-backfield coach. Bus came to the Vikings after a long career as a college head coach at Bradley, Kansas State, and Drake, where he coached Karl Kassulke. He also served some time as backfield coach for the Denver Broncos from 1965–1966. Bus was a very congenial person, an old warhorse. When Burns was cranky, Bus would give you a smile. He served as a father figure for many of the players. He focused most of his attention on coaching the little things, and he was very patient in his teaching of the fundamentals.

The offensive line belonged to John Michels. He fit the mold of an All-American guard at Tennessee at only 185 pounds. Before he made the move to Minnesota in 1967, he was Bud Grant's number-one assistant in Canada. His job was to mold five big hulks into one unit that moved together. His style was that of a typical marine D.I., a real stickler for detail, who would get right into the pits and show you how it was done. He was a good fundamental teacher of the game, but his real strength was to be able to turn off the tough-guy routine when needed and relate to the players as individuals. John made players who didn't often see the spotlight feel important.

The defensive line coach was Jack Patera, who later became the head coach with the Seattle Seahawks. Jack was the defensive line coach for the LA Rams' Fearsome Foursome for three seasons. He then went on to become defensive line coach for the New York Giants before coming to Minnesota in 1967. His job and real talent was to be able to keep his group of really talented athletes on a high fever pitch and coordinate their actions on the field. He knew how to appeal to the pride of these players and throw down challenges for them to perform at higher levels when needed.

CHAPTER FOURTEEN

PRESEASON GAMES

To prepare for the 1969 season, we played six preseason games. For most players, that's about six too many. Veteran players would rather have every game count. While Bud always wanted to win every game, he often treated preseason games like a team scrimmage. We would maintain the same practice schedule even on game days, and sometimes that meant having two-a-day workouts before an evening game.

Preseason games can be valuable in that they give the players a chance to hone their skills in combat, and new players a chance to experience participating in the NFL. The games weren't really a proving ground because Bud made it clear that players make the team in practice. We tried to use every player in the preseason games. Grant followed a quarterly rotation system. The starters played first and third quarter, while reserves played second and fourth quarters.

Preseason Schedule

August 2	at Miami Dolphins (Tampa)
August 9	Denver Broncos
August 23	at St. Louis Cardinals (Memphis)
August 30	at New York Jets (Winston-Salem)
September 6	New York Giants
September 13	at Cleveland Browns (Akron)

GAME ONE: MIAMI

We opened in Tampa with the Miami Dolphins. The preseason was the only time all year we'd play against AFL teams until the Super Bowl. It also was a time when we'd go to non-NFL cities that were trying to get a franchise, such as Tampa, Winston-Salem, and Memphis.

The Miami game was typical of many of the games we'd play during the season. I started the game and had a rough first quarter. I hit a Miami defensive end in the hands with the ball and he rumbled twenty-five yards with it for a touchdown to put us behind 10–0. But we settled down and put together three long drives, and by halftime we were leading 24–10.

In the second half, Gary Cuozzo came in and lit up the board for two more scores. During this game, we scored on seven of eleven possessions. By the fourth quarter, we were being accused of running up the score by throwing long bombs. But by then it was backup quarterback Bob Lee airing out his arm and practicing his trade in a game situation. The final score was a convincing 45–10, with our defense only yielding three points.

A number of players were in heated battles for their positions at the start of the game. Bobby Bryant was pushing Ed Sharockman, and Charlie West was challenging Karl Kassulke. The most interesting battle was between Dave Osborn and Clint Jones. Up until game time, Bud hadn't decided on a running mate for Bill Brown. The solution: he flipped a coin and Ozzie won. Just another talent of the man from Cando.

GAME TWO: DENVER

We played the Denver Broncos a week later at the Met. It was a game I should have missed. Early in the second quarter, I dropped back to pass and tried to set, and my knee crumpled underneath me. I spent the next several weeks with an ankle-to-thigh cast that really itched. Sports medicine was still very primitive in those days. The doctors weren't really sure what was wrong with my knee except that it was old, so they decided to immobilize it with a cast. With one of those high-tech braces they have today, I probably would have been back on the field the next day. We still taped everything, and I'm not sure what hurt worse, getting injured or pulling that tape off after a game.

A great team is able to keep its stride. Gary came in and easily led the team to a 26–6 victory. Actually, it was the defense that made this an easy win. It was their second straight week without giving up a touchdown. All the work they had done in order to get more interceptions was starting to pay off. The linebackers, who hadn't intercepted a pass in twenty-one games, snagged two—one by Lonnie Warwick, who thought it was one of my lame ducks he was looking at, and one by Jim Hargrove. The corners grabbed another two to make a total of four for the day.

GAME THREE: ST. LOUIS

Ten days later in Memphis, the offense put together one of its best games. We ran the ball well and passed it superbly. Coach John Michels was given the game ball for great pass protection provided to quarterbacks Cuozzo and King Hill. Even in a total team effort, great individual play is important. Gene Washington was driving the St. Louis defense crazy. They were double- and triple-covering him, yet he still caught four passes for 109 yards and a touchdown. This opened up the field for backs and tight ends to run free and have a field day catching the ball.

A lot of defenses would consider the St. Louis game a great day, but the defense finally broke and gave up its first touchdown in three games. The defense did even up the score with a touchdown of its own. Early in the first quarter, Jim Marshall knocked the ball loose and Gary Larsen returned it for a touchdown. The defense also exceeded its interception goal with three for the day. It's tough to watch any game from the sidelines, but it was fun to watch my teammates ring up a 41–13 victory over the Cardinals.

GAME FOUR: NEW YORK JETS

We stayed in the sunny south to take on Joe Namath and the world-champion New York Jets in Winston-Salem. This turned out to be a very frustrating game. The Jets' offense passed and ran the ball at will and at one point led the game 24–7. With 9:26 left in the game, Broadway Joe left the game to rookie quarterback Al Woodall, who promptly ran nine minutes off the dock. We were only down 24–21 midway through the fourth quarter, but we never got our hands on the ball again.

As in any close game, every player can think of one play here or one play there that might have made the difference. The defense seemed about a half a step off from making a number of interceptions that the Jets turned into long plays. One of these plays was a seventy-six-yard fly pattern to Don Maynard for a score. Our preseason record now stood at 3–1, and we were learning from our wins and now from our losses.

Every day since my knee injury, I'd been after the trainers to remove my cast. They said I'd have to wait for Dr. Lannin, the team doctor, to come down to Mankato before they would do anything. I don't have that kind of patience, so my "Gringo Chauffeur" Dale Hackbart drove me about ninety miles to Minneapolis to get this thing taken care of. The doctor wanted to be cautious and wait a while longer before doing anything. I had played with this loose knee throughout my career and I knew I would never play this season if I stayed in a cast any longer, so Dale Hackbart and I drove over to a local service station and got some cutting tools and did a little bit of our own surgery with some sharp tire snippers. I reported the same day to Fred Zamberletti and started the rehabilitation process. Dale's been in the tire business ever since.

GAME FIVE: NEW YORK GIANTS

The lifespan of a coach can be as tenuous as the lifespan of a player. On some teams, a streak of bad games means the coach is sent packing. Nine days before the regular season, Giants coach Allie Sherman was replaced by Alex Webster. Sherman had eight strong seasons and had won three Eastern Division titles. But the fans were restless, and management gave way to the pressure. The general manager rationalized the change by saying that the team was in business to please and entertain the fans.

So in his first week, Webster brought his New York team to the Met. During this game, Bud went away from his normal substitution policy and flooded the field with reserves. At the end of the game, we were ahead 28–27 with two minutes to kill. Our forty-man team gained valuable game experience and we came away with the victory.

This game was a good test of our depth. The Giants were trying hard to win this game for their new coach and kept their first team in for most of the game. Fran Tarkenton, the starting quarterback for the Giants, played the entire game. He found himself flat on his back while our first line was in, and he was only able to rally his team late after we had cleared our bench.

GAME SIX: CLEVELAND BROWNS

In the final week of the preseason, we moved on to play Cleveland in Akron, Ohio, for the annual Rubber Bowl game. This was our first of three meetings with last year's Eastern Conference champions. Teams often win games because the breaks seem to go their way, but good teams make their own luck and capitalize on good fortune. We scored on two touchdown passes when Cleveland defenders fell down.

The game winner turned out to be a seventy-yard pass to Bill Brown, who was not known as a breakaway runner. On that pattern, Brown was the clearout guy and the primary receiver was tight end John Beasley. But I spotted Brown quickly, and he was wide open. As I threw the ball, I was knocked flat, but I could tell we had scored by the roar of the crowd.

The Cleveland game was a good preseason test for us. We were playing against a first-rate team and they were out ahead of us early, but we proved we could play a full game by coming back to win 23–16. We had reestablished our momentum.

We ended the preseason schedule with a 5–1–0 record. Unfortunately, the only prize for this record was that we were allowed to start the regular season 0–0–0. Our defense had played magnificently and had started to achieve goals of increasing interceptions and stopping the run. On offense we were starting to run and pass more efficiently, beginning to come together as a cohesive unit.

No one had spoken the words "forty for sixty" yet, but the underlying spirit was there. The team was finally trimmed to forty, with four players on the Taxi Squad, and we were off to New York City for the start of the regular season.

CHAPTER FIFTEEN

THE 1969 REGULAR SEASON

In the arena mettle is tested, in the arena time is arrested.
We strain and struggle together, feeling ever the acute pressure.
In the arena our souls are stripped naked.
In the arena great effort seems fated, the games made losing or winning.
Touching swift glory in passing.
In the arena sport can be abused.
In the arena athletes often are used.
There is always injury, pounding, and pain, yet we strive, conquer, and gain.
In the arena fans cheer, clap, and boo, in the arena we condition for truth.
There's much cliché, cost, and scandal.
But forever one more challenge to handle.
In the arena excellence is the key.
In the arena we are inspired to destiny, in the arena we are ideals to be.

        —Ned Averbuck, "In the Arena"

"The credit belongs to the man who is actually in the arena, whose face is marred by dust and sweat and blood; who strives valiantly . . . who knows the great enthusiasms, the great devotions; who spends himself in a worthy cause, who at the best knows at the end the triumphs of high achievement and who at worst, if he fails, at least fails while daring greatly, so that his place shall never be with those cold and timid souls who know neither victory or defeat."

        —Theodore Roosevelt,
        Citizenship in a Republic

We were ready to step into the arena, hungry for a championship. Over the next fourteen weeks we were about to face the best teams in the NFL, each with its own credo and hopes for glory. It was now forty for sixty for fourteen games.

In the arena, under fire, the true nature and character of individuals and a team show through. A team's strengths become evident and its weaknesses become transparent. It's a test to see if the forty will become one or if the one will become forty. Every game is a test of teamwork and a test of individual values. Through each week of the season, it was evident that our shared values were helping us develop into a championship-caliber team. Each week we learned an important lesson that helped us move on to the next, higher level.

The quintessential values of what makes championship teams can be demonstrated well by reviewing and retelling the Vikings' 1969 season game by game. Championship teams such as this one must be learners who are resilient and committed to change. A key quality is consistency of effort, along with shared values and concordant shared goals. The team members must communicate with each other on all levels to the maximum extent possible. Every player can thereby exhibit his talents and leadership skills when his number is called.

Each lesson learned and told here can be applied to and associated with other arenas of life, from the office to the schoolyard to the family. These games depict lives dedicated to excellence, achievement, and self-examination. They demonstrate values that are participatory, qualitative, and passionate. A championship team requires members committed to a process.

The game-by-game insights that follow, which I was privy to as a member of the 1969 Vikings team, reflect many years of personal exploration of the success of this team. Looking back now almost fifty years later, what were the inner dynamics of the first Vikings team to experience the victory of winning the NFL Championship?

What effect did the 1969 Vikings team have as an organization, and what did it do to create a culture of winning for the team and its fans? Maybe it means that coaches, friends, writers, teachers, pro analysts, organizational personnel, and players worked together with serendipity. As the quarterback, I have insights into what got those results, and had significant responsibility in producing them. My interpretation of our survival and eventual dominance in terms of results is based on the concept of perceived contributions. The players always know who gets the job done.

The 1969 team as a group was unusually close and perceptive of what went on around it. We knew how to obtain results with the weapons we possessed. We saw, felt, and heard each other. We were unified in our commitment to making the team win. We communicated; we dressed, hurt, and laughed together. We also built from within slowly, continuously making the adjustments to create a team that was always better, not necessarily in our skills but in our values. With our shared commitment to making the team win, we consistently won and gained something well beyond the immediate elation of victory. The 1969 season reveals efforts of a team that found real meaning in its work.

1969 Regular Season Schedule

September 21	at New York Giants
September 28	Baltimore Colts
October 5	Green Bay Packers
October 12	at Chicago Bears
October 19	at St. Louis Cardinals
October 26	Detroit Lions
November 2	Chicago Bears
November 9	Cleveland Browns
November 16	at Green Bay Packers

November 23	Pittsburgh Steelers
November 27	at Detroit Lions
December 7	at Los Angeles Rams
December 14	San Francisco 49ers
December 21	at Atlanta Falcons

WEEK ONE: AT NEW YORK GIANTS

TEAM	1st	2nd	3rd	4th	FINAL
Minnesota	3	14	3	3	23
New York	3	7	0	14	24

Good Teams Learn from Their Losses

All professionals want to start fast and finish strong.

This was going to be our season. We rolled into New York's Yankee Stadium for our first league game with the New York Giants. We had beaten the Giants in the preseason, and we were excited and confident. After coming off the bench the week before to quarterback the Vikings to a come-from-behind victory, I thought I had regained my starting spot. On Wednesday, Bud told us that Gary would be the starting quarterback. He had been playing most of the preseason games while I was injured, and I guessed it was Bud's decision to maintain continuity. Gary had also prepared well for this opportunity.

By the end of the third quarter, we had amassed a 23–10 lead. Gary hit two long bombs, one to John Henderson for forty-seven yards and one to Gene Washington for forty-eight yards. We caught the Giants blitzing twice, and they paid for their boldness. On defense, our rush was fierce. The giants were keeping seven and sometimes eight men in to block, and yet Marshall, Eller, Page, and Larsen still were getting to Giants quarterback Fran Tarkenton. The front four knocked down Tarkenton three times and forced him to run to safety another seven times.

The Giants were down but not out. With 4:48 left on the clock, Tarkenton hit Don Herrmann with a sixteen-yard pass to make the score Vikings 23, Giants 17.

On the next series of downs, Cuozzo hit Gene Washington on a short pass, but Spider Lockhart's jarring tackle popped the ball loose. The Giants got the ball back on our thirty-six. With fifty-nine seconds left in the game, Tarkenton dropped back to pass. The big rush was on, but instead of eating the ball, Tarkenton threw a desperation pass into the corner of the end zone. Touchdown! The Giants had ended up with two men in the same area, which had confused the Vikings defenders for a second—just long enough for Don Herrmann to make the final score Giants 24, Vikings 23.

Throughout the game Paul Dickson, a giant of a man figuratively and literally, paced the sidelines with me. Two grown men, suited up and taped, waiting for our call. Both of us were ready to perform. We threw ourselves into cheering and doing whatever we could for our teammates, but we ended up internalizing our frustration as the game slipped away. Although Paul and I had started as hostile strangers three years ago, months of practice and dedication had created a mutual respect and admiration for each other. Although neither of us had a chance to play, Paul and I pulled for our friends and fellow warriors, swallowing our pride and the frustration of riding the bench. We learned that being part of a team meant giving the man on the field 100-percent support.

We thought we'd played well enough to win. We had outrushed and outpassed the Giants. Gary Cuozzo had a fine performance, completing seven passes to Gene Washington and three to John Henderson. The Giants had turned the ball over more often and had been penalized twice as much. Tarkenton had spent the entire afternoon running for his life. Yet, we had lost.

If we had shrugged this loss off to bad breaks, or to Tarkenton getting lucky at the end, we would have missed an important lesson. The game films show that at key points in the game, we'd had a momentary loss of focus and concentration that had led to immediate Giant scores. We had missed tackles, fumbled, and failed to execute properly at the wrong times in the wrong places. Individually these mistakes weren't enough to cost us the game, but collectively they added up to a one-point loss.

Even with our mistakes, we were still ahead after fifty-nine minutes. But the game of football is sixty minutes long, and we came up one minute short. We needed to endure one more minute to win this game.

To a lesser group, this type of loss could have been monumental. It could have led to a cold season of doubt and defeat. But we learned an important lesson from this defeat: every NFL team is good enough to beat you if you don't pay attention to the details, avoid mistakes at critical times, and concentrate for an entire game. We learned that the difference between winning and losing can be as small as one play. We had to choose to bring ourselves together by sacrificing ourselves for the team. I think we learned these lessons so well that we were able to teach it to our next twelve opponents.

WEEK TWO: BALTIMORE COLTS

TEAM	1st	2nd	3rd	4th	FINAL
Baltimore	0	7	7	0	14
Minnesota	14	17	14	7	52

"Be Ready When Your Number's Called"

It was great to be back home with the Minnesota fans within the confines of Metropolitan Stadium. We had waited an entire year to get another crack at Baltimore. We lost to the Colts in a very tough, physical game in the 1968 Western Conference Championship game, 24–14. Some of the critics thought we were outmanned in that game. Those same critics also claimed that the Jets didn't stand a chance in Super Bowl III.

One year later, it was still the same NFL Champion Baltimore team that won fifteen games in 1968. They still had quarterback Johnny Unitas, defensive end Bubba Smith, and middle linebacker Mike Curtis. You might say the Colts had our number: in fourteen tries, our record against the Colts was 2–11–1. Baltimore came into this game with a perfect 6–0 preseason record, but they had also lost a close season opener. So, in a way, it was going to be a test to see who could bounce back from a disappointing loss and who was going to play a complete sixty-minute game.

During practice that week, we didn't spend any time dwelling on the loss to the Giants. Coach Grant told us a team must be able to look forward and play today's game, not last week's. I was sure that Cuozzo was going to start against the Colts. He had played an admirable game against the Giants, and as an understudy to Unitas for four years, he knew the Baltimore system and their weaknesses well.

But you have to be ready when your number is called. On Wednesday, Grant told the quarterbacks that I would be starting. I think I may have gotten the call because of my performance against Baltimore in the playoffs the year before. When Bud made the announcement, I started to say something to the effect that Gary had not been the reason for the Giants loss, but Grant cut me off cold—nothing to discuss. Being the champion he is, Gary was as encouraging to me as I had been to him. We all had the same goal: beat Baltimore. Forty for sixty!

After studying the film, we decided that we weren't going to win with a ball-control game or by trying to establish the run. Our game plan was simple: launch an all-out air attack. Every time we got our hands on the ball, we were going to put it up. We felt we could take advantage of the Colts' blitz and their overcommitment to play the run.

The plan started to come together early. On the fourth play after the opening kickoff, I hit Dave Osborn in the end zone for eighteen yards and a touchdown. Our defense quickly got the ball back. On our first play, like a lightning strike, Gene Washington caught a ten-yard pass and streaked past the defense for seventy-three yards and another touchdown. The game was still new, but we were ahead, 14–0.

The game settled into a defensive struggle until midway through the second quarter. After we fumbled at midfield, Earl Morrall completed two quick passes and the Colts were now down by only seven. But the game never got closer, and this would turn out to be the Colts' last gasp.

On the next series, we put together an eleven-play drive topped off by a twenty-one-yard scoring pass to Bob Grim. We followed that drive with a field goal and another touchdown pass to Kent Kramer. We left the field at halftime leading 31–7. The passing game was in high gear: we had completed eighteen of thirty passes for 306 yards and four touchdowns.

We obviously decided not to change anything at halftime. All week we planned to put the ball in the air for the entire sixty minutes. Back on the field, lightning struck for the fifth time on a forty-two-yard bomb to Gene Washington. With only two minutes gone in the second half, we were beating the NFL champions 38–7. We kept passing and added one more touchdown, and I went to the bench for what I thought was for the rest of game, leading 45–7.

By the fourth quarter, the Colts had been knocked out and our entire forty-man roster was getting a chance to join in the fun. I was back on the sidelines cheering my teammates, but my number came up again. Cuozzo had been knocked silly by the Colts' front four and I was forced onto the field again. (Later we found out that Cuozzo had sustained a broken nose.)

We quickly moved down to the fifteen-yard line, and I hit Jim Lindsey for a seventh touchdown pass. After that, Bob Lee came in to mop up on a 52–14 shellacking of the Colts. We weren't piling it on; we just didn't have any running plays in our game plan.

The all-out passing attack produced an overwhelming victory, which included tying a league record of seven touchdown passes in a single game. We also surpassed five team records: most points scored (52), most total yards (622), most passing yards (530), most first downs (34), and most pass completions (36). We gave out two game balls that day. I got one for the aerial circus and tackle; Doug Davis got the other for keeping Bubba Smith off my back.

In this game we proved to ourselves that we could beat anyone, including champions. A great plan came together at the right time. Our line dominated the pits. Grady Alderman, Milt Sunde, Mick Tingelhoff, Doug Davis, and Jim Vellone provided an impregnable pocket of safety for me to throw from. It was their effort and coordination that made the pass game more productive than it had ever been for the Vikings. The defensive unit created turnovers and gave us that opportunity to perform.

WEEK THREE: GREEN BAY PACKERS

TEAM	1st	2nd	3rd	4th	FINAL
Green Bay	0	0	0	7	7
Minnesota	6	7	3	3	19

Legends Die Hard

Every game in the "Black and Blue" Division was an all-out war with no prisoners taken. The three-time NFL Champion Packers still had legendary players. Under the tutelage of head coach Phil Bengtson, their proud team included players such as Bart Starr, Jim Taylor, Ray Nitschke, Paul Hornung, and Willie Davis. They were the team we feared most. We would play them twice, and we felt we had to beat them twice to win our division. They were still angry at us because we had dethroned them as Central Division Champions the year before.

After a win over a team like Baltimore, it's easy to get overconfident, to look too far down the road and forget the opponent right in front of you. We played this game at Memorial Stadium at the University of Minnesota. It was the first time a professional team ever had played a game in a Big Ten stadium. Met Stadium was a converted baseball stadium that was small by league standards. On the other hand, Memorial Stadium—called the Old Brickyard—is a classic horseshoe stadium that seated more than sixty-five thousand people. That put an extra fifteen thousand Vikings backers in the stands.

When you play a team as often as we played the Packers, you know each other's strengths and weaknesses too well to try to win with finesse or trick plays. Instead, you try to tee it up and play a head-to-head, bone-crunching game. We played this game with a controlled discipline that had been emblematic of the Packers themselves. This game belonged to the defense and our special teams.

On defense, the Purple People Eaters—Alan Page, Jim Marshall, Carl Eller, Gary Larsen, and Paul Dickson—lived up to their name by sacking Bart Starr eight times and recovering three fumbles. The Packers were continually stymied by mistakes and penalties in key third-down situations and just never seemed to get on track. The defense played a near-perfect game and came within five seconds of recording our first shutout.

In the Baltimore game, the offense hit on almost every big-play opportunity. In this game, the big play seemed to constantly dribble off our fingertips. I missed two long passes to Gene Washington that would have been sure touchdowns. Nevertheless, we were able to put together enough offense to pin the Packers on their side of the field. This was one of those unusual games where Bob Lee was never called on to punt. Fred Cox provided all the scoring we'd need. He kicked four field goals, two in each half.

The week before, we had learned that we could light up the scoreboard from any position on the field. We had the offensive firepower to beat anyone. Against Green Bay, we learned that our defense could dominate and win if we didn't make mistakes and beat ourselves. A great defense is aggressive and attacking in such a way that it creates chaos and confusion in the opposition's offense, which ultimately leads to victory. We won this game through the same controlled discipline that had created the Packers legend. Legends die hard, but we were going to be the next kings of the hill!

WEEK FOUR: AT CHICAGO BEARS

TEAM	1st	2nd	3rd	4th	FINAL
Minnesota	7	0	7	17	31
Chicago	0	0	0	0	0

Trust is a Team's Foundation

Our goal was to get better each week of the season. However, against Green Bay, we had made more mistakes than we had against Baltimore. A critical penalty or a missed assignment kept us from cashing in on numerous scoring opportunities. We knew the Bears weren't going to be as generous.

It was a rainy, gray, overcast day, perfect for playing the Monsters of the Midway. This meant we could get down in the muck and go eyeball to eyeball, mano a mano, to see who would flinch first. A typical Chicago game would make your muscles hurt for weeks.

When you prepare for the Bears, you practice all week for the blitz: in other words, Dick Butkus coming full speed, loaded for a Viking. After a week of practice, you could see him red-dogging in your sleep. The blitz is an all-out, big-play defensive maneuver. If the offense can't block it, it leads to big losses and a very long day. However, if the blocking is perfect, it creates the opportunity for a big offensive play.

Coach Burns and Coach Michaels showed us the film on Chicago's 4–3 overshift and blitz. In this formation, Butkus would slant and come all out. When this happens, a small crack can be opened up between guard and center. If the halfback can hit it at full speed, he'll have clear sailing to the end zone. This is what happened when Dave Osborn ran for a touchdown and left Butkus foaming at the mouth— described in more detail on page 67.

During the week, Mike Riley (a former Bear) was activated to replace an injured John Kirby at linebacker. Riley quickly became one of the forty when he blocked a punt and ran it back for a twenty-six-yard touchdown to put us into an early 7–0 lead. It was another example of every player finding a way to make a contribution. John Beaseley caught a touchdown in the second quarter to increase our lead.

For the rest of the first half, we hammered away at each other. The Bears found a way to stop Osborn and Clint Jones until the fourth quarter, when their combined thirty-five carries resulted in a touchdown for each man. Meanwhile, we found a way to stop Gale Sayers.

While the offense and special teams rolled up thirty-one points, it was the defense that really put on the pressure. They sacked Bears quarterbacks thirteen times and finally had their first shutout in the team's nine-year history.

We won this game because we had learned to believe in our coaches, our system, and ourselves. From this belief a bond of trust develops that every player is going to do his job on every play. All teamwork is based on trust: trust in yourself, your teammates, and the coaches. Trust is one person committed to others. It is a support pillar, firm and strong. Trust is based on understanding, time, respect, effort, honesty, and knowledge. The key ingredients are an openness and acceptance of others. Trust leads to cohesion with teammates and a confidence in leadership. Fidelity and reliance bond together as trust grows.

Talent is overrated—you win over the long haul with character and trust. Losing tests trust, and the outgrowth of nurtured trust is winning. All beginnings are difficult, but when trust develops, the team has no limits. Good coaches trust the game to the players because the players have trusted the coach during training and practice.

WEEK FIVE: AT ST. LOUIS CARDINALS

TEAM	1st	2nd	3rd	4th	FINAL
Minnesota	7	7	7	6	27
St. Louis	3	7	0	0	10

Every Game is a Big Game

The St. Louis Cardinals were a team the Vikings had never beaten in the regular season. On a player-by-player basis, they had as much talent as any team in the league, but they were torn by infighting and racial tension. They were a team affected by the societal problems of the late 1960s, and as a result, they never found a core strategy, system, or tempo to unify them. The Vikings, on the other hand, were able to insulate themselves to a degree that we were able to concentrate on football.

We had beaten St. Louis 41–13 in a preseason game on a hot August day in Memphis. We had beaten Baltimore in a romp and gone toe-to-toe with Green Bay and Chicago, and they had both flinched first, but St. Louis was not going to be easy.

Shortly before halftime, we were being severely tested. The Cardinals were leading 10–7 after St. Louis defensive tackle Bob Rowe intercepted a pass and ran it back seventeen yards for a touchdown. The Cardinals were moving the ball with short, quick passes that kept our defense from putting on the same kind of pressure they had in the last four games.

We'd run into a buzzsaw, and now our poise and confidence were being challenged. The Vikings had never won four games in a row. This could be the end of our streak. But championship teams don't panic; they know how to keep their cool and go out and do what has to be done.

Ed Sharockman was great at this. Before every game he'd get jittery, even physically sick. But with the opening kickoff, he was able to transform himself into an icy professional. He was emblematic of what we were becoming: professionals with power, poise, and purpose.

After falling behind, we responded with twenty consecutive points: two touchdown passes to John Henderson and two Fred Cox field goals. As the last field goal cleared the uprights to put us into a commanding 27–10 lead with only 1:58 left, I could hear Karl Kassulke yelling, "Do we sing tonight?" As true competitors, the songs are surely happier when you win. We didn't sing well, but we were starting to sing often.

Every win and every loss counts the same in the final standings. I think we learned that we had to concentrate on every game as though it was a big game, or our season would slip away. Our poise and our conviction carried us, and after five games we were 4–1. We were starting to build momentum. Each week that we played like a unified team, the tighter and stronger we became. We had learned another lesson, and we had overcome another hurdle.

Professionals realize there is a mindset that works in football games. It goes beyond the high spirits and getting "psyched." It's a cool, calm, confident aura that great teams exhibit in winning efforts. The Vikings were getting into a poised groove from which we controlled the energy and direction of the game. We were performing consistently.

WEEK SIX: DETROIT LIONS

TEAM	1st	2nd	3rd	4th	FINAL
Detroit	0	3	0	7	10
Minnesota	3	21	0	0	24

It Pays to Plan for Special Situations

The Detroit Lions came to the Met feeling they could whip us and be in position to win the division. We were 4–1 and the Lions were 3–2. Detroit was the fourth member of the Black and Blue Division, anchored by an aggressive defensive unit led by Alex Karras, Mike Lucci, Wayne Walker, and Lem Barney. On offense they featured All-Pro tight end Charlie Sanders, running back Nick Eddy, and quarterback Greg Landry.

It was an offensive and defensive war, but this was the day our special teams kept Detroit off balance, pinned back, and finally defeated. In the first half, Bob Lee punted the ball three times, pinning the Lions inside their twenty each time. Our kickoff coverage was the best it had been all season. On the kickoff returns, the Lions barely got past their own fifteen. To add to the Lions' poor field position, their punter Lem Barney had a heavily taped leg and, as a result, averaged only thirty-one yards on seven punts. To top it off, Clint Jones and Charlie West combined for 110 yards in punt and kickoff returns. We started almost every drive at midfield. Because of our special-teams play, Detroit had to play a great game to hold us to twenty-four points.

We took a lot of pride in our special-teams play. We practiced every possible special situation, and we used our best athletes on our punting, kicking, and return teams. Players with a little bit of madness and reckless abandon make the opposition think twice about returning a kick. Players such as Bill Harris, Dale Hackbart, Karl Kassulke, Jim Lindsey, and Mike McGill thrived on this type of play. We also let other teams know that if they made a mistake on special teams, we'd make them pay.

Throughout the season, we won games by blocking punts, recovering onside kicks, knocking down extra points, and running back kickoffs and punts for touchdowns. On many teams, kickers are outcasts. On our team, Fred Cox and Bob Lee were first-class citizens. When it's forty for sixty, everybody is part of the total team success. There are no special teams, only special situations. The coach said it, and we believed it.

Football is a game of territory and field position. The NFL puts a premium on specialization, especially in the kicking game. Like other parts of the game, kicking requires an adeptness and proficiency that are fluid and artistic. Snapper Mick Tingelhoff, holder Paul Krause, and kicker Fred Cox worked endless hours mastering the timing and developing a level of excellence that eliminated mistakes. This gave the entire team a high level of confidence every time the kicking team came onto the field.

Our defense played another stellar game for the fourth week in a row. The only touchdown Detroit scored came on a tough interference call on Earsell Mackbee late in the fourth quarter. Detroit got the ball on the nine, but it still took the Lions four plays to score. Nevertheless, Earsell got the game ball, partly for his aggressive play but also for his three interceptions.

In our second game with Detroit later in the season, the Lions again would find a way to beat themselves with poor special-teams play. Winning teams don't always have the punters who can boom the ball sixty yards or kickers who can kick fifty-yard field goals, but they all have a sure-handed return man, centers who can snap the ball perfectly, cover men who won't let the opposition escape, and holders who always give the kicker a fair shot. Great teams win on special teams, and they never beat themselves.

WEEK SEVEN: CHICAGO BEARS

TEAM	1st	2nd	3rd	4th	FINAL
Chicago	0	7	0	7	14
Minnesota	7	10	7	7	31

Fundamentals Pay Off

The Minnesota fans truly became our twelfth man during our seventh consecutive home sellout. Our sixth consecutive victory was cheered by 47,900 fans. It was perfect football weather for playing the Bears: forty degrees with light rain and a strong wind blowing from the North.

Chicago had been plagued with a series of bad breaks and strange plays all year. In our first game with the Bears, we'd blocked a punt for a touchdown, and they'd blocked a Fred Cox field-goal attempt that we caught and ran for a first down and eventually scored. We felt we weren't thirty-one points better than the Bears and that they would be the most physically punishing team we'd play all year. It was evident throughout the game that the Bears were feeling the pressure to win or die in the Central Division race. Part of their hope rested on Gale Sayers. This was his first real game after a severe knee injury and he managed to run for 116 yards, but he didn't seem like the Gale Sayers of old. It used to be if there were two men in the open field, he'd beat both of them; now he could beat only one.

In this game we played good, sound, fundamental football, while the Bears again made just enough mental mistakes to lose the game.

On Chicago's first possession, Paul Dickson submarined to stop Bears quarterback Bobby Douglass on fourth and one. We took over, but after two dropped passes our drive stalled. However, the Bears were called for running into the kicker and we responded with a twenty-yard scoring pass to Gene Washington.

In the second quarter, the Bears helped us get our second score. On a fifty-yard Fred Cox field goal attempt, the Bears were called for having twelve men on the field. This gave Freddy a second chance and he sailed it right through the uprights. We had scored ten points immediately after two mental mistakes by the Bears.

This game had its strange plays too. After the Bears' first touchdown, Clint Jones mishandled a short Mac Percival kickoff. The ball skidded and bounced away, and finally was covered by Charlie West in the end zone. The officials claimed that Jones had kicked the ball on the two-yard line, which is a fifteen-yard penalty. The Bears claimed that the penalty should be from the point of the infraction, which would give the Vikings the ball on the one. The officials, however, ruled that the infraction should be stepped off from the point from which the play originated. So the Bears had to kick again from the Vikings' forty-five. The ball sailed out of the end zone and the Vikings took possession on the twenty.

With just fifty-two seconds left in the half, the Bears made another key mistake. Bob Lee punted the ball to Cecil Turner, who was immediately hit by a bone-crunching tackle from Bill Harris. The ball sprang loose and was recovered by Bob Grim at the Bears thirteen-yard line. A quick pass to John Beasley, and we were ahead 17–7.

The Bears had made three fundamental mistakes that had immediately led to our seventeen points. On the other hand, we were playing a sound game on both offense and defense. We had built a winning streak by getting ahead and forcing the other team to pass. In the first seven games of the season, we had given up only six first-quarter points. That would allow us to put on an all-out pass rush that would wreak havoc and force more mistakes. The Bears had put themselves in a hole, which put the bull's-eye on Bobby Douglass's back. By the end of the game, he was sacked six times for a total loss of seventy-eight yards. The Bears' passing attack for the game netted only twenty-six yards.

The key offensive play that really opened up this game and quickly put us ahead 24–7 was a sweep by Clint "Cadillac" Jones. We knew we could run outside on the Bears if we executed perfectly. In the huddle, I called for a twenty-eight sweep on two. As Mick Tingelhoff snapped the ball, he fired off the line and knocked down the linebacker. Guards Jim Vellone and Milt Sunde pulled in unison to the left to create a running alley. Tackles Grady Alderman and Doug Davis fired straight out to neutralize the Bear rush, and tight end John Beasley moved down the field diagonally to seal off the Bears' secondary.

With everything working perfectly up front, the Cadillac took the handoff and sprinted through the open hole, out into the open, and down the sidelines for an eighty-yard touchdown. Good, sound, fundamental football had created the longest run in the NFL in the last five years.

The closest a team comes to perfection is when it acts as one mind, mastering the fundamentals and subduing misjudgment and miscues. We had succeeded in this quest, while the Bears had failed for the second time.

WEEK EIGHT: CLEVELAND BROWNS

TEAM	1st	2nd	3rd	4th	FINAL
Cleaveland	0	3	0	0	3
Minnesota	10	17	7	17	51

Planning and Positioning Leads to Excellence

After a big win over the Bears we were now 6–1, the best start in the club's history. The Bears had made a lot of mistakes, and it had cost them the game. Cleveland, on the other hand, were a championship-caliber team, and we knew they weren't going to beat themselves. This was a great Cleveland team that dominated the Eastern Conference year after year. The Browns featured an explosive offense built around wide receiver Paul Warfield and running back Leroy Kelly.

This was one of those rare Sundays when a plan comes together and every member of a team plays as one. We didn't award a game ball for this game; there were too many heroes. It was as close to a perfect game as possible. It was our seventh straight win, and it came against a team that we would later meet in the playoffs for the NFL Championship.

We got the game films for Cleveland really late that week, and it was almost time for us to get on the game bus before we were able to spot a weakness in Cleveland's defense. We noticed that on first down, the Cleveland corners would come up tight to be prepared to play the run. So we decided that the best way to beat Cleveland was to abandon the run and throw mid- and long-range passes on first down. The plan worked to perfection. In this game, the offense scored the first nine times it had the ball.

Drive 1	Fifty yards in six plays, sixteen-yard TD pass to Washington
Drive 2	Fifty-seven yards in five plays, thirty-two-yard Fred Cox field goal
Drive 3	Fifty-nine yards in eight plays, ten-yard TD pass to Washington
Drive 4	Seventy-eight yards in seven plays, twenty-eight-yard Fred Cox field goal
Drive 5	Fifty-three yards in eleven plays, one-yard TD pass to Washington
Drive 6	Seventy yards in eleven plays, five-yard TD run by Osborn

Drive 7   Eighty-five yards in fifteen plays, one-yard TD run by Jones

Drive 8   Eighty yards in eight plays, thirty-two-yard Fred Cox field goal

Drive 9   Three yards in two plays, two-yard TD run by Lindsey

The defense didn't spend much time on the field that day, but they were on long enough to intercept Bill Nelsen four times and hold Leroy Kelly to only twenty-four yards rushing. On special teams, Fred Cox was a perfect three for three on field goals, Charlie West had a fifty-five-yard punt return to set up a score, and lonely Bob Lee didn't get a chance to punt until the last minute of the game.

I've always been criticized for throwing wobbly passes that look like lame ducks. But it's important to remember that this game of football isn't figure skating. There are no style points. You only get points for touchdowns. In this game, I threw a two-handed shovel pass and an alley-oop pass, both for scores. On the other hand, I have thrown some really tight spirals in my life—and both of them were intercepted.

This game sent a message to the league: "The Vikings are for real and this team will not beat itself."

When a young player chooses to dedicate his time and energy to football, he always has the vision of playing the perfect game, every assignment carried out with unbroken perfection. This game was close to that dream, almost like catching the perfect fish in Hemingway's *The Old Man and the Sea* or finding the perfect pearl in Steinbeck's *The Pearl*. After three years of developing team communication and leadership, the team had come to full blossom in this game.

WEEK NINE: AT GREEN BAY PACKERS

TEAM	1st	2nd	3rd	4th	FINAL
Minnesota	3	0	3	3	9
Green Bay	0	7	0	0	7

Life Can Be Trouble

Some days the Vikings would soar, and on other days we would crawl, strive, and struggle for every inch of territory. This game was a reminder of how quickly perfection fades. This game was clawing and cruel, like a gang fight for turf. It was obvious that the Packers hadn't read our press clippings from the week before. They knew us too well to believe we could manhandle them as we did Cleveland. They wanted to prove to us that life can be trouble.

Green Bay started the game blitzing and using a stunting five-man defensive line. The Packers' pressure kept us off balance, and except for a short field goal, all we could do was trade possessions throughout the first quarter.

Midway through the second quarter, Jim Marshall fell on a Bart Starr fumble deep inside Green Bay territory. Trying for the score, I threw a pass that was intercepted by safety Doug Hart, who raced eighty-five yards for a touchdown to put the Packers ahead 7–3.

Toward the end of the first half, Karl Kassulke blocked a Mike Mercer field-goal attempt to put us in good field position. It turned out to be an important play in determining the final score.

Bud felt we needed to try something different at this point, so he pulled me out of the game and put in Gary Cuozzo. On a lot of teams, benching a quarterback can create a quarterback controversy, but Bud handled it well. He said that no one would have questioned a baseball manager for pulling a pitcher on a bad day. Sometimes a change can give a team the spark it needs, and unlike in baseball, you can always put the starter back in.

Later in the third quarter, Bud's judgment came under question when he decided to kick a field goal from fourth and a foot at the Packers' five-yard line when we were down 7-3. In a game where scoring opportunities were rare, the fans felt this might be our only chance to score. But Bud was prepared for this type of situation and knew what he wanted to do.

It was only the second time all year that we would enter the fourth quarter trailing. On our first possession we were able to move the ball down to the Green Bay twenty and kick a field goal for a slim 9-7 lead. As the minutes ticked off the clock, we were holding on for dear life. It was time for some extra courage to pull out a win. Bart Starr had driven the Packers down inside the Vikings' five-yard line with less than two minutes to play. Bobby Bryant, the NFL's leading interceptor with eight, stepped up to provide what we needed by picking off a Bart Starr pass to seal the victory.

We were one play away from losing a game in the last seconds of play. After a blowout win against Cleveland, this game was a good reminder of why it's important to play a full sixty minutes. Life can be trouble. Any competitive effort requires dealing with problems, and recognition of that fact puts you in position to make important decisions. Bud made the tough decision to go for the field goal on fourth down. He was confident that our defense would hold up for the full sixty minutes and the offense would come up with the winning points—even if the game went into extra innings with a relief pitcher.

We were now on an eight-game winning streak, which was the longest ever by an expansion team. If we were able to beat Detroit the next time around, we would be the first team to have a Central Division sweep.

WEEK TEN: PITTSBURGH STEELERS

TEAM	1st	2nd	3rd	4th	FINAL
Pittsburgh	0	7	7	0	14
Minnesota	7	10	14	21	52

Every Player Counts

Pittsburgh was a team that was struggling to find its identity and chemistry. The Steelers were about at the stage we were at in 1967, and they soon would find the players and the leadership they would need to become a dominant team in the 1970s—but it wouldn't happen this day.

Bud showed his confidence in me by letting me start this game, even after Gary had led us to a victory over the Packers. But it just wasn't my day. Part of a quarterback's job is to know when to take risks and when to play it safe. In the first quarter of this game, I tried to force the ball downfield and threw three interceptions.

I wasn't getting the job done. I felt the way a pitcher feels when he just doesn't have his good stuff. I told Bud that I thought the team might be better on this day with Gary at the helm. For the second straight week, Gary came off the bench to direct the Vikings to our ninth straight victory.

It was a wild game where big plays on offense, defense, and special teams led to another lopsided score. The Vikings drew first blood when Paul Krause stepped in front of a Terry Hanratty pass and ran it back for a seventy-seven-yard touchdown. Then we quickly struck again for a field goal to make the score 10–0.

Pittsburgh was not to be outdone. On the ensuing kickoff, Don McCall broke loose at the five-yard line and ran 101 yards with a kickoff return. This was the first time since Bud Grant came to Minnesota that a team was able to return a kickoff for a score against the Vikings. As a result of this kickoff return, Fred Cox started kicking line drives on the ground. By a strange twist of fate, three of these kicks hit line-men on the first line of defense, and we recovered two of them. This really kept Pittsburgh deep in its own end and on the defense.

We ended the first half with a perfectly executed two-minute drill. We took the ball sixty-nine yards in eleven plays capped off with a one-yard run by Bill Brown. This gave us a more comfortable lead of 17–7 going into the locker room. We added another touchdown at the start of the second half and seemed to be pulling away at 24–7.

Midway through the third quarter, and we had just forced Pitts-burgh to punt. Pittsburgh's punter, Bobby Walden, lofted a punt that landed short and took a wicked hop that hit Bobby Grim, and the Steelers recovered the fumble on our fourteen. Three plays later, the score was 24–14.

As Pittsburgh kicked off, disaster almost struck again. Charlie West took the ball on the fourteen and dashed out to the forty, where a pad-popping tackle sent the ball into the air. An alert John Beasley grabbed the fumble in midair and rumbled sixty yards for a touch-down. Instead of the score being 24–21, it was 31–14, and we had bro-ken Pittsburgh's spirit.

Oscar Reed scored two fourth-quarter touchdowns, and Bob Lee came in to throw a last-minute score to John Henderson. It was a 52–14 victory, and every man had made a contribution. This was the third time this season we had scored more than fifty points. But unlike the Baltimore and Cleveland games, we didn't dominate the game until late in the fourth quarter, and our big plays came on special teams rather than on long drives.

This was a game in which every man counted and every man seemed to be making the big play when it was needed. All three quarterbacks played, and five different players scored touchdowns. Fred Cox and Dale Hackbart each recovered an onside kick, and Paul Krause, Ed Sharockman, and Roy Winston each had interceptions.

A winning organization is just like change itself. Sometimes it takes years to develop, and other times in a quixotic moment it jumps up and happens. In both cases, the right ingredients must be blended and fused in the right situation. The Pittsburgh Steelers' time was yet to come. They would win four Super Bowls in the 1970s, when the last few pieces of the puzzle were in place.

For now, in 1969, the Vikings were much further ahead in their development, but you had the idea that even with the lopsided score Pittsburgh was going somewhere, mostly because of the young players who played with dedication and enthusiasm. We won because of our experience, team unity, and a common feeling that this was our year.

WEEK ELEVEN: AT DETROIT LIONS

TEAM	1st	2nd	3rd	4th	FINAL
Minnesota	7	3	7	10	27
Detroit	0	0	0	0	0

There Are Some Things You Can't Control

We all like to think we can control our own destinies and that we can overcome every obstacle through hard work and perseverance. My old high school coach Al Lewis taught us that luck happens when opportunity meets preparation. But even within that philosophy, it's important to recognize that there are some things you just can't control. You accept them and make the best of the situation. If you've ever been stuck in a Los Angeles traffic jam at rush hour or circling O'Hare Airport in Chicago for an hour waiting to land, you know what I mean. Playing in an outdoor stadium, there's one thing you just can't control: the weather.

It was Thanksgiving Day, and we were about to play Detroit for the Central Division Championship. We were 9–1 and Detroit was 7–3. A victory would clinch the Central Division Championship for the second straight year. We arrived in Detroit with only three days' rest from the Pittsburgh game. It was Lake Michigan cold, and the field was covered with snow. Even for the most dedicated and motivated players this was no one's idea of fun, but teams must constantly play through drudgery and hardship.

Cold-weather and bad-weather games are different; they can feel like playing on eggshells. Everything slows down, yet you can't let the elements interfere with your concentration and execution. If you let the weather bother you, you'll start to rationalize and make excuses for poor performance. The weather soon becomes "I don't feel good" or "My jersey is too tight" or "My biorhythms are off." You can't control the weather, so you have to forget about it and play your game.

In bad conditions, a defense has an opportunity to take over and control the game, and our defense did just that. Midway through the first quarter, the Lions were backed up in their own end and forced to punt. Paul Dickson broke through the line and blocked the punt to set up the offense on the Lions' sixteen. Three plays later, Ozzie dove over from the one for the game's first score.

At the end of the first half, the Lions mounted a long sixteen-play drive, taking them inside our twenty. With twelve seconds left, they lined up for a field goal, and this time Carl Eller reached up and blocked the kick. It seemed that the Lions' holder was confused about where to spot the ball, and the placement was too close to the line.

After exchanging the ball for most of the third quarter, Nick Eddy tried to run around right end and fumbled, and Jim Marshall recovered on the Lions' twenty-three. Five plays and a six-yard pass to Oscar Reed later, and we were moving away at 17–0. The Lions were letting the weather get to them. They just weren't able to execute on the icy field, and we were taking advantage of every opportunity.

The final straw came in the fourth quarter, when Alan Page forced a fumble and Jim Marshall picked it up and started running through the snow toward the end zone. As Marshall was about to be tackled, he lateraled back to Page for a forty-five-yard scoring play. The snow was so heavy at this point that you could hardly see the players, but Page and Marshall, in the spirit of true Norsemen, made it look as though they were having more fun the worse the weather got.

By the end of the game, our defense and the weather had taken most of the fight out of the Lions. We were trying to control the ball in the fourth quarter to preserve our defense's hard-earned shutout. I noticed that the Lions' defensive ends were beginning to lose leverage by letting the weather dictate their footwork, so I called for an end sweep. Without telling anyone, I kept the ball and ran by the defensive end, who had lost containment, for a key first down that kept our defensive unit off the field.

Detroit tried one last time to break the shutout with four seconds to play. But our special teams were determined not to let it happen. The game ended as we blocked our third kick, a nineteen-yard field-goal attempt.

There are things you can't control, like the weather, which means you need to pay attention to those elements that you can. This means working on the fundamentals, such as footwork and being more exacting in the execution of your assignments. The preparation will pay off in good luck and an opportunity fulfilled.

In 1969, the Vikings became a team without any real weaknesses. If there were any holes, they were quickly plugged by someone moving forward to assume the responsibility. Our cocaptains Jim Marshall and Grady Alderman exhibited a quiet fire that raised and motivated our level of play on this day. Our team captains led the way by demonstrating a commitment and stubbornness not to let anything, including the elements, stand in our way. Everyone was ready to participate to the fullest because of Jim and Grady's leadership.

WEEK TWELVE: AT LOS ANGELES RAMS

TEAM	1st	2nd	3rd	4th	FINAL
Minnesota	7	10	0	3	20
Los Angeles	0	3	3	7	13

It's Not Good to be Alone, Even in Paradise

After being snowbound in Detroit, the palm trees and bright lights of Hollywood can seem like paradise. It's a natural reaction when you get off the plane in Los Angeles to put on your dark glasses and pretend you're safe and secure. Despite the warm weather and the Hollywood glitz, we knew we were here for mortal combat. But it's not good to be alone, even in paradise. Friendship creates a closeness that crosses all obstacles. Each becomes better through each other. One is none! Through the courage of fighting battles together, the Vikings had become a team of friends. We had developed a sense of fairness and empathy for each other. If one hurt, we all bled. If one succeeded, we all cheered. This type of camaraderie generates a force of goodwill that pervades the whole team.

In California, I was back among family and friends. I'd procured tickets to the game for half of East Los Angeles, and we were set to bash it out with the Rams in a preview of the Western Conference Championship Game. We entered the game with a ten-game winning streak, and the Rams were rolling with an eleven-game winning streak. One streak had to end. It was the Purple People Eaters versus the Fearsome Foursome. I knew that this would be a physically brutal game. In my first game as a Viking in 1967, the Rams mauled and pummeled us 39–3. The Fearsome Foursome, led by Deacon Jones and Merlin Olsen, each took one of my legs and treated me like a chicken bone—making a wish at my expense.

The Rams were a solid veteran team with an awesome defense and an explosive offense that featured supertalented quarterback Roman

Joe in his mother's arms in Santa Fe, New Mexico, 1938.

Joe's mother, Florencia Eufracia Garcia Kapp, in 1971.
Her kids called her Flo, and she called herself Florence.

The Hart High School football team, 1954. Coach Al Lewis is at the top.
The varsity roster: J. Percivalle, B. Woodson, D. Garcia, J. Pryde, L. Webb,
B. Wertz, T. Wood, B. Keahy, B. Jones, J. Fisher, R. Lee, G. Neighbors,
D. Bovee, D. Fields, J. Wyse, R. Boyle, S. Garret, G. Darr, J. Kapp,
B. Harper, G. Cox, R. Howard, L. Nicholson, L. Nutter, O. Pascoe,
J. Lotspeich, G. Haggart, M. Scannel, D. March, R. Moore, J. Wise,
D. Tibbets, T. Keck, R. Stoneceipher.

The Cal football team, 1958 Pacific Coast Conference (PCC) champions. This was the last team from Cal to play in the Rose Bowl.

Front row: Bob Duey, Pete Domoto, Ken Meade, Jim Ferguson, Bob Kinney, Emerson Byrd, Grover Garvin, Ted Dinkler, Terry Jones, Jack Hart, Joe Kapp, Hank Olguin.

Second row: Tom Cloutier, Steve Bates, Jim Burress, Bob Cox, Jerry Bogue, Don Piestrup, Jack Yerman, Jerry Lundgren, Pat Newell, Andy Segale, Walt Arnold, Mike Prado, Frank Doretti.

Third row: Tony Perrin, Roland Lasher, Henry Giudice, Dick Bertero, Bill Cooper, Dick Carlson, Dennis Wiegand, Wayne Crow, Jim Green, Charlie Holston, John Michael, Gael Barsotti.

Top row: Tim McLaughlin, Bob Carlson, Van Kecklin, Bill McComb, Ed Burns, Larry Parque, Bob Gonzales, Charlie Johnson, Bill Streshly, Gret Thomas, Frank Sally, Doug Furuta, Tom Bates, Dave George, Skip Huber.

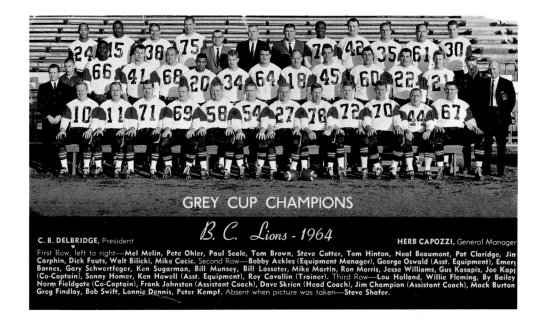

GREY CUP CHAMPIONS

B. C. Lions - 1964

C. B. DELBRIDGE, President   **HERB CAPOZZI**, General Manager

First Row, left to right—**Mel Melin, Pete Ohler, Paul Seale, Tom Brown, Steve Cotter, Tom Hinton, Neal Beaumont, Pat Claridge, Jim Carphin, Dick Fouts, Walt Bilicki, Mike Cacic.** Second Row—**Bobby Ackles (Equipment Manager), George Oswald (Asst. Equipment), Emery Barnes, Gary Schwertfeger, Ken Sugarman, Bill Munsey, Bill Lasseter, Mike Martin, Ron Morris, Jesse Williams, Gus Kasapis, Joe Kapp (Co-Captain), Sonny Homer, Ken Howell (Asst. Equipment), Roy Cavallin (Trainer).** Third Row—**Lou Holland, Willie Fleming, By Bailey, Norm Fieldgate (Co-Captain), Frank Johnston (Assistant Coach), Dave Skrien (Head Coach), Jim Champion (Assistant Coach), Mack Burton, Greg Findlay, Bob Swift, Lonnie Dennis, Peter Kempf.** Absent when picture was taken—**Steve Shafer.**

British Columbia Lions football team, 1964 Grey Cup champions.

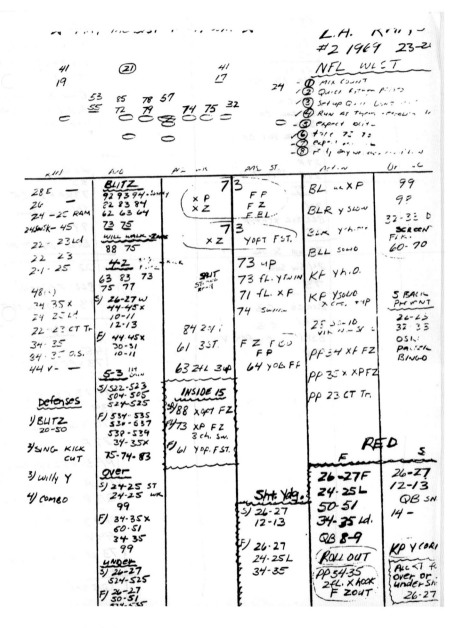

Joe's homemade play sheet in preparation
for the 1969 LA Rams playoff game.

FRONT ROW: John Beasley, Alan Page, Paul Dickson, Jim Marshall, Carl Eller, Ron Yary, Steve Smith, Gary Larsen, Doug Davis

SECOND ROW: Larry Nelson, ass't. trainer, Ed White, Earsell Mackbee, Bob Lee, Milt Sunde, Paul Krause, Jim Hargrove, Grady Alderman, Jim Lindsay, Mike McGill.

THIRD ROW: Jim Eason, equipment mgr., Gary Cuozzo, coach Jack Patera, coach Bob Hollway, coach Jerry Burns, head coach Bud Grant, coach Bus Mertes, coach John Michels, Mick Tingelhoff, Bobby Bryant, Bookie Bolin.

FOURTH ROW: Fred Zamberletti, trainer, Mike Reilly, Joe Kapp, Jim Vellone, Gene Washington, Kent Kramer, Dale Hackbart, John Henderson, Lonnie Warwick, Wally Hilgenberg.

FIFTH ROW: Ray Earley, ass't. equipment mgr., Oscar Reed, Bob Grim, Ed Sharockman, Karl Kassulke, Dave Osborn, Bill Harris, Clint Jones, Roy Winston, Bill Brown, Charlie West, Fred Cox.

Minnesota Vikings football team, 1969 NFL champions.

Joe drops back versus the Chicago Bears, 1969.

Joe barks out signals, 1969.

"Hey, you're offsides, Lions!" 1969.

A 1939 LaSalle, the official limo of the 1969 Vikings.

Joe Kapp, Alan Page, Jim Marshall, and Carl Eller in 1992.

Joe and Burt Reynolds during production of *The Longest Yard*, 1973.

Cal's Kevin Moen crashes into the Stanford Band at the end of the Play, 1982.

Gabriel and wide receiver Jack Snow. To beat the Rams, we felt we had to accomplish three things: minimize mistakes, control the ball, and eliminate LA bombs.

The Rams entered this game leading the league with forty-seven sacks, and they also hadn't given up a touchdown in three games. We knew that if we were going to have any success throwing the ball, our offensive line had to control the line of scrimmage. The line responded with their best game of the season by neutralizing their front four. Coach John Michaels called the offensive line hogs because good linemen always root, dig, drive, and keep their wide bodies close to the ground.

We won the toss and elected to receive. Charlie West took the opening kickoff seventy-eight yards, just to remind the Rams not to drop their guard. Our offensive line took over and ripped open big holes in the LA front. We ran four successive running plays, topped off by a four-yard touchdown run by Dave Osborn.

In the second quarter, we managed to put together a long eleven-play drive for a touchdown and a fourteen-point lead. Then both teams traded field goals to make the score 17–3 at halftime. We were winning this game on the ground, and we were controlling the ball. Bill Brown was ripping through the line and was averaging almost seven yards a carry.

Our running game dominated the second half as well. We were keeping the ball away from the Rams and eating up the clock. As a team, we rushed for almost two hundred yards, averaging almost 4.5 yards per carry. We had only seventy-two yards passing, but that was all we needed.

Not to be left out of the action, I had a chance to run with the ball five times, including an eighteen-yard run where I used safety Richie Petitbon as a low hurdle. The critics liked my running style about as well as they liked my artistic passing. Jim Murray of the *LA Times* said I had the gracefulness of Dagwood Bumstead trying to catch a bus.

But again, it's the results that count; football is a game of substance. Style doesn't matter if you get the job done.

The game was a struggle for physical advantage and psychological supremacy. During the game, I fully realized that people who have been through the fire together have a bond and friendship that never waver. An energy is created when every person from the ball boy to the owner, from substitute to head coach, must devote and give themselves entirely to the team. Otherwise the team is lessened and held back. Making a commitment and fulfilling it with friends is an exhilarating and enduring experience.

WEEK THIRTEEN: SAN FRANCISCO 49ERS

TEAM	1st	2nd	3rd	4th	FINAL
San Francisco	0	0	0	7	7
Minnesota	0	3	0	7	10

Remember, There Ain't No Santa Claus

Our record was now 11–1, and we were Central Division Champions for the second straight year. It would have been nice to celebrate with an easy game in front of the home crowd. But Vikings aren't meant to play in the sun and the warm ocean breeze, or to get an early Christmas present. Games like the 49ers game help you realize that there ain't no Santa Claus, and there ain't no red-nosed reindeer. You can't expect gifts. Nobody gives you anything in the arena. You have to take the responsibility to get it yourself.

Just before we took the field, the flamethrowers were out trying to clear off the yard markers. The weather at game time was a snowy nineteen degrees, and it was predicted to get worse as the game progressed. Groundskeeper Dick Erickson and his crew did an excellent job of making the grass field playable, but it was going to be a hard day at the office.

We decided to rely on our rushing attack that had worked so well in the Rams game. We felt that in these conditions, running the ball would be the best way to eliminate mistakes. San Francisco, on the other hand, felt it could take advantage of the poor footing to launch an aerial attack. The 49ers' quarterback, Steve Spurrier, threw for 279 yards. They were throwing a lot of quick outs in front of the corners, believing that the corners couldn't react in time to stop the play.

Through three quarters, it looked as if no one was going to score. We had managed a field goal, but we were barely hanging onto that 3–0 lead. Even in the snow, we knew we could always rely on Fred Cox. He knew how to handle the responsibility of his position and never wavered when the game was on the line. You simply can't win games in the fourth quarter without a responsible kicker like Fred.

At the start of the fourth quarter, the snow had eased up and Spurrier put the ball up eight consecutive times, including a six-yard touchdown pass to put us behind 7–3. On the next series, we came right back. A quick pass to Beasley for fourteen yards put us at midfield. As we came up to the line for the next play, I noticed that they had single coverage on Gene Washington. The play was supposed to be another pass to Beasley, but I never looked at him once. I just dropped back and let it fly. Gene caught the pass on the twenty, about ten yards behind the 49ers defender. He raced into the end zone for a fifty-two-yard score. It was his first touchdown catch in three games, but it came when we needed it.

Earsell Mackbee decided to play Santa Claus and make this win our early Christmas present. He stopped San Francisco's next drive by recovering a fumble, then stopped them again with a brilliant interception and a thirty-eight-yard return. We might not have believed in Santa Claus, but we did believe in players such as Earsell Mackbee, Fred Cox, and Gene Washington.

WEEK FOURTEEN: AT ATLANTA FALCONS

TEAM	1st	2nd	3rd	4th	FINAL
Minnesota	3	0	0	0	3
Atlanta	0	7	3	0	10

Save for a Rainy Day

We left the snow and cold for Atlanta and the sunny south. We'd always rather play at home, but a little warm weather in December can be a welcome relief. When we took the field, though, the sun was gone and it was a miserable thirty-four degrees, and the rain was turning to ice as it hit the ground.

Bill Brown said this was the coldest game he ever played. Bob Berry said the same thing. You can imagine how cold the rest of us were if Brownie was cold. It was the combination of rain and low temperatures that made this game unbearable. The minute you were hit, you'd be knocked into a pool of water that would freeze to your jersey as you got up. Bill was in the shower for half an hour after the game trying to get his feet to turn from blue to pink.

More than just the bad weather was waiting for us; former Vikings Norm Van Brocklin, Bob Berry, and Paul Flatley were eager for a chance to beat up on their old friends. The weather was the same for both teams, but in the muddy conditions we fumbled five times—despite only fumbling nine times in the previous thirteen games combined—and threw up three interceptions.

Atlanta did a better job holding onto the ball than we did. The Falcons fumbled only twice and had one interception, but our defense shut them down, allowing only 111 yards total offense. The game-winning play happened midway through the second quarter. I was hit and the ball popped loose. Claude Humphrey picked up the loose fumble and ran twenty-four yards for the game's only touchdown. We let this game slip and slide away, losing 10–3.

When you put so much into a game it always hurts when you lose, but we had wins in the bank. To have a reserve gives a team the opportunity to get through the tough times. We had won our division and were headed for the playoffs for the second year in a row. We were beginning to believe we belonged there. We had improved each game during the season. We had the momentum of a twelve-game winning streak.

The Vikings' regular season ended the way it began—with an unexpected loss. Bud Grant was asked if he thought this loss was going to affect the team in the playoffs. He said, "It might have an effect on a high school or college team, but this is a professional team. This team will approach the game pretty much with the same state of mind as they have all along. They'll put out 100 percent."

The Vikings played hard in every minute of every game because we were a team of pride and honor. We had a strong feeling of self-worth and pride in what we had accomplished in fourteen games. We had adhered to our principles and values, and they had taken us through both good and bad times. In the end, we were all winners because of what we had done together.

A SEASON TO REMEMBER

In looking back over these fourteen league games, I feel again the satisfaction that came with our second division championship. Our team had demonstrated group development and growth, but also the attainment of the primary hallmarks of excellence. We reflected self-worth, integrity, and wisdom as individuals and as a unit. The team values and lessons learned along the way led to a quiet confidence, inner strength, and stability.

We learned how to function as a forty-man unit. Every man had a role to play and was ready when his number was called. Game after game, different players came to the front to make a key block, run, or interception that turned the tide in our favor. But even more important, different individuals came forward to lead us with a demonstration of their key values. Bill Brown showed us what it meant to be tough. Paul Dickson showed us what loyalty and friendship meant. Bobby Bryant portrayed courage on every play. Alan Page taught us how to be resourceful.

We also learned how to play a complete sixty-minute game. We had learned how to come out of the locker room prepared to play and to take an early lead. We learned how to maintain a lead in the fourth quarter and how to come from behind when it was needed. We were like a relentless prizefighter who would keep coming for fifteen rounds.

This was the type of season most teams can only dream about. We were 12–2, but we were only a few ticks of the clock and seven points short of a perfect 14–0 season. We had taken on the NFL's best—Baltimore, Cleveland, and Los Angeles—and we had knocked each one of them out before the final gun. Our success was a living testament to what a team can accomplish when forty individuals play as one.

CHAPTER SIXTEEN

THE PLAYOFFS

The Frozen Battles
for New Orleans

THE ROAD MAP

Once a team reaches the playoffs, becoming Super Bowl champions requires winning three straight games against the best teams in the world. At this level, every team has great talent, good coaching, and a strong organization. Their team unity and goals have been tested under fire, and they have all come up winners. Unfortunately, all but one of these teams will lose one game. Every game is sudden death.

The 1969 playoffs were packed with experienced teams. In the AFL, the teams that played in the first three Super Bowls were back again. Kansas City and Oakland, losers of Super Bowls I and II to Green Bay, were on top at the end of the season. The New York Jets were the defending world champions and winners of Super Bowl III. In the NFL, Dallas, Cleveland, and Minnesota were back for a second try, along with a strong Los Angeles Rams team.

I had the opportunity to compete for Canada's Grey Cup, the Super Bowl, and the Rose Bowl. From this experience, I have learned that the team that comes out on top in a three-game playoff series is the team that can accomplish five keys to success.

1. *Sustain momentum*

Teams can play on their emotions and rise to a peak to win one game, but it's almost impossible to keep the adrenaline pumping all out for three weeks and three games. The players can't go out there and "win one for the Gipper" week after week. A winning team finds a rhythm or pace that helps them sustain their momentum. Each player has to find the right tempo and routine for himself. Victory at this level requires patience, poise, self-confidence, and endurance.

2. *Play error free*

The better teams know how to make their opponents pay for their mistakes. The team that doesn't throw interceptions, doesn't fumble, doesn't miss tackles, and doesn't blow assignments will always win. In each of our three playoff games in 1969, the team that played with the least number of errors won the game.

This striving for security can often lead to some very conservative game plans. Both teams come out of the locker room determined not to make a mistake. They're so cautious it looks like dancing teddy bears. However, when you play with top-level competition, you often have to take a risk or go for the big play in order to make something happen. It's a matter of being alert for the right opportunity and having the good judgment to know when to take a risk and when to throw the ball away to safety.

3. *Keep focused*

Playoffs quickly become a media circus, which intensifies after each round. Obscure players become celebrities and all-pro players become gods. It becomes difficult, if not impossible, to keep daily routines, get in a normal week of practice, and focus on the task at hand. Maintaining balance and concentration in this environment is particularly difficult.

Most teams need to experience the pressures of a playoff at least once before they are able to grasp the brass ring. Teams such as Dallas,

Kansas City, Oakland, Baltimore, and Miami all lost in the Super Bowl before they were able to win.

4. Stay healthy

By the time a team gets to the playoffs, they've already played twenty games between preseason and the regular season. There isn't a player on any team who isn't bruised and battered. At this point, the trainer and the team doctor become as important as a quarterback and a fullback. Trainer Fred Zamberletti and Dr. Don Lannin did an outstanding job of keeping us all up and walking. It's a lot like having a good shade-tree mechanic who knows how to keep an old '57 Chevy running with baling wire and chewing gum.

It's also interesting that teams that play all out on every play tend to be the healthiest teams. When you don't let up, you usually are the one delivering the blow rather than taking it, and you seldom get hit by surprise. Nevertheless, it still takes great spirit, proper training, and good fortune to have forty players ready to play sixty minutes of NFL playoff football.

5. Get the ball to bounce the right way

A football is a strange object that bounces unpredictably, wobbles when you throw it, floats like a knuckleball in the wind, and squirts around when a thousand pounds of beef drop on it. We play on ice, in snow, in mud, and even sometimes on carpet. Sometimes they paint the lines too high and it's easy to trip over them.

What I'm trying to say is that the game of football isn't an absolute; it's a game of chance and a gamble at best. There is a certain randomness, like the spin of a roulette wheel or a toss of the dice, that can turn happiness into sorrow, glory into embarrassment, and victory into defeat. However, great teams are always ready and prepared when the ball does bounce their way. When an opportunity presents itself, they seize it and use it to their advantage.

SIXTY MINUTES: THE MOMENT OF TRUTH ARRIVES

"Truth is the cry of all, but the game of a few."

—George Berkeley

In the arena, the clock can be a relentless opponent or a friendly ally. As each second ticks away, an opportunity is made or gone forever. Every player and every team has the choice to play all out for sixty minutes. It takes courage, endurance, experience, poise, and loyalty to play a complete game. It doesn't just happen. The moment becomes our yardstick of success and failure. In football, life is upon us. It coerces us to be urgent. There is only here and now, no delays, no rain checks. We are like cannonballs propelled point blank. The hour of the Rams and the Vikings was upon us.

Every player must face the truth and reality of time. A player's career is short, and there are only a limited number of chances to win a championship; there are only so many big games. Football is a physically competitive business, and every player needs to understand that every game could be his last. No one is immortal. When you fully understand this fact about time, you learn how to go full out with reckless abandon and to savor every minute of every game. There's no point in playing the game or working at the game of football if you're just "putting in your time" for a paycheck.

Time also has a way of creating champions. In any sport, the players who want the ball in the closing seconds of a big game, who take charge and make the big play when the game's on the line, become the heroes. As kids we idolized these players and repeated the big game over and over. It was the bottom of the ninth, the seventh game of the World Series, the bases were loaded, and the count at three balls and two strikes. It was the twenty-foot jump shot at the buzzer to win the NCAA basketball championship. It was the eighteenth hole at Augusta National with a four-foot putt to win the Masters. We had played in a playoff game the year before against Baltimore and had come up losers. As a team, they made the big plays in the pinch. We had been there once, and now we knew what it would take to win.

Our strategy throughout the 1969 season was to make sure that we were as close as possible going into the fourth quarter. We knew we were going to play the last fifteen minutes as hard as we possibly could, and our opponents quickly found out that a fifty-nine-minute effort would leave them a yard short at the end.

The recipe for a great game is a lot like making good salsa. It has to be a careful blend of spice, heat, and sweetness. Great games are morality plays that reveal real-life lessons. In Super Bowl III, the Jets and the Colts replayed the story of David and Goliath with a modern dash of spice, but no less surprise.

Our first playoff game against the Los Angeles Rams was a different kind of story, a story of two heavyweights standing toe-to-toe in the snow waiting to see who would blink first. Like Frazier and Ali, the title would be awarded to the one who was still standing at the final bell.

All the elements for a great game were there. The teams had finished the regular season with the two best records in the NFL. We were 12–2, and the Central Division champions and the Rams were 11–3 and the Coastal Division champions. Both teams featured awesome defenses. The game could have been a horror film entitled *The Fearsome Foursome Meets the Purple People Eaters*. The defense that smelled blood first would win.

On offense, we featured a balanced attack that led the NFL in scoring. The Rams played a more wide-open style directed by Roman Gabriel, who won the NFL's Most Valuable Player award that year. The Rams and the Vikings were dangerous teams that had big-play people on defense, offense, and special teams. All in all, a great matchup.

If there was an element of revenge, it belonged to the Rams. We'd beaten them in the regular-season game in Los Angeles sunshine to break their eleven-game winning streak. Gabriel made an interesting comment about the first game when he said that "the Rams' offense didn't go for the full sixty, we sputtered in the second half." Both teams had lost their last game of the regular season after they had won their division, but the money was already in the bank. Now it was time to cash in.

The week before the game, most of the press focused on the weather. The forecast was for temperatures in the teens with a possibility of snow. Could the Rams make the transition from Malibu Beach to the Arctic? It makes for good reading, but I don't think cold weather makes all that much difference for an experienced team. To prepare us for the cold, Bud Grant told us stories of how the Eskimos kept warm up on the D.E.W. line.

Cold weather does slow the pace of the game, and it tends to keep the score down. Every hit stings a little bit more, and it's a little bit harder to catch your breath. The cold is a test of endurance. The winner can be decided in the fourth quarter when one team is thinking about football and the other team is thinking about keeping warm.

Preparation

We had a normal week of practice, keeping the tempo of the regular season intact. We all realized that it was too early to start celebrating. This week everyone was a little more serious and a little bit more courteous. I think we all knew what had to be done and wanted to give everyone a chance to prepare for the game in his own way. There is a concentration needed to bring a total convergence of energy into one effort. You can feel a sense of purpose.

Because of the cold weather during the week, our practice site was moved to the University of Minnesota Field House. This allowed us to work both inside and outside depending upon what we needed to accomplish. When we worked outside, everyone except for Brown and Osborn would hide several layers of sweatshirts under our jerseys.

We all looked like penguins waddling in the snow. As a result, the workout becomes slow motion, but it's still good practice for playing in adverse conditions. I had played eight years in Canada and considered myself an expert on bad-weather quarterbacking.

During the week, I was showing Bob Lee, our young quarterback, the secrets of playing in snow and cold. Imagine that you were walking on eggshells. You have to be conscious of every step and exaggerate every action. I showed him a slow-motion handoff, taking the ball carefully from center and then watching it into the running back's hands. I should have taken my own demonstration a little more seriously—maybe I wouldn't have fumbled on the second play of the game on a handoff to Bill Brown.

Most successful teams learn early that when you get into big games you should stick with what got you there. You've got the same players and the same system you had the week before, so it's extremely difficult to change now. Your strengths must be executed and weaknesses shored up. This is a time when I think coaches can easily become shortsighted and take steps that will seem inconsistent and unfair to the team. More than that, it is often difficult to keep perspective when the season can end with the loss of one game—decisions feel all the more pressured.

It's easy when preparing for a team like the Rams to talk yourself out of your routine or system. As you watch the films, you start to say, "Nope, you can't run around them, you can't run at them, you'll never have time to throw that pass." Before long, all you think you can do is stand in the huddle and quiver. Good teams have to believe that they can beat anyone with their own strengths.

Digital video, laptops, and tablet computers are now the norm in this country, but in 1969 we still watched black-and-white game films on old, beat-up projectors. Every time you wanted to look at a play in more detail, you had to stop the film and run it back by hand. The team usually had only two or three copies of the film for all of us to share. The coaches would monopolize the films until about Wednesday when they had their game plan mapped out. This meant that the quarterbacks would have only a couple of days to figure out how to read the defense and attack its weaknesses.

I had the reputation as a quarterback who would draw plays on the bare ground using a stick or improvise on the run. But before every game, I used to draw up a plan of attack that incorporated what the coaches wanted to do and what I felt I needed to do to make it all work. I would list what I felt would be the keys to the game and the key plays that I wanted to call. Once I had the plan set on paper, I would try to visualize that game as it would unfold. I called it "cooking"—preparing the ingredients necessary for victory and finding the best way to blend them. (See Joe's game preparation sheet in the photo insert.)

For this game, I could see myself standing in the cold trying to avoid the rush of Deacon Jones, Merlin Olsen, Diron Talbot, and Coy Bacon. I also could visualize the situations where we'd get the ball and put together a long-sustained drive with runs by Brown and Osborn and passes to Washington, Henderson, and Beasley. I could also see what we needed to do on third and long and fourth and short. By game time, all my uncertainties were gone because I'd already played every possible situation. I had seen the game, conceived the script, envisioned my role, imagined and projected all realizations. By game day, we were ready.

I condensed what I felt I had to do onto one sheet of paper. Then, during the game, I'd stash it in either my belt or my hat for easy reference. I called it my security blanket. For the Rams game, I wrote down eight keys.

1. Mix the count

One way to keep an aggressive front four back on their heels is to mix the count and break up the cadence. All week we practiced calling the plays on long counts, overdoing it. I'd get these funny looks when I'd call a count on "nine." Long counts have to be practiced because a long, jerky count requires even more concentration from the offensive line. This is a way of controlling the tempo, using time and our knowledge of the snap count to our advantage.

2. Make quick-rhythm passes

The Rams never gave you enough time to set up and throw, so our plan was to throw quick-rhythm timing passes. This means throwing the ball before the receiver has made his break, to a spot where the receiver should be, not where he is that moment. This type of passing is based on exact execution and deep trust. A total sense of cooperation between the quarterback and the receiver. The blockers appreciate the fact they don't have to hold their blocks for quite as long. It gives them another tool to change the rhythm and take a cut at their opponents.

3. Set up quick and don't get caught

A sack for a defensive lineman is like a shark getting the smell of blood. To avoid this, I needed to get back quickly and throw more quick-rhythm passes. I also wanted to decrease the margin of error by consciously throwing certain balls more to the outside shoulder, or a little long. For a pro quarterback, this is easy to do. It's like Jack Nicklaus planning to play a draw or a fade. I concentrated on quickness of footwork and throwing motion.

4. Run at them and establish the draw

One way to defeat great defensive linemen is to use their aggressiveness against them. Running right at a Deacon Jones or a Merlin Olsen takes away some of their ability to run rampant all over the field. We needed to freeze them with the draw play and have patience if it didn't work the first few times. Bud Grant always liked to keep running the same plays. He felt that you got better at them. By the end of the game, you have plays that the defense has a tough time stopping. Practice makes perfect, even during the game.

5. *Expect blitz*

I knew it was part of their game plan to put as much pressure on our quarterbacks as possible. If we neutralized their line, I knew I could expect their linebackers and safeties to pick up the slack. I should not be surprised to see them all attacking. By expecting the unexpected, I could keep my mind in control and assure good performance.

6. *Take 75–73*

It is necessary to be specific in your plan in order to achieve specific results. The terminology "75–73" represented quick-out patterns that I wanted to make sure to focus on throughout the game.

7. *Expect something unusual*

The Rams had been a big-play defense all season. I just wanted to make a special note to myself to be alert for the unusual. Keep cool, make them guess, do not commit yourself too early.

8. *Be ready for any weather condition*

This was to remind me to visualize different weather situations as I did my pregame run-through in my mind. The weather was bad only if we allowed it to be. Besides, Vikings love the cold.

THE GAME

It's now Saturday afternoon, December 27, 1969. The temperature is a balmy twenty-one degrees and groundskeeper Dick Erickson and his crew have done an outstanding job of clearing the snow and making the field playable. There are 47,900 fans in ski caps and mittens awaiting the opening kickoff. Our focus is clear: get the job done. Reach for a higher plateau. Cut the rope and be free to be the best you can be for the next sixty minutes of your life.

First Quarter

Bruce Gossett boomed a kick down to our goal line and Charlie West weaved his way back to the twenty-eight-yard line. Fair field position, but no time to be reckless. On the first play of the game, I hit John Henderson on a quick out for twelve yards. Then it happened: as I was about to hand off to Bill Brown, the ball popped in the air and we turned it over to the Rams.

On the very next play, though, our defense seemingly bailed us out: the Rams tried a screen pass that was intercepted by Carl Eller, who dashed forty-six yards for a touchdown. The whistles were blowing, and the referees waved their hands furiously. Minnesota was off-sides—it was the Rams' ball, first and five at the forty-one. An early test of our character. One minute we were cruising on a high, and the next minute all the wind was knocked out of our sails. The momentum swung back to the Rams, and eight plays later they scored on a three-yard pass to Bob Klein. Rams 7, Vikings 0.

We took the ensuing kickoff and put together a long, sustained march of seventy-five yards in ten plays. We mixed quick outs with Bill Brown and Dave Osborn running up the middle. At one point we completed four passes in a row, including a twenty-seven-yard strike to Gene Washington at the four-yard line. Osborn vaulted into the end zone and it was a new ball game. Rams 7, Vikings 7.

Second Quarter

The game sputtered as the defenses stiffened. We all began to settle in for the second quarter. The Rams put together another impressive drive but missed a field goal from thirty-eight yards away. Throughout this game the Rams were able to drive the ball, but they came up empty too many times.

Going away from our game plan, I went for the bomb instead of taking the quick outs. I wasn't paying attention to the agreed-upon and practiced game plan. As a result, we got only three plays and the offense was back on the bench.

The Rams put together yet another long drive, sixty-five yards in thirteen plays. The Rams were successful four times on third down on this drive. However, our defense didn't break, and the Rams had to settle for a thirty-five-yard field goal with five minutes left in the half. Rams 10, Vikings 7.

Another three and out! We weren't coordinated, and we weren't concentrating; we had to do better.

Using up almost four and a half minutes, the Rams drove again—fifty-six yards on eight plays. The final touch was a running pass by Gabriel to Billy Truax in the end zone. With only seconds before half it was Rams 17, Vikings 7.

We frittered away the closing ticks of the clock with a holding penalty and a fumble. Time to get in the locker room and regroup. This was not what we wanted. But we had time and the truth was, we could still win—we would will it!

The Rams had played another good first half, and it was no longer forty for sixty. It was now forty for thirty. We were only ten points behind, but so far the Rams had outrushed us, outpassed us, and kept the ball for most of the half. On both defense and offense, we couldn't seem to make the big plays. Alan Page made the comment that the Rams were running into the "one" hole, which is just inside of where Alan lined up. It was neutralizing his line charge in the same way we had planned to neutralize Deacon Jones.

Halftime

All coaches at every level have the same thing to say as you enter the locker room at halftime. "Okay, get some rest! Get off your feet! Relax!" Bud, as you would expect, would say nothing. He would immediately start taking off his parka and strip down to his T-shirt. He looked like an ice fisherman who just came into the lodge.

We were all looking each other in the eye. No one was looking down. There was not a lot being said, but a lot of communicating was going on. We had a new awareness of a common purpose. We had thirty minutes left to get the job done. The unspoken word was a powerful force. The truth was, we had time. The sense of urgency and common purpose filled the air.

At the end of the halftime, all the players got into their groups with their coaches to make any last-minute adjustments. On offense, we didn't change any blocking assignments. We knew we had to go back to the quick outs and running up the middle. We knew we could score if we just got the ball more often and made better use of it. We'd only had five possessions and twenty-four plays in the first half. The defense was confident they could shut teams out and that they had won games by themselves in the past. There was no room for doubt. Each of us, each of the forty, had to contribute. We all had to get the job done.

Third Quarter

At the start of the second half with the heightened sense of responsibility and resolve, more of our players became sideline cheerleaders. I was running up and down the sidelines cheering our defense: "Get back that seed, get us that seed!" Paul Dickson, an eleven-year NFL veteran, looked like an eleven-year-old boy.

The defense quickly shut down the Rams, and we got the ball back on our own twenty-eight. Helped by an interference penalty, a roughing penalty, and a forty-one-yard bomb to Gene Washington, we moved the ball down to the Rams' one and Dave Osborn vaulted over to make the score. Rams 17, Vikings 14.

Our defense had found its rhythm. They were taking on the Rams' offense, and the pass rush was paying off when it counted. Rising to the occasion, they shut down the Rams for the rest of the third quarter, despite the fact that I threw two interceptions. Fortunately, I threw the interceptions deep in Rams' territory. On the first interception, John Beasley was the primary receiver. Instead of looking for the secondary receiver, I tried to rifle it in to Beasley. Then, on the second interception, I didn't spot Richie Petitbon, who was covering Beasley.

The risk-reward theory is no better tested than the decisions quarterbacks must make in the heat of the battle. There is rarely any gain without the pain that comes with it.

Fourth Quarter

The dance was over, and now the bullfighter had to move in for the kill. The moment of truth was at hand. All the years of practice had prepared the warrior to face those few seconds. The air was filled with excitement and fear. It was now forty for fifteen. There was no turning back.

After my second interception, the Rams put together another drive of sixty-four yards in six plays, but they were stonewalled on three successive pass plays and had to settle for a twenty-seven-yard Gossett field goal. Another opportunity unfulfilled. Rams 20, Vikings 14.

We retook possession on our thirty-five after a short kick and a great return by West. Behind the blocking of Tingelhoff, Alderman, Sunde, Vellone, and Yary, it was Brown straight ahead for five . . .

. . . complete to Henderson for twenty . . .

. . . Brown off tackle again for one . . .

. . . pass to Brown for twelve . . .

. . . Osborn spun for three . . .

. . . I scrambled for twelve . . .

. . . and then Osborn vaulted us to the two-yard line.

At this point we were all huffing and puffing, but Jim Vellone led us into the end zone to give us our first lead. Vikings 21, Rams 20.

We'd slugged it out for fifty-one minutes, but no knockdown

punches had been recorded, and they don't decide football games by judges' points. You could tell it was getting colder because more and more Rams players were huddling near their heaters. The game would be won by the team that could stay together for nine more minutes.

Fred Cox crushed the kickoff one yard deep in the end zone—a rare sight, indeed. Ron Smith tried to dash out but was sideswiped by Dale Hackbart with a loud crunch you could hear all over the field at the twelve. On the first play, Gabriel dropped back for a pass, but before he was even set he was hauled down by Carl Eller for a safety. Everyone in the stadium could feel that the Rams had just taken a hard right cross to the chin and were about to go down for the count. Vikings 23, Rams 20.

The Rams were staggering, but heavyweights don't go down or stay down easily. The Rams mounted a final attack from their own fifteen and drove the ball to midfield. On the next play, Alan Page couldn't get a good line charge, so he dropped back and stretched out his arms. Gabriel's line of vision was blocked, and he threw the ball right into Page's hands. With only thirty-nine seconds left, we ran two quarterback sneaks and the game was over.

Throughout the second half, both the offense and defense got better, just as we had done all season. We made enough mistakes in this game to lose it and enough big plays to win it. The real difference in this game was that as a team we made a commitment back in September to persevere the entire sixty minutes. This was the first playoff win in Vikings' history, which was really the start of a winning tradition that has lasted for over forty years.

Athletes strive to master the game. Every day you hope to come out and play perfectly, yet the dynamics of the sport make perfection impossible. But on December 27, 1969, a magic existed in icy cold Metropolitan Stadium that proved each Viking could reach an even higher level of play. On this day, the Vikings demonstrated willingness and ability to withstand pain and achieve a common goal, no matter the sacrifice. We faced the fire bravely together. Our loyalty to each other and the team was our motivation to perform above the pain and hurt, and in the end it made us even closer as a team. True loyalty is revealed only in times or games like these.

FIGHT FOR THE LAST NFL CHAMPIONSHIP

After the dust had cleared from our playoff game with the Rams, we had won the first postseason game in the club's history. Our determination and resolve had won the game. We didn't get rattled when we got behind early. We cut out our mistakes in the second half and we played a complete sixty-minute game. Bring on Cleveland! We were ready!

Being a professional football player was not a way to make a lot of money until the AFL started to seriously compete with the NFL for players. With the advent of the common draft and the restriction of players moving from one league to the other without compensation, salaries leveled off. What this meant is that playoff money could be a substantial part of a player's income. The winner of the NFL Championship Game was guaranteed between $3,000 and $8,000, which in 1969 was real money.

We had already beaten Cleveland twice in the 1969 season by lopsided scores, but those scores meant nothing now beyond giving us the confidence that we could beat them again. Even though we had defeated Cleveland 51–3, they were still a team that was now sixty minutes away from the Super Bowl—a team with a great history and tradition, and explosive offensive players like Paul Warfield and Gary Collins.

This was the first Minnesota game of the 1970s. The date was Sunday, January 4, 1970, noon Central Standard Time. The skies were clear, and the temperature was eight degrees with a light twelve-mile-per-hour wind. We took the opening kickoff, and everything fell our way. We delivered a knockout punch, and the game was all but over by halftime. The game was a living example of what happens when a team gets on a roll and makes its own momentum.

We got the ball to bounce our way on our first two drives of the game. After taking the opening kickoff and driving down to the Cleveland seven, I took the snap from center and turned to hand the ball off to Bill Brown. He had slipped and fallen on the ice and I was left with nowhere to go, so I followed the blocking and skated in for our first score.

For the third time this season, it just wasn't Cleveland's day. On the next series, the Cleveland corner Eric Barnes slipped on a patch of ice—Gene Washington threw on a burst of speed and I caught him in stride for a seventy-five-yard scoring pass. Twice the ice field had affected play, and twice we came up smelling like roses.

It wasn't long before Leroy Kelly fumbled, and we turned it into three more points. Then Bill Nelsen, under a fierce rush from Marshall and Eller, threw a pass right into Wally Hilgenberg's hands. Dave Osborn took it from there, busting off tackle for twenty yards to make the score 24–0 at the half. We'd played errorless football and had taken advantage of all the breaks. The Cleveland players had to feel that we had their number and there wasn't anything they could do to change that fact of life.

There is always a constant struggle between quarterbacks and defensive players. They keep knocking down your receivers, they jump all over your running backs, and they can't wait to sack you on a blitz. In this game, I had a chance to personally meet the Cleveland linebackers and to let them know how I felt. On a pass play with all receivers covered, I broke out into the open, and there was left-side linebacker Jim Houston waiting to take his shot. So instead of hook sliding, I put on all my moves—both of them—and took him on in a head-on collision. We both went down, but I got up and he didn't. My knee had caught Jim right on the chin, and he was out cold. Not a good idea for an Ohio State All-American and an All-Pro linebacker to be knocked out by a sissy quarterback. Apparently, Odin was working overtime.

It was incidents like this that gave *Sports Illustrated* the crazy idea that I was some kind of tough guy. They did a three-part series entitled "The Toughest Chicano," which did wonders for me back in the old neighborhood. "Hey, Kapp! You don't look like no toughest Chicano. I don't need no stinkin' helmet to be tough, I'll show you." Sometimes it's not healthy to establish this type of reputation.

Anyway, we put Cleveland out of their misery 27–7 and claimed the title of NFL Champions. It was a total team victory that meant a lot to us and to the Vikings' franchise.

SUPER BOWL IV: MEET THE KANSAS CITY CHIEFS

While we were beating the Rams and Cleveland at home, Kansas City won a game in New York and a game in Oakland to get into the Super Bowl. They beat two good teams on the road to make it to the big show. After the Jets' win in Super Bowl III against Baltimore, the contest between the AFL and NFL was being taken more seriously and becoming a nationwide spectacle. We were in for one week of hype and ceremony before we'd be in the arena.

There was almost more talk about the halftime show than the actual game. It was the only time that I can remember that each team was given a designated trumpeter at halftime. The NFL was going to be represented by jazz great Al Hirt, and the AFL boasted Doc Severinsen from *The Tonight Show*.

Preparing for Kansas City was more difficult for us than preparing for a team like Green Bay or Detroit, whom we played twice a year every year. We knew what the Packers would do on third and short, or what type of return Detroit would show us on kickoffs. Our only exposure to Kansas City was three game films and a 1968 preseason contest. The Chiefs were a finesse team (which does not mean that they were soft) like Dallas that used multiple formations and always had a few tricks up their sleeve. Their coach Hank Stram fancied himself a master strategist and an innovator. He was always meticulously dressed with sport coat, vest, and tie. Quite a difference from Bud Grant, who tried not to attract too much attention to himself.

On offense, they would start in a stacked "I," with the tight end and both backs lined up directly behind the quarterback. Then they would shift into other formations. This formation is designed to give the defense trouble recognizing what's going to happen, but it also creates a greater opportunity for the offense to make mistakes.

On defense, Kansas City used an odd-man line that put a very active Curly Culp directly in the face of the opposition's center. At the corners, they played a lot of bump and run, trying to keep the opponents' receivers stuck on the line. This type of defense features a lot of one-on-one physical matchups where they feel that can beat the other team. The Kansas City offensive and defensive schemes weren't played a lot in the NFL, so we knew we would have to adjust and be alert during the game.

On the other hand, it's not that difficult to prepare for a Bud Grant team, whether it's for the Grey Cup or the Super Bowl. All you have to do to beat a Bud Grant team is to outexecute them. All you have to do is block better, tackle better, pass the ball better, catch the ball better, and eliminate errors. It sounds simple, but only three teams in twenty-two games had succeeded: a close loss to the Jets in preseason, a one-point loss at the final gun to the Giants, and a one-touchdown defeat to the Falcons in the mud. Chiefs head coach Hank Stram did a lot of talking after the game about the great strategy the Chiefs had for the game, but that doesn't give the players enough credit. They executed the key fundamentals on the field, and that made the difference.

All season long there is a pace and a tempo that develops playing each week. When that rhythm is broken, it can be tough to adjust. Kansas City had been through all this turmoil three years earlier in Super Bowl I, and that experience shouldn't be underestimated.

To Kansas City's credit, the Chiefs were able to overcome a rather major distraction and near crisis. The United States Senate was investigating the link between professional sports and gambling. Just two weeks before the biggest game of the year, it was leaked to the media that Chiefs quarterback Len Dawson was going to be subpoenaed. A few days later, there were news reports that Dawson had "associations" with known gamblers. Almost until game time, there were rumors that he might be suspended. It was plain untrue. Jim Finks came into the locker room after practice one day after the story broke. He looked pale as a ghost, as if he were really scared about something. He announced to all the players in a very serious and emphatic tone that there was nothing to the rumors about Dawson, and that we were to block them out of our minds as if we had never heard of them. I thought this was an extremely strange pronouncement. I don't think that we were thinking about the rumors at all until Finks made such a big point about it. I do think it had an effect on our performance in the sense that we had sympathy for Dawson, which is not the right emotion for football. Justice prevailed, and the innocent Len Dawson's name was cleared.

Being in the media's eye, athletes' lives are always under a microscope. We have the same vices and shortcomings as the average guy, but what we do on our own time can quickly become front-page news. Almost every office has a football pool, but any hint of impropriety on the part of a player or coach and everyone's buzzing. Gambling is of particular concern to professional sports because it bears directly on the integrity of the game. Fans want to know that what they see on the field is for real.

A bigger concern in football is the use or abuse of alcohol and drugs. The need for alcohol or drugs, in the player's mind, happens for three reasons. First, every player is in some degree of pain from the opening of training camp to the last game of the season. If you're lucky, the bruises and swelling go down before it's time for training camp again. If you're not so lucky, you'll end up with injuries that will last a lifetime. A shot of cortisone or a painkiller can be as normal a part of getting ready to play as taping an ankle.

Second, there's a big emotional roller-coaster that comes from being in the spotlight. A performer who goes onstage every night experiences the same phenomena. Players are sky high on game day, feeding on the excitement of the game and the fifty thousand screaming fans. When it's over, there's a low or empty feeling, a void that needs to be filled. Finally, most football players are young men in their twenties with money in their pockets who feel like they are invincible, like nothing can touch them.

All three of these factors can lead to trouble and even tear a team apart. That's why teammates need to look out for one another. We were known to have a tequila or two, and we weren't always saints when we went out to blow off some steam. But we would look out for each other and not let anyone drive home drunk. It's important that teams recognize when a player has a problem and help him, instead of looking the other way.

In the midst of all the talk about gambling, the oddsmakers had installed us as thirteen-point favorites. Even after the Jets downed Baltimore, they still refused to believe that an AFL team could compete with an NFL team. It was silly pride more than reality. As great a team as the Vikings were and as great a season as we had, we still should not have been so heavily favored to beat the Chiefs. They were a great team with great players and a higher payroll. The Chiefs only gave up twenty points in three playoff games to get to the Super Bowl. The New York Jets had proven that NFL superiority was a myth the year before when they whipped the Colts in Super Bowl III, but the myth was still the common perception in 1969, and we were heavily favored.

Kansas City had a big, fast team that made for several physical mismatches. We didn't have anyone the size of Chiefs' linemen Aaron Brown or Buck Buchanan. Curly Culp was another oversized threat at nose guard. If we double-teamed him, we opened it up for Buck Buchanan. At wide receiver they had speedsters Frank Pitts and Otis Taylor. Quarterback Len Dawson was supported by Heisman Trophy winner Mike Garrett at halfback.

Kansas City's special teams featured a real weapon in kicker Jan Stenerud, who would later finish his NFL career as a Minnesota Viking. He was one of the first soccer-style kickers to play professional football, which ultimately resulted in the league moving the kickoffs back to the thirty-five-yard line and the goal posts back to the end line. With his leg, he was a threat to score every time the Chiefs crossed midfield, and seldom was the opposition able to run back a kickoff. Their punter, the great Jerrel Wilson, kept us out of good field position with his booming kicks that pinned us deep in our own end. Jerrel was as good a punter as there's ever been, but he seems to have been forgotten.

In one of Hank Stram's comments about the game, he said that the Chiefs never feared the Vikings physically. "The only edge the Vikings have is their team unity," he said. "They are the most unified team in the league." He recognized the value of forty for sixty, and he knew that when heart, determination, and toughness were measured, the Vikings got the top ratings.

SUPER BOWL IV: JANUARY 11, 1970

We had dealt with less than ideal playing conditions in Minnesota, but the Super Bowl was played after a tornado watch was lifted before kickoff. Overnight rains created a muddy field. It was cold, thirty-eight degrees, and raining. The sun would come out later in the game, but it shone more on the Chiefs.

At the start of the game, both teams were very tight and played conservative football. I could feel how flat we were near the end of the week, and this psychological dullness carried through the game. Our emotions were down, and our concentration was off.

The game started with Stenerud sailing the ball through our end zone. We marched the ball across midfield from our own twenty. From their thirty-nine we were still out of Fred Cox's range, so we had to punt when our drive stalled. Kansas City came back to our forty-one, which gave Stenerud a chip shot of forty-eight yards to put the Chiefs up 3–0.

We played even through the rest of the first quarter until we were called for pass interference while covering Frank Pitts. Boom— Stenerud popped through a thirty-two-yarder to make the score 6–0. We lost field position on a fumble, which ultimately led to a twenty-five-yard field goal to make the score 9–0.

We were still in the game because our three mistakes had cost us only nine points. But on the ensuing kickoff, we fumbled and the Chiefs took over on the nineteen. Six plays later, Mike Garrett ran in from the five-yard line to make the score 16–0 at halftime. Kansas City was doing what a team had to do to beat us: playing a flawless game.

Sixteen points is not a big lead with thirty minutes to play, and we knew we could come back if we played an error-free second half. In the locker room I knew we needed a wakeup call. I got up and said that we needed to get mad and take back the game. For a minute, it looked like the Rams game all over again. On our first possession of the second half, we put together a ten-play, seventy-yard drive capped off by a four-yard touchdown run by Dave Osborn to make the score 16–7.

But we just couldn't live with prosperity, and we couldn't stop making mistakes. Kansas City bounced back on the next drive. The Chiefs worked the ball out toward midfield thanks to a fifteen-yard personal foul against the Vikings. On the next play Dawson threw a short hitch to Taylor, who then raced to a forty-six-yard touchdown. Kansas City 23, Vikings 7.

That was all the scoring. In the fourth quarter we gambled trying to come back, and I threw two interceptions, stopping our drives. Then Aaron Brown knocked me out of the game with a separated shoulder. We just didn't get the job done. Fumbles, interceptions, key penalties, and missed tackles killed us. There are no excuses in a game like this. Kansas City just lined up and outexecuted us.

On offense and defense their schemes and formations were ahead of their time. Dale Hackbart still chuckles about how convoluted the Vikings defensive plan was for their multiple formations. The day before the game, the coaches decided to play basic zone because there was still so much confusion about the adjustment schemes. They deserved to win. Unbeknownst to his team, Hank Stram was miked for the game by NFL Films. His performance on the sidelines has become an NFL classic. As much as I hated watching Hank Stram strut around like a rooster calling all his players "boys," he was right: we were flat as hell.

Defeat hurts, but it can also make you strong. It makes you hungry to try again. Kansas City peaked and had its finest hour, then faded for twenty years. The Vikings had laid a final piece in the foundation for an ongoing winning tradition. In the next four decades the Vikings would repeat as division champions sixteen more times, make it into the playoffs twenty-four more times, make it to the NFC Championship eight times and return to three more Super Bowls—an enviable record that few teams could match.

CHAPTER SEVENTEEN

THE BOSTON MASSACRE

After the Super Bowl, I had played out my option year with the Vikings. It was time for a new contract. In the NFL in 1970, there were no renegotiations before the contract was up. There was no free agency when a player completed the terms of his contract because of the Rozelle Rule, a.k.a. the Ransom Rule, coupled with collusion among the owners not to sign players that had played out their options. This rule required a team signing a free agent (who had played out his option) to compensate any team losing a free agent with players and/or draft picks of equal value. If the teams couldn't agree, then the commissioner would decide the matter. This discouraged teams from signing free agents because they wouldn't know what the signing would cost them in terms of lost players or draft picks. In short, no free agency at all.

What should I be paid? What was I worth? We had the first Vikings playoff team in 1968. We were NFL Champions and had played in the Super Bowl in 1969. Even at that time it was reasonable to expect a raise. Jim Finks offered me a two-year deal under the same terms as my original Vikings contract. In my mind, he was offering a pay cut.

Boxed out, I held out and did not report to training camp while Mr. Cook tried to negotiate with Jim Finks. At least by then I had Mr. Cook to deal with Gentleman Jim. The Saint Paul paper, owned by Vikings team owner Tony Ridder, reported that "Joe Kapp demanded $1 million!" I did not hold out for a million dollars. I had earned a raise, not what amounted to a pay cut. Mr. Cook argued for a substantial increase from the $300,000 original Vikings contract. He may have made a case for a million dollars, but I doubt the Vikings ever came close to that. As a result of the failed negotiation, I was signed by the Boston Patriots, who were forced to give Minnesota their first-round draft selection from 1967 and their first-round draft choice for 1972. How does a player who is not under contract get effectively traded? If Minnesota did not want to sign me, why couldn't I sign with a team of my choice? It was simple; the system did not allow for that (as described above). I didn't say it or show it at the time, but it hurt to be "traded" from the Vikings. It felt like our team had been taken away from me. We were a game away from being world champions. I felt that we would return and win a championship for Vikings fans, just like we had done with the BC Lions in 1964 after losing the Grey Cup in 1963. The Vikings fans deserved a Super Bowl championship.

A group of kids at school told my son that I was a traitor. I can't blame those kids; some fans both then and now see players holding out for a fair deal as disloyal money grubbers. I don't know if that is a testament to the NFL's masterful manipulation of the press, or fans' resentment of men making a living playing kids' games. Maybe it's both.

But the bottom line is that negotiating cost my family and me. All the Kapps loved Minnesota. I loved playing for the Vikings. The camaraderie on our team was as good as it gets. I'll always wish we had another season to get it done.

Whenever a quarterback joins a new team, the fans anoint him franchise savior. This was especially true for Patriots fans. The team was coming off 3–10–1, 4–10, and 4–10 seasons, and morale was at an all-time low. The Pats had only been to the playoffs one time in their eleven-year history. As a quarterback, you have a tremendous responsibility in rebuilding the team. Boston was going to be the biggest challenge yet.

Adding to expectations was the three-year, $600,000 contract Mr. Cook negotiated for me. His efforts made me the highest-paid player in the NFL at that time. As usual, I missed training camp, preseason, and the first three games. Billy Sullivan, the Patriots owner, was so desperate that he offered me the head coaching job as well. I was thirty-two years old and in my prime. I still considered myself a player. I didn't see how I could play quarterback and coach forty players effectively. Basketball is the most compatible for a player-coach. Looking back, I should have considered it more seriously for many reasons. For one thing, our coach Clive Rush acted like he was on drugs. I have no idea what the real reason was, but he lived on his own wavelength. Likewise, I should have negotiated for an ownership interest in the Patriots. Given Billy Sullivan's desperation and money troubles over the years, it might have been possible. I guess subsequent Patriots owners Victor Kiam and Robert Kraft beat me to it!

The Pats may have been better than their record suggested. Our head coach was supposed to be an offensive guru. In 1969, he was the New York Jets' offensive coordinator whose game plan helped to defeat the Baltimore Colts, 16–7, in Super Bowl III. Within days of that epic win for Broadway Joe Namath and the Jets, the Pats hired him as their head coach. When I looked around the Patriots' locker room, I saw a lot of impressive-looking players. Gino Cappelletti was a great receiver and kicker. Fullback Jim Nance and halfback Carl Garret were bigger and faster than Bill Brown and Dave Osborn, my great Vikings teammates. John Morris, our center, was also talented but even bigger than Mick Tingelhoff. But the general atmosphere was sour. Years of losing and a lack of leadership from players and coaches killed team morale. At our first offensive meeting, Nance and Garret were dozing. My first act of leadership was to blast them with spitballs. I knew from the beginning it was going to be a long road.

Head Coach Rush's first act of leadership was to switch all the offensive linemen to different positions. This produced disastrous results. I pleaded with him to let the linemen return to their natural positions. Finally, he relented. He chose to tell me when we were standing next to each other using the locker room urinals. I was so excited I turned to look him in the eye to thank him. Unfortunately for Clive, I had not finished urinating.

In a coincidental twist, the first Patriots game I suited up for was against the Kansas City Chiefs. We were competitive in the game for a while, but ultimately lost 23–10. My memory of my season with the Patriots is very foggy, but I do remember playing the Baltimore Colts in the middle of the season. Colts middle linebacker Mike Curtis dropped a late hit on one of our players, right in front of our bench. Instinctively I ran up to Curtis, cussed him out, and challenged him! I looked behind me expecting to see an army of jacked-up Patriots backing me up against this animal Curtis. Nada. I was alone. I wasn't used to this. On the Vikings or the BC Lions, this never would have happened. It was clear we were not a team yet. We had a long way to go. The Colts were heading to a Super Bowl V victory against the Cowboys. We weren't.

In 1969, the Vikings went 12–2 and were the NFL Champs. In 1970, the Patriots went 2–12 and were the AFC East bottom dwellers. In my eleven games with the Patriots, I threw three touchdown passes and seventeen interceptions. But I hadn't given up. In my first year with the Vikings, we finished last in the Central Division and ultimately turned things around. As would be expected, the press was rough. Dick Stockton, a local sports anchor at the time, said that I was a good cheerleader but not much of a quarterback. My son was ridiculed in grade school. The kids said, "Your dad stinks. The Patriots stink." We did.

Everybody on the Pats knew we had a job to do. I went about the business of building more rapport with my teammates. We worked out in the offseason together. I took our guard Lenny St. Jean to Ecuador with me to shoot a marlin-fishing expedition for *The American Sportsman*. We shared a team trip to Falmouth on Cape Cod where the families came along. I saw a better attitude on our team brewing. Coupled with the talented players on our roster, I thought we would be a much-improved team in 1971.

Gino Cappelletti was a great player. I spent a lot of time trying to persuade him not to retire and come back for just one more season. I failed, but Gino and I had a lot of fun together. He was quite a character and a great ambassador for Boston. Everyone knew Gino. One night we were having dinner in a little restaurant in Boston's North End. He had me get up and walk over to meet this little old man who was seated at a table with about four or five other Italian guys. After we sat back down, I asked him the man's name again. He said, "That's the Don." "Don who?" I asked naively. After an exceptional fifteen-year playing career, he went on to become the much-beloved radio voice of the Patriots for thirty years.

Our 2–12 record in 1970 yielded the Patriots the first pick in the 1971 draft. They selected Stanford's Heisman Trophy–winning quarterback, Jim Plunkett. Jim was also a Chicano who had a Latina mother like me. I was not concerned about losing my starting job. I had always been a starter and expected to be the starter in 1971. My many years in football taught me that you can't compete to your full potential if you're worried about losing. You don't have to like it, but all competitors lose sometimes. A true competitor does not let the fear of losing, or getting hurt, or being traded or demoted effect his or her performance. Those thoughts are distractions that will not help an individual or a team win. In fact, I planned to help

Jim any way I could, but I never got the chance. Jim did fine without my help, of course, going on to quarterback two Super Bowl wins for the Oakland Raiders. Other than the QBs in some of the no-huddle offenses, Plunkett was probably the last QB to call his own plays on a regular basis in the NFL. He is another guy who has not received his due as a pro.

Heading into our 1971 camp, I was optimistic about our team and ready to go. Then they called me into the office. I needed to sign a "standard player contract." They said all players had to sign this contract. I said that I already signed my contract. They insisted that all players were required to sign the standard player contract, including those with legally binding deals. I called Mr. Cook. He said the contract was illegal. They could not force me to sign it. My gut and my lawyer were telling me this was wrong, so I refused to sign the contract. They kicked me out of training camp. The front-page newspaper headline was "Kapp Quits!" This stung me. It was completely false! Throughout my life and career, I prided myself on not quitting, no matter how far we were behind in a game or the standings. There was a gang of reporters on our front lawn when my son got home from school. His only question was, "Why not sign the piece of paper, Dad?"

The standard player contract required the player to give up all his rights to self-determination as a football player. The player could not negotiate with the team of his choice even after he met all his contractual obligations and was no longer under contract with the team. All players were required to sign it. The NFL said the standard contract terms were not raised when I signed at the beginning of the 1970 season because there was no collective-bargaining agreement in place at the time. Mr. Cook advised me that the standard player contract violated federal antitrust law. Mr. Cook said if the NFL and the Patriots did not relent, we would challenge it in court. It was an illegal contract. The NFL and the Patriots did not relent. We filed suit in Federal Court in San Francisco. I hoped for a quick resolution so I could join my teammates in training camp. That did not happen. The Patriots and the NFL were being obstinate. My family and I moved to Belmont, California, a suburb of San Francisco, to be near Mr. Cook and the trial court.

CHAPTER EIGHTEEN

TRADING SHOULDER PADS FOR LEGAL PADS

The Monopoly vs. Joe Kapp

I don't go looking for fights, but they do seem to find me. When they do, I stand up for myself. That's what my mom would do. That's what she taught me to do. A bully is a bully whether they're wearing a jersey or a pinstriped silk suit. In 1970, the easiest thing for me to do would have been to sign the contract, just like I had for the previous twelve years, and like other hardworking football players had done from the beginning of time. But with Mr. Cook's advice, I felt that it was time to stand up against the powers that had turned me into a migratory football worker. I was angry. I had signed a contract in good faith. I had always honored the terms of any contract I signed. I played to win. And I wanted to play to win again, as soon as possible. But I had to fight for what I thought was right. And, yes, I would do it again today.

Few if any professionals in America would stand for the kind of treatment that professional athletes received back then. The reality is that things are better today, but there are still improvements that should be made. Football is the only major sport with no guaranteed contracts, even though it is the most brutal and debilitating team sport. If a football player gets hurt or has a down season, his team can cut him, and is generally not obligated to pay the player for the balance of his contract. A $20 million contract may only be worth a fraction of that amount.

Also factor in that a typical football player's career is short, even under the best of outcomes. Many will suffer lasting physical and neurological consequences of the game, often requiring expensive medical care for the rest of their lives. Fully guaranteed contracts would help players and their families to survive what might be a long road ahead. Moreover, if you look at the money the players make for the team owners, the players deserve more security. And I don't know many team executives who had to worry about being sacked at the office by the Fearsome Foursome or the Purple People Eaters!

On average, a player's career in the NFL is only three and a half years. A player is not eligible for a pension unless he plays for four years. Compounding the problem, the NFL's pension plan pales in comparison to all three other major sports'. The system is set up to cut players before they have the opportunity to earn all the money on their contract or have their pensions vest. With more than 120 Division I college or minor-league teams, there is a constant supply of young talent. This minor-league system is its own self-sustaining league and does not cost the NFL a penny to operate. The steady supply of players allows teams to get rid of more expensive veterans without too much concern about reduced team performance.

In my case, I was hijacked to Canada by my personal coyote, Gentleman Jim. After that, Pete Rozelle refused to let me sign with the Houston Oilers even though I had met my obligations with the BC Lions. Then Gentleman Jim shipped me out to Boston after we had built an NFL champion Vikings team. I had a signed contract with the Patriots. The NFL's standard player contract was surplus and illegal. It was time to take a stand for my family, myself, and all the other dedicated football players who would follow.

In 1970, the NFL owners steadfastly justified the Rozelle Rule as a necessity to maintain competitive balance in the league. To me, it was deeper than that. While they may have believed free agency would doom competitive balance in the league, I believe they wanted to maintain control over player salaries with a cobweb of monopolistic rules to protect their profits. After my lawsuit, it took nearly twenty years of labor strife and other legal action to gain limited free agency for the players. To this day, the law has always been on the player's side, but the issue is complicated by the reality of collective bargaining and the stranglehold the owners maintain over the NFLPA. More importantly, given the history of the NFL, players have been conditioned not to understand their value to the enterprise. Ever since my playing days, I have wondered why players can't own teams, and why players from all professional leagues—NFL, CFL, NCAA (yes, it is pro football too), and Arena Football—don't form a single union. I have also wondered why Division I NCAA Football does not compensate its atheletes with at least insurance plans that extend beyond playing eligibility.

On December 20, 1974, I won a summary judgment after being on the sidelines for over three years. Mr. Cook was right. The court concluded that the standard player contract, the Rozelle Rule, and the draft were unconstitutional and amounted to a restraint of my trade. The court described the NFL's actions as a "cobweb of collusion."

This ruling was a landmark decision because until our case, the NFL rules had never been invalidated. Because I had been locked out of the league since 1971 and the federal court confirmed that my trade was restrained, it seemed obvious that I was damaged by the NFL. Now it was just a matter of determining how much the NFL would have to pay me in damages, if anything. Standing on our summary judgment, I assumed my attorneys could negotiate with the NFL for a fair settlement of damages. I was wrong. Despite the summary judgment, the NFL refused to pay any damages to me. We would have to prove damages to a jury.

In the spring of 1976, we went to jury trial on that single issue of my damages. The NFL, led by future Commissioner Paul Tagliabue, had to defeat me. They hoped to capitalize on a jury's suspicion of any plaintiff seeking money, especially one they portrayed as a disgruntled, ungrateful quarterback who was seemingly enriched by the NFL system, not victimized by it. The league had the reach to influence public opinion of me and my case through the media. The league used their huge war chest to assemble an All-Pro team of attorneys. They retained former San Francisco mayor and renowned trial lawyer Joe Alioto to handle the trial work. His defense strategy was to portray me as a money-grubbing, malcontent journeyman quarterback who orchestrated the whole suit because I did not in fact want to play, but instead wanted a big payday for no work.

My attorney was Cal sports hero and World War II Army veteran Chuck Hanger. We needed to tell the opposite story: that I was a good quarterback who was hijacked, traded, voided, suspended, and locked out of my livelihood through the unfair NFL practices. Further, we needed to show that these practices impaired my and other players' ability to earn security and fair wages, which was not good for America in general. To present my case, we needed to call opposing players and my teammates to support my reputation as a player who loved the game and gave it his all for his team. The NFL's power to intimidate potential witnesses was on full display. I called San Francisco 49ers legend John Brodie for help. His people told me he was unavailable for the next four months due to participation in an EST symposium, a.k.a. Erhard Seminars Training, the popular self-help movement. Rams defensive tackle Merlin Olsen, who was once paid to attack me in the pocket, was willing to testify for me. But Merlin told me straight up that he thought it would mean losing his job as the number-one television analyst for a major network. I did not want to be responsible for that. Brodie had a network job as well that I did not want to disturb.

Two of my former Vikings teammates answered the call. Gary Cuozzo, our backup quarterback, and Gene Washington, our star wide receiver, came forward. Gary testified that I was a tremendous leader in the same category as Johnny Unitas. He added that I had the most significant effect he'd ever seen in turning a mediocre team into a great team. He didn't know if the Vikings could have made it to the Super Bowl without me. Gene Washington was equally supportive. He testified that I was an excellent passer, and he rated me ahead of the great Fran Tarkenton and all the other quarterbacks he played with in pro football. He called me a catalyst who put together the terminology and feeling of "forty for sixty." I felt tremendous gratification.

In his defense of the NFL, Joe Alioto paraded a high-profile list of local and national stars to make his case and smear my good name. Al Davis was brought in to testify about how doing away with the Rozelle Rule would be devastating to competitive balance in the NFL. Davis would later hire Alioto himself to sue the NFL when the league resisted his move to Los Angeles for a better deal. Restraining my trade was okay with Al Davis, but restraining Al Davis's trade was not okay with Al Davis. Billy Sullivan was brought out to say that a favorable verdict for me put his ownership of the Patriots in jeopardy. Ironically, Mr. Sullivan sang his jeopardy song from the first bar of his Patriots ownership to his last when he was forced to sell the team.

Then, after presenting this NFL doomsday defense, Mr. Alioto pointed his finger at me. He called another Bay Area hero, Oakland Raiders quarterback and place kicker George Blanda, whose twenty-six season tenure in the NFL still stands as a record today. George testified that I was an average quarterback, not an upper-echelon NFL quarterback. The Miami Dolphins and Baltimore Colts head coach Don Shula gave the same assessment as George Blanda. Shula went so far as to say that I had qualities as a quarterback he would instead like to see on special teams; recklessness and aggression. To Shula, I was nothing more than a special-teams player. That made me proud! That was a high compliment because I appreciated the heart and toughness of special-teams players. In pulling all the stops to protect the

NFL, Shula denigrated an entire unit critical to the success of any football team.

Alioto strutted around the courtroom like a noisy rooster as he called me out and charmed the jury. Mr. Cook was incensed over how effectively Alioto was whipping us, and he expressed his criticism so intensely that I thought our trial lawyers were going to cry. Then the jury came back. We all had reason to cry. We got our butts kicked. The jury didn't give us a red cent. Goliath won. I think Joe Alioto succeeded in making me look like a prima donna to the jurors who were skeptical of giving money to a plaintiff, especially a man paid to play a boy's game. Perhaps they believed I should have played under the standard illegal contract while my lawyers fought in court for the deal I signed. That didn't seem right to me. The Patriots and I signed a deal I planned to honor. Mr. Cook likely thought if I played and suffered a career-ending injury, it would have prejudiced my case because an injured quarterback who can't play isn't worth anything.

We appealed the decision. We lost those too. Looking back on it, I would have done it again. A bully is to me what a red cape is to a bull. I attack. I don't know whether it's a strength or a weakness, but when you grow up the way we did, it's a reflex, one that I never got over.

Even though I didn't recover any damages, the summary judgment against the NFL in my case set precedent for the *Mackey v. NFL* case and all the subsequent cases that have found the NFL's rules to be clearly in violation of American antitrust law. John Mackey, the great Baltimore Colts tight end, stood up for himself and others too. Mackey successfully challenged the Rozelle Rule and the rest of the NFL's "cobweb of collusion," and ultimately won an injunction against these practices in the Federal Court of Appeals. His case is the seminal case on this issue because it was a complete trial on the merits and then an appellate court decision. I love football and the players who risk all to keep the game alive for fans. If my case helped them to gain the right to shop their talents like other Americans to earn fair compensation for themselves and their families, I am proud of that.

If the NFL rules are illegal, why is there not unlimited free agency today? The answer is collective bargaining. Over the years, the rights that other Americans enjoy have been bargained away in the interests of a better deal. Ed Garvey, the NFLPA Director at the time of my lawsuit, was a good man and did his best for the players. But in the end, as I must say again, it is the players that have to be tough enough to earn the consolations. It is the players that need to have solidarity, and not just NFL players but all professional football players: NFL, CFL, NCAA, and Arena Football. If they joined together, they would have a lot more bargaining power. Every single player in every league is subject to the same physical dangers. When most of the starting quarterbacks—except for Jim Kelly and Boomer Esiason—crossed the picket line in 1982, the owners knew there was no solidarity, and the bargaining power and the strike were lost. There have been some, maybe even many, improvements in pay, practice, and training camp limitations, but it is still a mug's game!

CHAPTER NINETEEN

TOUCHDOWN IN TINSELTOWN

I would be landing in Hollywood soon. With the help of Minneapolis local good guy Mark Zelonovich, who was a good friend and publicist, I was able to break into commercials and acting. My first contacts with anything related to show business were following Super Bowl IV. Kansas City Chiefs quarterback Len Dawson and I were in a commercial for Gillette. In 1970, Mark set up another ad for me with General Mills for Wheaties cereal. Shortly afterward, I was asked by somebody at General Mills if I had representation. I said I did not. They asked if I would use the William Morris Agency. I said, "Of course, have Bill give me a call!" Like most or all football players at the time, I was looking for work in the offseason. I would go from migratory football player to migratory bit player.

In the meantime, I was living out of my suitcase in Northern California. I had never uprooted from Vancouver because I still had business there: Joe Kapp's Time-Out Lounge & Peanut Gallery. My good friend, Juan Valencia, was managing the restaurant while I was working to get my acting career going. The restaurant was doing better than I was. We had a lot of action in our bar. Many NHL players and other celebrities were frequent guests. The Boston Bruins were notorious for refusing to let the bartender close, and they could be very persuasive.

One night, at our restaurant in Vancouver, I had the opportunity to meet the famous opera singer Montserrat Caballe, who was well known in the world of opera for her work in Europe, the US, and

South America. I asked her, "Madame, do you ever get butterflies?" She answered, "My dear young man, if you don't get butterflies, you can't hit the high notes." I carried that one with me.

No player, actor, or entertainer has zero anxiety. When I go into a big game—and to me, every game is a big game—emotional butterflies offer me the freedom, enthusiasm, and reckless abandonment football requires. Some players are known for playing with ice in their veins. Not me—I played hot. I rode my emotional butterflies. As I got older and wiser, I understood that emotional butterflies are an asset off the football field too. They've helped me to face challenges in daily life. The key is to get those butterflies to fly in formation. This is controlled freedom. You're riding an emotional wave. You can enjoy and manage the ride. I have been told I played football like I loved the game. I did. That's the way I was taught. Sports are supposed to be fun. I let my boyish enthusiasm carry me on the field whether we were winning or losing.

Those butterflies came to Hollywood with me. I needed to perform in a new arena. I began working with the William Morris Agency in Los Angeles. My agents Ronnie Meyer and Robert Stein got me my first real acting role in the television movie *Climb an Angry Mountain*, which starred Fess Parker and Stella Stevens. Fess and I became good friends. We worked with Father Walter Schmidt on his annual fundraiser for Santa Clara University.

I would fly down to Los Angeles from Northern California or Vancouver for an appointment with Ron or Robert that would typically last about twelve minutes. They were handsome guys who looked like movie stars. With my mug, I would ask them what they needed me for—they should book parts for themselves. But they were great guys who got me a lot of work, mug and all! I worked on many TV shows like *The Rookies*, *Adam-12*, *Emergency*, *Police Woman*, and other

TV movies. I was typically cast as a thug or a villain. I got to work with some great people.

As in football, you have to go where your opportunities are. Not all the parts or the productions were memorable. At that time, disaster movies like the acclaimed blockbuster *Towering Inferno* were in vogue. Everybody wanted to make the next hit disaster movie. I was in a knockoff called *Smash-Up on Interstate 5*, which was more disaster than movie. However, it was fun. I got to meet a young up-and-coming star named Tommy Lee Jones. He was a great guy, and he had played football for Harvard. Tommy Lee and I were trading football stories when the star of the movie, Robert Conrad, jumped in. Forget Harvard, the CFL, the NFL, or the Super Bowl—Robert regaled us with endless stories of his high school football exploits. Tommy Lee and I just looked at each other and grinned.

In 1973, PGA great Lee Trevino, a.k.a. Super Mex, had a short-lived show called *Golf for Swingers*. Add that one to Super Mex's many titles! The show featured Lee golfing with celebrities, including Sammy Davis Junior. I loved Super Mex. He was a terrific Tejano guy and loads of fun, but Sammy was in a league by himself. After taping an episode, Sammy invited me to an intimate dinner with few close friends. There were twenty of us! Our dinner turned into a two-day party. Sammy had a big heart that way.

I did seven big-screen movies, including *The World's Greatest Athlete*. I got to live the dream of every athlete at the time: I dumped a trash can over the caustic Howard Cosell's head. Some of my other big screen efforts included *The Longest Yard, Two-Minute Warning, Semi-Tough,* and *Breakhart Pass*.

The director I enjoyed working with the most was the great Robert Aldrich. Bob really knew how to use my acting "talents." In 1974, we started filming *The Longest Yard* at the Georgia State Penitentiary in Glennville. What a head coach in sports Bob would have been. He was a great teacher and mentor. Bob A. really appreciated my assistance in choreographing the football scenes. I helped come up with some of the football gags, such as the scene in which Burt Reynolds's character fires the football into the groin of Ray Nitschke's character, and the famous neck-breaking clothesline tackle followed by the stadium announcer's line, "I think he broke his fucking neck!" We watched the dailies of the football footage every night together. Bob knew all about our lawsuit against the NFL because he was the head of the Director's Guild and was involved in the labor movement.

We were at the prison for eight weeks straight without much to do in our time off. We really developed great camaraderie, not only among the cast and crew but also with the inmates and the prison staff. We had lots of fun. I became close friends with Ed Lauter, who expertly played the movie's sadistic Captain Knauer. Day after day, Eddie entertained us with his great impressions of all of the classic Hollywood legends: Humphrey Bogart, Clark Gable, Burt Lancaster, John Wayne, Jimmy Cagney, you name it. Eddie even coached me up enough that I was doing pretty good Clark Gable and Burt Lancaster impersonations myself. And it got to the point that we would ad lib conversations impersonating Golden Age Hollywood stars.

One night I wanted to play a joke on my old BC Lions pal Big Mike Cacic, who was a huge John "the Duke" Wayne fan. I got Eddie to call Big Mike up as the Duke and ask him if he would he like to try out for a spot in his upcoming western. Big Mike was very respectful to "Mr. Wayne" but when he came back on the line with me he said, "God-damn it, Kapp. You can't fool me! I know that was Rich Little!"

Of course, there was also plenty of fun on the movie set too. The whole locker room would have to be cleared out whenever Burt swapped his football helmet for his hairpiece, and vice versa. This was our daily fire drill. Sometimes, my old Packer nemesis and friend Ray Nitschke flubbed his lines. After a long streak of flubs, Nitschke announced the reason: Bandito, a crew member with mustache and goatee, was distracting him. After another long streak of Nitschke line fumbles, Nitschke called out: "Cut, cut, cut!" Director Bob Aldrich deadpanned, "If Mr. Nitschke wants to cut, then we will cut." Bob didn't play pro football, but he knew enough not to get in the way of a fuming middle linebacker.

Burt Reynolds was a very down-to-earth guy. He invited me and my wife Marcia for a visit to his place in Savannah for Thanksgiving dinner. He and his girlfriend at the time, Dinah Shore, showed us a night of real southern hospitality. Burt handled himself well on the football field too. He was a running back at Florida State with genuine athletic ability. His famous sense of humor was evident throughout the film. Aldrich's ability to blend Burt's performance with the supporting cast of many real ball players and convicts was masterful. I am really proud of the film. One day, Burt and I got to talking about who we wanted to be when we grew up and the old films we watched, like *The Jim Thorpe Story*. Burt said, "The difference between you and me, Joe, is that you wanted to be Jim Thorpe and I wanted to be Burt Lancaster, the guy who played Jim Thorpe in the movie!"

One weekend, the fun down in Georgia got a kick-start in the most unlikely setting, a Ramada Inn. I had pulled a few strings to get Dick Fouts, my BC Lions teammate, a part in *The Longest Yard*. We were in the bar enjoying some drinks and some laughs amongst vacationing families, and what looked like business travelers with sprayed hair in loud, double-knit leisure suits. We didn't fit in at all. Dick was a six-foot-five All-Pro defensive end with a huge natural hairstyle. In the seventies, huge hair meant huge. He was also sporting one of those huge, lobster-shaped turquoise necklaces over a turtleneck. I wasn't helping things with my baggy Mexican-style shirt and huaraches. We looked like a hit squad in an action flick.

The guys in the loud leisure suits sitting next to us got even louder. Then they insulted our clothes, Dick's necklace, and my huaraches.

They made it perfectly clear we didn't belong, that we were not welcome in Savannah, Georgia. What ever happened to southern hospitality? I somehow lost control of my margarita. Some of it spilled on one of them. Chaos erupted! These little men attacked Dick and me like a pack of wild chihuahuas. Within seconds the cops arrived and dove into the ring. Dick was a gentleman. He held up his hands up politely to be handcuffed. I wasn't a gentleman. I kept on fighting. The cops beat me up pretty good. To prove their point, they slammed my leg with the police car door. Beat up and bloody, I wanted to save my badly stained shirt as evidence.

It turns out *los poquito pendejos* who bit our ankles were off-duty cops. Talk about home-field advantage. I was charged with assault, battery, battery on an officer, and inciting a riot! The next morning, the producer, Al Ruddy, had our backs. He got us released on our own recognizance, got us a lawyer, and drove us back to Glennville. When we reentered the prison and were back on the job, the inmates greeted us with a loud standing ovation. They had heard about our little skirmish with the police down in Savannah. For a moment, Dick and I felt like we were back on the field with the BC Lions after our Grey Cup win.

The production company hired an attorney for me named Stanley "Spud" Karsman. He was a pro's pro and a real southern gentleman. With Spud leading the charge, I took it to the box. We presented our case of self-defense. During my trial, Spud had great command of the courtroom. He could read every move of the prosecutor and the judge like a great defensive back reading an offense. The jury was sent out to deliberate. After the longest ten minutes of my life, they came back with their verdict on all counts: not guilty! Within seconds of the clerk reading the verdict, I heard the judge's deep southern drawl: "Mr. Kapp, can I have your autograph?" That's southern hospitality! I obliged. I am always happy to sign an autograph when I can, especially after a win!

After the verdict, I asked Spud what I should do about being beat up and framed by bad cops who were in cahoots with the alleged victims. Spud said, "Joe, I think you ought to get on a plane back to California as soon as possible." I took Spud's advice and have not been back to Georgia since. However, Georgia has not heard the last of the Kapps. My granddaughter, who is a talented artist, will attend the Savannah College of Art and Design (SCAD). In fact, she will be living next to the site of my dust-up with the leisure-suit lynch mob. The Ramada Inn buildings are now part of the SCAD campus!

I had the good fortune of working with Burt Reynolds again, along with Kris Kristofferson, in the football movie *Semi-Tough*. It was really more a rip on the self-help movement than a football movie. I played Hose Manning, a quarterback. Then I played a waiter on a train in *Breakhart Pass*, a western with an all-star cast including Charles Bronson. I was featured in a dramatic death scene. It was fun to shoot. But it landed on the editing-room floor like an incomplete pass. This was the beginning of the end in Tinseltown—my parts were getting smaller.

Breakhart Pass was filmed in Lewiston, Idaho, where most of the cast was put up at the Ponderosa Hotel. There was so much smokin' and dopin' going on that they threatened to kick us all out. To patch things up, we helped to arrange a charity basketball game. I coached the team. We had fun, even if I missed a layup. I can only imagine what Pete Newell, my Cal basketball coach, would have thought.

In 1977, I was able to work with Bob Aldrich in the comedy crime story *The Choir Boys*. I played a big vato—that's a big Mexicano dude. It was a small part. I didn't care. It was fun. Bob A. always created a great atmosphere on the set. I got to reconnect with actor Charles Durning.

He was very kind and generous with his acting advice. In 1979, Bob A. cast me in *The Frisco Kid*. Once again, he needed a big dude to play Monterano. But the part was written for a big Italian railroad worker. When I asked Bob A. about it, he said, "Don't worry, we'll just make the Wop a Cholo!" Bob A. respected everybody, but he had a blunt sense of humor. My scene was with comedian Gene Wilder. He was a very cute and funny guy, even though his character Avram enjoyed hitting my toe with a sledgehammer.

Likewise, it felt like Hollywood was taking a sledgehammer to my acting career. As the parts got smaller and fewer, I tried my hand on the production side of the business. I teamed up with George Litto, a renowned talent agent turned producer. George was instrumental in bringing together the creative elements for some great movies.

I helped George Litto produce *Over the Edge* and earned an associate producer credit. I was able to raise over a million dollars in production money from my good friends in Vancouver. The movie was Matt Dillon's first picture and also starred Vincent Spano, who has had a strong career as well. At the time, Vinnie was being pressured to change his last name to something more "show business." I encouraged him not to and to be proud of his Italian heritage! The film was not a big success in the US, but ultimately earned enough money to pay back the Canadians, I think.

Had Bob Aldrich lived longer, I might have had a few more movie roles. But Hollywood faded into the rearview mirror. It was fun. I met some great people and made some lifelong friends. But I was heading north. I was going back to my roots, back to the center of the universe.

CHAPTER TWENTY

THE CALL OF THE BALL

The Golden Bear Comes out of Hibernation

In 1982, my alma mater wanted me back. Cal invited me to become head coach of the football team. I could not resist the call of the ball! Some quarterbacks I've talked to stopped listening to the football to move on to enjoy great success in other careers. Not me—Old Joe missed the game of his youth. Once again, Judge Holden's words in *Blood Meridian* explain it best: "Men are born for games . . . play is nobler than work . . . the worth or merit of a game is not inherent in the game itself but rather in the value of that which is put at hazard." The game was in my blood. Life trained me to accept and attack the challenge. I was a bear in a straitjacket without it. The physical and mental challenges of football, the danger, the stakes, the camaraderie, the wins and losses—all test and fuel the human spirit like nothing else. For me and many other former football players, it is difficult to find another calling as satisfying as the game itself. As a coach, perhaps what I learned on my journey as a migratory football player could help young players to realize their full potential on and off the field. I know how much my coaches helped me to become the man I was. It was my turn to give back whatever Old Joe had learned, and to do it for my beloved Cal Golden Bears was a dream come true.

I was ready to be a head coach in the Pac-10. However, many disagreed with my assessment. They said I had been out of the game for eleven years, I had no coaching experience, I was too old school, and

I was a renegade. I never figured out how you could be both a renegade and too old school. Despite this, Cal's Athletic Director Dave Maggard believed in me. He and I go back a long way. I first met Dave hosting him during his recruiting visit to Cal in 1958. Although coveted as a football player, he went on to become a track and field star at Cal who set the school's shot put record prior to his graduation in 1962. He qualified for the 1968 Olympics, where he placed fifth in the shot put. He returned to Cal as a track and field coach prior to being named Athletic Director in 1972.

When Dave hired me, he took a lot of heat from the skeptics, especially about my lack of coaching experience. I thought it was a nonissue. I considered myself a student of the game. I broke down game film of every professional game I ever played. I was a quarterback who called all the offensive plays starting in high school and through twelve years of pro football. I felt that as a quarterback, I was a coach on the field. I tried to be a good example for my teammates. There was plenty about coaching at the Division I level that I did not know, but I was not worried about it. I could and would learn what I needed to learn. I was confident I could do the job.

Cal was 2–9 in the 1981 season under head coach Roger Theder. He was an excellent coach but was using an offense called the Run and Shoot, developed by Mouse Davis. This offense emphasized putting receivers in motion and having them adjust their routes on the fly in response to what the defense was doing. Run and Shoot was a precursor to the spread offenses that are run today. The spread offense has the quarterback in the shotgun formation and positions multiple receivers to spread the defense horizontally from sideline to sideline. Like many spread offenses, Cal's Run and Shoot did not utilize a tight end. The problem with this approach was that we had an All-American tight-end candidate named David Lewis. We planned to use David in his natural position. As a coach, I believe you have to find out what talents your guys have and put them in the best position to help the team. If necessary, adjust your system and schemes to the skills of your players. In that regard, football has a position for almost everyone with the heart and toughness to play the game. A football team needs big guys, as well as smaller guys. It's the ultimate team sport. I think that's why football fans identify with the game so much.

Cal was also returning twenty-three of twenty-four starters, so I really believed that we could win right away. However, there were many doubters. The announcement of my hiring was a surprise to many. I stepped into a whirlwind. I knew there were outstanding coaches on Roger's staff. I wanted and needed continuity. Many of the 1981 coaches were looking for jobs outside of Cal, even if they wanted to stay—or said they wanted to stay in order to hedge their bets.

On one of my first recruiting trips with Al Saunders from the 1981 coaching staff, he stopped the car after about an hour of driving and talking. To my surprise, he exclaimed, "Coach, you fire me up so much!" A few days later, Al Saunders told me that he was quitting for a job at the University of Tennessee. Of course, he said it was for the good of his family. I loudly demanded that he give me his keys to his office. He was taken aback, but I expected loyalty. Maybe that's what "old-school" means. I was a lifelong Cal Golden Bear with deep loyalties to the school and the program. I didn't understand the commitment of coaches for hire. I was naive. Adding to our problems, Ray Sherman and Mike Haluchak left the program too.

Thankfully, my old friend and Cal Rose Bowl teammate Bill Cooper agreed to come on board as our assistant head coach and linebackers coach. Had it not been for Bill, I would have been fired after the first year. He was the only coach who remained with me for all five of my years in charge. He was our rock and held the program together. To come to Cal, he had uprooted his family from southern California, where he was a high school administrator and a very successful football coach. He was well suited to help recharge the program. He also knew Cal better than anyone. We needed to share and promote the

Cal experience with recruits. Cal alums like Bill were in the best position to do that.

Ron Lynn was the 1981 defensive coordinator and was considered to be an outstanding coach. I really wanted Ron to stay because most of my energy would be focused on the offense. With Ron and Coop on the defensive side, I would not need to worry. Ron showed up late for our first meeting by a couple of minutes and I confronted him, but he stood his ground in a way that earned my respect. We were able to sign him up for the 1982 season.

In the end, Ron Lynn and volunteer coach Ed Hall were the only guys to stay from Roger Theder's 1981 staff. Larry Kuharich, the son of NFL and Notre Dame Head Coach Joe Kuharich, was a fanatic about joining our coaching staff. During blizzards back east, he would hike to a phone booth to call me and lobby for a job. The only thing that could stop him was running out of coins to feed the pay phone. I liked his attitude; he was fearless and totally committed to helping our program. We signed Larry as our offensive backfield/quarterbacks coach. He called most of the plays in 1982 and 1983.

My old teammates Pokey Allen of the BC Lions and Charlie West of the Minnesota Vikings were brought in to coach our defensive backs. Charlie wanted even more responsibility. He volunteered to coach our outside linebackers and coached our special teams, which we renamed the Special Forces.

Our players loved Bill Cooper and Charlie West. Coop wore so many hats on our staff—as an academic liaison, fixer of my missteps, team spokesman, recruiting counselor, and player-development coordinator—that it is a wonder he had time to coach the inside linebackers. Coop got more players hired in the summer and after graduation than a Manpower agency. With all that on his plate, it's no wonder he would smoke a pack of cigarettes during games from his seat up in the press box. After Cal, he went back to Mira Costa High

School in Manhattan Beach, California. He was such a great coach that the school named a scholarship and the field after him.

In 1983 Charlie West went to the Denver Broncos and coached in the NFL for another eleven years. Our special teams were never as good. Before Charlie left, he had recruited an undersized center from Verbum Dei High School in Los Angeles. The rest of our coaches had no confidence in this recruit and got in Charlie's face about it. Charlie was ready to fight over it. The other coaches feared that Charlie was going to get us all fired. In his defense, I said, "Of course we were going to get fired!" We didn't get fired for signing this recruit. His name was Hardy Nickerson. He emerged as our best player during our five years at Cal: a three-time MVP, and one of the greatest players in Cal football history. After Cal, he was an All-Pro who played sixteen years in the NFL. So much for "experienced" evaluators of talent.

The final coaching staff included Sam Gruniesen, offensive line; Nate Wright, wide receivers; and Ed Lambert, running backs. Al Borges was our other volunteer coach with Ed Hall. We also brought in some guest coaches from the Oakland Raiders: Fred Biletnikoff, Tom Keating, and Art Shell. We were very fortunate to inherit a great trainer, Bob Orr, and the best equipment manager in the business, mi hermano, Big Mike Arellano. I will never forget our first game at Colorado when the clear blue skies turned to a cold downpour. Big Mike calmly opened a trunk full of rain gear as if he knew the deluge was coming. These guys were completely dedicated to our players, the university, and our team.

I liked our coaching staff and our players. I was so sure the Bears would realize our dream of winning the Rose Bowl that I vowed not to drink a drop of tequila until we did. I wanted the players to know that winning took sacrifice and that, as their coach, I was willing to do more than just preach the importance of sacrifice. I said adios to my old friend Jose Cuervo.

As the coaching staff settled in, our quarterback Gale Gilbert announced that he intended to transfer. He was an exceptional talent. We believed we could build a solid team around him. The bottom line: Gale was skeptical that I would be able to coach him to the NFL, which was his priority and ultimate goal. After a lot of discussions and help from Raiders coach Tom Flores, Gale decided to stay. Muchas gracias to all! Gale went on to play in the NFL for the Seattle Seahawks, Buffalo Bills, and San Diego Chargers.

The season started with a high-energy pep rally in the Greek Theatre. The theatre was packed. I was on stage, and my goal was to rev up the students. I led off with the classic "C-A-L" cheer. I shouted, "Gimme a C!" The crowd roared, "C!" I shouted, "Gimme an L!" The crowd roared, "Hunh?" My butterflies weren't flying in formation. I admitted my mistake to the thousands of Cal scholars, who gave me a pass. I rallied and correctly spelled *Cal*. As you would expect from a dear friend and ally, Coop has told this story repeatedly. At least he would always give me credit for correcting my error without missing a beat. Despite my failed spelling bee in front of thousands of Cal fans, we went on to have a great season, finishing with a record of 7–4, climaxing with our historic win against Stanford in the Big Game, which featured "the Play," which I will break down in detail in an upcoming chapter.

I valued everyone on our team for their unique contributions, on and off the field. In particular, Gale Gilbert had a great season. Wins and losses are the measure of a quarterback. He also came up big in the Big Game. Dwight Garner and Ron Story were our hardworking tailback and fullback respectively. Fullback Ed Barbero's time had not come yet, but he would prove to be as hard a runner as we had at Cal. Wes Howell, a guard on Cal's basketball team, joined us on the football team to make great catches, along with Marriet Ford and David Lewis. Andy Bark displayed his potential to become the dominant possession receiver on the '83 team. Our offensive line was anchored by Harvey Salem. It was solid.

However, it was the defense that led us to our winning record. Our linebacker Ron Rivera proved why he was on his way to becoming the 1983 Pac-10 Defensive Player of the Year. I did yell at him one time to run off the field . . . but only once. He was a very coachable, curious, unselfish, and dominant player. Ron said that Roger Theder and I had a tremendous positive impact on his life, and he had a tremendous positive impact on mine. In 1983 against Texas A&M, I chose to take a field goal off the board due to a penalty. We fumbled the next offensive snap and Texas A&M recovered. My decision looked very bad until Ron tore through the line and tackled their tailback for a game-winning safety. Have you ever heard of a football player making a game-winning safety? That is how dominant a player Ron was for Cal. At the time of this writing, he is the Cal all-time leader in tackles for loss. Ron went on to a long, successful career in the NFL as a linebacker with the Chicago Bears and as head coach with the Carolina Panthers.

Reggie Camp was a dominant defensive lineman who manhandled Stanford in the 1982 Big Game. Richard Rodgers was a defensive backfield mainstay and Special Forces captain. Defensive back Ahmad Anderson was a team leader and never let me be complacent. He was the embodiment of the Berkeley free-speech movement. Most players would not speak up to their head coach, but Ahmed did it often on many subjects like player treatment, team morale, and academic issues. It made me proud. Strong safety Kevin Moen was a team leader and a hard hitter—so hard we nicknamed him the Undertaker.

Later, Gary Hein was one of our scrappy defensive backs and a rugby standout too. Once he intercepted a pass in practice and was charging toward the end zone. I didn't want him to score. I jumped on the field to stop him, trying to make a point that I was still in the players' fight even as a coach. Gary did what we coached him to do.

He knocked me flat. We did not always have the best teams, but we hit—just ask Gary! He went on to play for some great Cal rugby teams, and the Eagles (the United States National Rugby Team).

I was proud not only of our players, but also of the rest of the staff. In 1982, I was voted Pac-10 Coach of the Year and the *Seattle Times* National Coach of the Year. Those awards were simply a reflection of everyone who contributed to our success.

The 1983 season was a disappointing 5–5–1, but resulted in upsets over Texas A&M, Arizona State, another victory over Stanford, and a tie with then third-ranked Arizona. Equally important were the losses of three coaches: Larry Kuharich departed for the USFL's San Antonio Gunslingers, Sam Gruniesen left for the USFL's Los Angeles Express, and Nate Wright left to become the head coach of Central High School in the San Diego area. Ron Lynn had left for the USFL after the 1982 season. Our defenses were never as good. So, in 1984, Cal was really starting over. We lost coaches and had few returning starters. The biggest loss was Ron Rivera, who was heading to the Chicago Bears. It is hard to discount the loss of a strong team leader and dominant talent. If the 1983 season was disappointing, the 1984 season was a catastrophe. We fell to 2–9 and lost to Stanford. The Cardinal's Brad Muster ran for over 250 yards against us, then went on to rush for the Chicago Bears and New Orleans Saints.

While the turnover of players and coaches is the nature of college football, Cal needed to establish recruiting pipelines. Continuity in player recruitment is required for long-term success. We were fighting an uphill battle to retain coaches. From their viewpoint, moving on made sense. Their pay at Cal was approximately $30,000 a year. Second, the USFL created a bunch of pro coaching jobs. Many if not all of the coaches that reach the Pac-10 level aspire to be professional football coaches. It's the natural professional progression.

In hindsight, I regret not doing more to get better salaries for our coaching staff when I was most popular after our 1982 season. Chalk it up as a learning experience. I didn't fully appreciate the problem and the effect it was having on our coaching staff. Maybe they did not like Cal as much as I did. Either way, it was my mistake. It would have helped them and our program if I could have done more. And there were some coaches who did not like my style. Nate Wright and others, including former players, were critical of me. It was reported that as far back as my playing days, I had a general dislike for assistant coaches. It is not that I disliked them, it was just that I felt that they sometimes did not know as much as the players they were coaching. Defensive coordinator Denny Schuler wound up suing Cal for wrongful termination. I still stand by my decision in that case.

We had a lot of returning starters in 1985, and the thought was that it could be a rebound year. We added freshman running back Marc Hicks. He was a throwback player who could do it all: run, pass, and punt. Marc shared the punting duties that year with a great Cal and Major League baseball player named Jerry Goff—the father of now-legendary Cal and LA Ram QB Jared Goff. Besides Marc's physical skills, he had the relentless enthusiasm I love to see in a player. We knew Marc Hicks was a phenomenal tailback. He was used in what we called the C formation, and he showed that he was special. Unfortunately, as time went on, it became clear that Cal wasn't the ideal academic environment for him. He ultimately transferred to Ohio State to play for the Buckeyes. We showed signs of life and went 4–7. We beat USC at home, 14–6, and lost to Stanford, 22–24. Brian Bedford came off the bench in the second half and engineered a great comeback, only to have us miss a field goal late in the fourth quarter.

Expectations were higher for the Cal Bears coming into the 1986 season. The previous year we had beat USC and kept our losses close.

Brian Bedford was our starting quarterback. In our opener on the road, we struggled against Boston College and lost, 15–21. Losing the opener in college football is really damaging to a team's psyche. Adding to the weight of loss itself, sports writers were turning up the heat to have me fired. Freshman Troy Taylor was named the starting quarterback and showed a lot of guts and promise. David Ortega started as a freshman on that team and went on to become Cal's all-time leading tackler. After we were blown out by Washington, I was asked by *SJ Mercury* writer Mike Antonucci if I was going to quit or resign. I pointed to my head and said, "You look into my mind." Then I pointed to my heart and said, "You look into my heart." Then I pointed to my zipper and said, "Why don't you look into this?" I did not unzip my pants. This became known as the zipper incident and turned up the heat to the high setting for the rest of the season, until I was fired after our eighth game against Oregon. The incident did cause some humorous reaction, with the student section chanting, "Win one for the Zipper!"

1986 was my final season. On November 1, we lost at home to the University of Oregon, 27–9. Our record was 1–7. Thereafter Dave Maggard lamented, "I can't find any support for you, Joe." My first reaction was, "Find some!" But I knew he meant the alumni and administration had given up on me. Because I could not give up, I forced him to fire me, which he did. I then challenged Dave to fire all the assistant coaches, which, to his credit, he did. However, we were to stay on and finish out the season. But Old Joe was a lame duck.

On November 22, 1986, I coached my final game for Cal, the Big Game. The Cardinal was ranked sixteenth in the nation prior to the game. They were twenty-one-point favorites coming to Berkeley to face us. Kevin Brown was named the starting quarterback after Troy Taylor had been injured the week before against USC. Kevin played great, and I wondered if I should have named him starter sooner. Wide receivers coach Mike Rasmussen called a great game, including an option reverse that went for a forty-seven-yard Mike Ford touchdown. We upset the mighty Cardinal, 17–11. I was overwhelmed by our team's heroic effort. It is still the biggest upset in Big Game history. I consider it the biggest farewell present a team could give their coach.

Being fired by my alma mater was painful. Since I first saw the campus as a boy, Cal was the center of the universe for me. But I understand nothing lasts forever. I have nothing but gratitude for all the opportunities Cal offered me as an undergraduate football and basketball player, and as a head coach. Dave Maggard was a man's man for taking a chance on me, even though I didn't look at it that way. He took on the naysayers to give me the opportunity to coach the Bears for five great years. I learned many lessons from all of our staff and players. As a coach, I attempted to support them in earning their degrees. I tried to help them get jobs and transition into their adult lives. I hope they gained something from my efforts that made their lives better. I know they forever enriched mine. Unfortunately, Old Joe did not get to enjoy a reunion with his old friend Jose Cuervo as head coach of his beloved Cal Bears.

CHAPTER TWENTY-ONE

THE PLAY

Fun and Games at Work

Of all the great moments coaching our Cal Golden Bears, my favorite has to be the Play. Our team did something unprecedented, unexpected, unrepeated, and unforgettable. And we did it our way.

My time coaching at Cal featured one iconic moment in the history of college football, and truly even all of American sports. On November 20, 1982, the Play ended the Big Game between Cal and Stanford at Memorial Stadium in Berkeley.

Bay Area sportscaster Joe Starkey called the Play "the most amazing, sensational, dramatic, heart-rending, exciting, thrilling finish in the history of college football!" Since then, wherever Old Joe goes, people want to talk about it, especially the Cal Berkeley faithful. It's an honor. I'm proud of what our team accomplished that day, so I'll break it down in detail for you.

As always, before the game I shared the bullfighter's prayer with the officials: "Que Dios reparte la suerte" (may God spread/divide the luck). The Play was neither all luck nor a freak accident. It embodied everything I had been called out for by critics for most of my career. Since my playing days, skeptics have said my techniques and methods aren't by the book; I don't grip the laces, I throw off my back foot, I improvise too much, I'm not an Xs and Os guy. I'll take it. That's the way I've always approached the game since I played football with lettuce heads on the fields of Salinas. As a pro, playing under suboptimal conditions and subzero temperatures had forced us to be resourceful, even if it meant winning ugly. It's more fun for everybody, and sometimes being able to think on the fly when everything is falling apart is exactly what it takes to win. Our coaching staff at Cal worked to instill that resourcefulness into our players. Being prepared enables you to believe in yourself, improvise your way through chaos, and enjoy it.

To the naked eye, that fateful, life-changing kickoff return may seem like a random series of laterals, delirium, and a rush of unsuspecting band members, but it was much more than that. The game of Grabazz started back when I played in the Canadian Football League and continued throughout my career with the Minnesota Vikings. As a coach, I brought it to Cal. In Spanish it's "Grabazzo," and in English it's "Grab Ass." It was a game of few rules, other than lateraling the football backward to your teammate. There were no offsides, and most importantly, it was something that gave lineman the opportunity to touch, run with, and lateral the football. At Cal, we played it at noon on Sundays. It was a way for the entire team to break a sweat, stay sharp, and have fun! Players who keep the fun in the fight perform better.

At home in Memorial Stadium that fateful day, things were looking golden for the Bears with less than a minute left in the game. We were up, 19–17. Both teams had played a great game. Stanford's legendary quarterback John Elway shone, but the game film showed that Gale Gilbert shone even brighter. And every man on our team felt like they were contributing. That's team spirit.

In Stanford's final drive, our defense had the Cardinal pinned down on their own thirteen-yard line, fourth and seventeen. Then John Elway came up big with a twenty-nine-yard completion to Emile Harry, then another clutch completion to Mike Tolliver. Fullback Mark Dotterer's run put the Cardinal in field-goal range. Elway called time-out with eight seconds left on the clock. Their placekicker Mark Harmon drilled a thirty-five-yarder through the uprights. The

Cardinal was on top 20–19, four seconds from pocketing the Axe, the trophy that goes home with the winner of the Big Game.

Had Stanford bled another four seconds off the clock prior to the field goal, nobody would be talking about the Play. Stanford had called timeout with eight seconds left. Later, Elway said he wished he called the time-out with four seconds left. Head Coach Paul Wiggin, to his credit, took the blame for not bleeding more time off the clock before calling the time-out. By leaving eight seconds, Stanford also left themselves a second field goal attempt if they botched the first one. Strategically, leaving eight seconds could be justified. Stanford did not lose the game because of their QB or coaches strategy decisions; they lost because they only played with complete focus for fifty-nine minutes and fifty-six seconds.

With four seconds still on the clock, Stanford players and fans celebrated on the field. They were hit with a fifteen-yard penalty for unsportsmanlike conduct for excessive celebration, to be assessed on the kickoff. They had to kick from their twenty-five-yard line instead of their forty-yard line.

After their amazing comeback, the Cardinal had given our hungry Golden Bears time and yards. Our attitude was to rise up and get as tough as we needed to be! Charlie West called for our "Hands Unit," our player package for onside kick returns. Our Special Forces captain Richard Rodgers's final words to the troops were keep the ball alive and don't fall with the ball! Grabazz was about to be field-tested to take home the Axe.

But we lined up for the kickoff down two Bears. In all the hysteria, two guys did not hear their number called. We lassoed running back Scott Smith, who rushed onto the field. Then, at the very last second, defensive back Steve Dunn was sent out to make eleven. But that sequence left a gap in the front row. When Kevin Moen noticed we were short a player, he moved back from the second row. His great football instincts gave us a chance.

Stanford squib-kicked the ball along the ground, and it went through the gap caused by the impromptu substitution of the initially missing tenth and eleventh players. The ball took a clean hop to Kevin, who received the kick on our forty-five-yard line. Had Kevin not had the presence of mind to drop back prior to the kick, he would not have been in position to cleanly field it, the ball would have gone over his head, and we would have had a more difficult if not impossible return. But Kevin took just two steps before he was surrounded by Stanford white shirts. He looked to the short side of the field, spotted Richard Rodgers, and tossed an overhand backward pass to him.

Richard took one step and flipped it to Dwight Garner. Steve Dunn, who was standing out of position after having been rushed out to field eleven players, made a key block. Without it, Richard's flip would have been unsuccessful. Dwight was devoured by Stanford defenders, but he managed to flip the ball back to Richard just before his knee hit the ground. Dwight took one step before five defenders collapsed on him. After a few yards, Richard encountered a few Stanford defenders and numerous band members storming the field—everyone in the stadium believed the play was over, that our ball carrier had been tackled. Richard flipped the ball to Marriet Ford, who was in a perfect trailing position to catch the pitch around the fifty-yard line. Marriet was the fastest guy on our team. He advanced the ball about twenty-five yards before meeting Stanford defenders and yet more band traffic. In response, Marriet blindly tossed the ball over his right shoulder to Kevin who was hustling behind him. Kevin had the ball and twenty-five yards to go to get to the end zone. He raced through the band, scored the touchdown, jumped in celebration, and landed on Stanford trombonist Gary Tyrell.

There were several flags on the field, but there was never a whistle. The officials huddled. After what seemed like a long meeting, the officials confirmed the flags were on Stanford for again storming the field before the game was over, and I said to Tom Keating, "Let's get the hell out of here before they change their minds." They didn't. The Play survived a committee meeting of officials. They made sure God divided the luck.

The Play was in some way a redemption of a lifetime of wins and losses, goofiness and grit, and my compulsion to embrace the eccentric to give our team a chance to win. I never cared about what it looked like, or what anybody thought, as long as I played within the rules and did my best. You owe it to the game, your team, the fans, and yourself. At Cal, the goal of our coaching staff was to pass along to our players the frame of mind necessary to imagine the impossible, believe in themselves, have fun, and execute when it was all on the line. Only a dreamer or madman would have expected us to turn four seconds on a long field into a game-winning touchdown. But our team believed. Our team loved giving their best for the Cal Bears for sixty minutes. Truth be known, one of reasons winning the Big Game was so rewarding was our respect for our opponent. In fact, I have met and become friends with many Stanford people both before and after the Play. That means something special to me, along with taking home the Axe!

In retrospect, some see the Play as inevitable, a preordained outcome. It wasn't. Our fate was tied to an oblong ball flipped between improvising players stampeding forward at high speed in heavy traffic. We could have botched it in dramatic fashion, especially against a team like Stanford. It is easy to imagine a pick-six, or a fumble run in for a score. But our players were willing to risk going down in flames to light up the scoreboard. To me, that's what sports, especially football, is all about. Reviewing the Play, you can tell that the guys had been playing Grabazz, not that they had practiced a specific five-lateral kick return. They just knew where to be in relation to each other if they were going to try and advance the ball by using laterals—particularly the last two laterals. When you watch pro and Division I teams, they rarely attempt more than three laterals. More commonly, teams desperately flail and toss forward laterals at the end of games. I say, take a moment and play some Grabazzo! The Cal Bears swear by it! And let's take the Play for the positive message that it represents rather than crying about whether replay would have reversed the masterpiece. The Play shows us all what we can do against all odds if we just keep trying and believe. See Peter Vogt's *The Play* documentary for the most comprehensive presentation of the Play ever produced.

I love the Cal Golden Bears. Win or lose, I am a Cal Golden Bear and always will be. Our school and our football program have much to be proud of, from a top-tier education at public-school price to the many Golden Bear football players who have done us proud over the years: Paul Larsen, Proverb Jacobs, Craig Morton, Ron Rivera, Hardy Nickerson, David Ortega, Tony Gonzalez, Aaron Rodgers, and Jared Goff, to name a few. Yet, overall, Stanford football has a significantly better record. Cal alums and casual fans have asked me why this is the case so often over the years. The bottom line is that Stanford has greater prestige than Cal. Stanford consistently ranks in the top five and Cal consistently ranks around twentieth in the national academic rankings. Nine out of ten top recruits with the right academic background will select Stanford. Without this educational background, the recruit will not be able to survive, let alone graduate, at either school. Because Stanford has historically had this type of recruit, the academic faculty has been more welcoming to football players who are essentially pre-qualified to succeed academically. Conversely, at Cal there is often faculty disdain for football players due to their perceived or actual lack of academic ability or interest. Some of this has been fostered by the admission of too many athletes that are legitimate Pac-12 players but not legitimate Cal students. Cal is not getting the same players and students that Stanford is getting, and that is why Stanford has been better than Cal over the entire history of the rivalry.

Some people think the answer is special admissions (meaning admitting recruits that are legitimate Pac-12 players but not qualified Cal students), but it's not. If you get too many special admissions, you might enjoy some greater success on the football field, but graduation rates plummet. This isn't morally sound and isn't fair to anybody. Cal needs a sound approach that is consistent with the academic status of the school.

Cal is a great university with so much to offer. Reasonable academic standards should not be lowered, but alumni need to lower their expectations until we can truly develop our program to last rather than to continually rebuild within the confines of the three- to five-year coaching cycle. They need to understand and accept that success in football is not as simple as hiring the right coach. The coach has to be committed to staying and be willing to diplomatically repair the divide between the athletic department and the academic faculty that has evolved over too many years. At Cal this is a long-term project that won't be resolved in the normal coaching cycle. Most coaches are not prepared for or interested in taking on this type of challenge.

Cal alumni need to be patient. It might take a coach seven or eight years to really build a program effectively. Rich Brooks at Oregon and Bill McCartney at Colorado were able to build solid programs because they were given the time they needed. While Cal should not trash their graduation rate to win football and basketball games, Cal should welcome former Cal athletes and staff to their graduate schools. Cal excels in graduate programs. Instead, too often we turn away loyal talent to other schools and discourage potential future homegrown coaches from staying at Cal. Cal must also do a better job of using their impressive and diverse alumni to recruit legitimate Cal student-athletes. Alumni should work to raise the extra money needed to recruit nationally, hire and retain good coaches, and most importantly, keep the athletic department solvent. Cutting or down-grading sports with glorious histories like baseball and rugby is not good for football, basketball, or women's sports. Success breeds success, and a solid history of commitment to athletic programs breeds trust in potential recruits. I would like nothing more than to see the Bears win the Rose Bowl or a national championship, but until then, we can appreciate and enjoy the other successes of all our talented Golden Bears teams on the field and in the classroom.

CHAPTER TWENTY-TWO

NEW FIELDS OF ENDEAVOR

The sad truth was that like any highly competitive job, playing football was all consuming, especially during the season. Maintaining a healthy balance between work and home was difficult. The game demands too much of you, especially if you want to win championships as much as I did. During my playing days, I was often pensive and irritable as I mentally prepared to go to war. And the NFL doesn't stop for the holiday season. We're part of the family entertainment, but it wasn't entertaining for my family. On Christmas day 1969, my first wife Marcia and my son J. J. had to watch me pacing around the house like a caged animal as I got ready for our playoff game against the LA Rams.

Marcia and I ultimately got divorced, but she was a kind woman, a loyal wife, and a great mother to J. J. Sadly, she passed away much too young in 2005. Marcia is loved and missed by all the Kapps who knew her.

In 1982, when I became Cal's head coach, I met my second wife. Bob Reuben, an old friend and Cal alum, recommended Jennifer Adams to run the football office. The Adams family had deep Cal roots. Both Jennifer's parents Joan and Bill are Cal alums, as is her older brother, Griff. Jennifer ran the football office for five years with tremendous skill and enthusiasm. We married in 1986 and settled in Los Gatos, California. However, talented as she was running the Cal football office, she has been an even better wife and mother.

After Jen and I married, my focus was on starting a family, not football. I didn't want to put my new family through the struggles of a football life. I was at the point in my life where I could afford to step away from football, at least for a little while. My brother Larry started Kapp's Pizza Bar & Grill in Mountain View in 1984. I joined in the venture in 1989. My Cal basketball teammate Ned Averbuck and I started a company offering teamwork training seminars called "Team Dynamics" for companies and nonprofits. In 1987, Emiliana "Emi" Kapp was born. In 1989, William "Will" Lorenzo Kapp was born. In 1992, Gabriella "Gaby" Kapp was born. As a father, I wanted to teach the same values my mother Florence wanted to teach me. Like my mother, who passed away in 2011, I wanted my kids to be well educated, self sufficient, and self sustaining. I never cared if they wanted to play sports or not; I just wanted them to stand on their feet, stand by their values, and stand up for people in need. I'm really proud of all of them.

BACK TO BC

In 1990, I returned to Vancouver, British Columbia, to become the BC Lions' General Manager. The call of the ball was powerful, especially for the opportunity to give back to the team and community that had been so good to me. My wife, Jen, supported this decision. At that time the CFL, including the BC Lions ownership, was not as stable as it is now. Murray Pezim bought the team in 1989 and declared bankruptcy in 1992. I was able to hire Larry Kuharich, who had been on our coaching staff at Cal, away from the Calgary Stampeders to be the Lions head coach. I brought in Mike Arellano, another member of our Cal staff, to be the assistant general manager. One of our best signings was quarterback Doug Flutie, who was a star at Boston College and played in the USFL and the NFL before coming to Canada. Flutie went on to a stellar career in the CFL quarterbacking multiple Grey Cup Champions and landing in the CFL Hall of Fame. Flutie is now considered by many to be the greatest player in CFL history. In spite of the solid hiring and great hopes for the 1990 season, Pezim fired Larry and me after the tenth game of the season.

If Canada can claim the largest football fields, the Arena Football League can claim the smallest. I would learn the difference. In 1992, I was hired as the head coach of the Sacramento Attack. The Attack was a league-owned team that was moved from Los Angeles before it ever played a game there. I brought in Pepper Mantanga from our 1986 Cal staff to be our assistant coach. We only had a short time to put a team together and install our offense and defense. To my surprise, most if not all of the other teams ran the exact same offensive system, even down to the terminology. I didn't want to see our quarterbacks getting Nitschke'd, like we did when I played for the Vikings, so we insisted on our own system and terminology. Given how quickly we had to put a team on the field, this was a big challenge. Richard Rodgers, who was a hero for Cal in the Play, was signed to anchor the defense.

The small field, tight passing lanes, and game speed can really tax a quarterback's decision-making ability and precision. Look at how successful Kurt Warner was when he left the Iowa Barnstormers and went to the NFL. He quarterbacked the Rams to their first Super Bowl championship. However, Kurt Warner was not on our Sac Attack roster. At one point during our season, I became frustrated with our quarterback's play. I gave serious consideration to suiting up and taking the field myself. Fortunately, Pepper had my back. He talked me out of it. Despite creating the Attack on a moment's notice, we managed to secure enough wins to make the playoffs. We lost in the first round, 48–23, to the perennial AFL powerhouse Detroit Drive, who went on to win the Arena Bowl that year.

After the 1992 season the AFL moved the Sac Attack to Florida, where it became the Miami Hooters. I knew my time had come. Football was in my past. The future belonged to my family, Kapp's Pizza Bar & Grill, and Team Dynamics with Ned Averbuck. However, I was always a soft touch when asked to be a guest speaker for charities. I was a fundraiser and Golf Tournament Host for National Hispanic University. Forever frustrated with the business structure of professional football, I became involved in the attempt to start the All-Star Football League with a single entity ownership structure, but we could not make it fly.

CHAPTER TWENTY-THREE

WISDOM FROM THE TRENCHES

Is there such a thing? Like my BC Lions teammate and lifelong friend Big Mike Cacic said, "Football is a mug's game." I agree. It is a mug's game. For whatever it's worth, here are a few topics that are important to a mug like Old Joe.

THE PAINFUL REALITY OF MEN
BEING BORN FOR GAMES

In 1979, I worked with songwriter Kris Kristofferson on the motion picture *Semi-Tough*. The extent of my "coaching him up" on the set was cutting up some foam padding to stick in his socks so his calves wouldn't look so skinny. I know he wasn't singing about football players, but the first line of his classic song "Sunday Morning Comin' Down" perfectly sums up how I felt after games, and how I still feel today when I wake up. Many of my former teammates feel the same way. The lyric goes, "I woke up Sunday morning with no way to hold my head that didn't hurt." When I wake up in the morning, I have pain in my head, joints, shoulders, neck, and knees. Sometimes everything hurts. Sometimes it is a dull ache. Sometimes it cuts like a knife. I also have a hard time remembering what I did five minutes before. This is because I had many concussions and numerous injuries playing nineteen years of full-contact football. Nobody in my family has had dementia or Alzheimer's disease. It is not the age of the body—it is the mileage on the body.

CONCUSSIONS

Any talk about injuries should start with concussions. I believe I had nine . . . or was it nineteen? Back in my era, we did not know that it was dangerous to play with or after a concussion; we did it with regularity and pride. Management encouraged it. Our ethic was to play through pain and injury. Despite greater awareness of the problem and greater efforts today, this mindset still exists.

One time I was knocked out by Dave Wilcox of the San Francisco 49ers. I was two yards into the end zone before he clotheslined me, and right in front of referee Jim Tunney. No call. Wilcox revealed later to longtime friend Dan Casey that the clothesline was payback for what he called an illegal pick play that we ran on the previous down. I don't think Wilcox was trying to knock me unconscious, even though in those days it was customary to knock down the quarterback at the end of every play. I took a lot of pride in playing through pain and injuries. With the BC Lions, I was hit so hard in an important CFL game against Calgary that my left hand went numb, and I only had clear vision out of my right eye. To regain feeling and vision, I was shaking my hand and scrunching my face. The Calgary middle linebacker, affectionately known as Thumper, a.k.a. Wayne Harris, thought I was taunting him. My teammates in the huddle would not let me leave, so I stayed in. We won. But like anybody who keeps playing after brain trauma, there is a price to be paid.

In the 1969 NFL Championship Game, I ran into Cleveland Linebacker Jim Houston and knocked him unconscious. Glorified by NFL Films, the collision has become a signature play in my career and has helped make my reputation as a tough guy. The truth is that it was a fluke. If he had tackled me fifty more times, I would not have knocked him out again. On the other hand, I was not going to slide. It was a freak accident, but as a result, Jim Houston got a concussion. No matter what is done to reform football, there will always be injuries.

I'M NOT ALONE

I am probably lucky as compared to many of my teammates and con-temporaries. Joe Namath has two artificial knees. Dick Butkus's knee is fused. Earl Campbell uses a walker. Tom Brown, the 1960 Outland Trophy winner and the middle linebacker of our 1964 Grey Cup team, went into the hospital for a knee replacement and came out paralyzed on one side of his body. "The Crusher" Neal Beaumont, also a mem-ber of the '64 Lions team, suffers from chronic pain.

The only player I know who was injury free and still has no com-plaints of pain is Ron Morris. Ron, you will remember, was a member of our 1964 Grey Cup championship team and is truly the most accom-plished and most underrated football player of all time. He excelled at multiple positions and often played three ways. He still holds the CFL record for touchdown receptions in a playoff game with four. He did all this without getting hit. It should be noted that his advice to my grandson Frank was that he should be a placekicker so that he would not get hit! He is often overlooked due to his incredible off-field hu-mility and on-field invisibility. He was never wide open—just open, all the time. No fanfare, no pain, and no injuries—that is the legend and the mystery of the Creeper.

A lot can be done to improve safety, but any real change seems unlikely given many of the responses of the NFL, NFLPA, and NCAA. While the NFL is promoting the teaching of safer tackling on some of the teams and in their Head Up public-relations initiative, they are still glorifying the force of the collisions in their mass marketing. It's a dangerous game, and men are born for games, whether to play or to watch.

RETIRED PLAYERS SETTLEMENT IS AN NFL "SPECIAL"

Recently, 4,300 former pro football players, including me, sued the NFL to get redress for brain injuries that resulted from our football work. The lawsuit was settled for millions of dollars. Many of us are skeptical that this was a fair settlement, considering the stratospheric popularity and prosperity of the NFL. We are also skeptical because other NFL funds supposedly available to former players for injuries have been inaccessible due to bureaucracy and many disqualifiers. How is a guy with dementia supposed to know when he got his first NFL concussion? The settlement specifically excludes retirees with chronic traumatic encephalopathy (CTE), the one condition that almost all former NFL players whose brains have been autopsied seem to have. I participated because I had a qualifying condition (Alzheimer's Disease). It is now clear that pro football has caused serious brain injuries to its players whose outstanding performances have enriched the NFL. The infamous cases of Mike Webster, Junior Seau, and Dave Duerson, who suffered tragic endings, are just the starting point. The NFL settlement included no admission by the league of their awareness of the head injury caused by the game. But we all know the truth. Unfortunately, the settlement takes the spotlight off of the issue. The NFL needs to be responsible for the dire health consequences of the game on its players.

OUR HEADS: A NEW MENTALITY IS NEEDED

Concussions are serious injuries, often with a lifetime of worsening consequences. We need to move away from the mentality that encourages hiding from or underreporting these injuries to stay in a game. No game is worth damaging your brain. As an example: it is unfortunate that 49ers quarterback Alex Smith lost his starting job to

Colin Kaepernick because of a concussion suffered in the 2012 season. On the other hand, the Kaepernick move may have been inevitable given his physical talents. Fortunately for Smith, his subsequent trade to Kansas City was a great opportunity for him. As an aside, there is too much emphasis on starters in football. All the players are important, and the "starter" needs to be secure enough to know that they can be effectively relieved. Competition is good for players and the game, but it creates some tragic dilemmas, and the potential for traumatic brain injury.

LESS IS MORE

When I was a sophomore at Salinas High School, I was handed a leather helmet with no face mask. I did not think anything of it. I played contact football for nineteen years and never had a helmet more substantial than a plastic suspension helmet with a one-bar face mask. The one bar was my choice. Football has moved to sturdier and sturdier helmets. The advent of the motorcycle-style football helmet with an impenetrable face mask has caused an epidemic of head trauma and other serious injuries to football players at all levels; the more secure a helmet, the bolder a player can feel about colliding with another player headfirst. The truth is that the greater the collision, the greater the entertainment value. It's similar to auto racing, where many fans look forward to the high-speed crashes.

AN OLD GAME HOLDS A MODERN ANSWER

Modern football helmets can give a player a false sense of invincibility. Players of all ages have been taught, or have learned on their own, to use their helmet as a weapon. Rather than wrap up a ball carrier, defenders launch their bodies like missiles with enough velocity to knock them down. It's dramatic but dangerous. "Spearing" with the head, as it used to be called in my time, has always been illegal in football. The NFL has made new rules that outlaw the intentional hit with a lowered helmet, but inadvertent hits like this are still inevitable. American football evolved from rugby, an equally physical game. Rugby players do not wear helmets or pads. The players make initial tackling contact with their shoulders, instinctively sliding their heads away from contact because their heads and faces are not protected. A rugby player is required to grasp an opposing player before knocking them down.

Football at all levels should follow rugby's example. First, eliminate the modern helmet. While it is true that they help to prevent skull fractures, they encourage dangerous play. Go with lighter ones with no face mask at all or eliminate helmets all together. Secondly, a player should not be allowed to leave their feet when tackling an opponent; they must have one foot on the ground when initiating a tackle. This will stop players using their helmet as a warhead on a human missile. Both football and rugby are dangerous games. Both cause the brain to bounce around inside the skull. The NFL and the NCAA, along with other football authorities, are desperately trying to legislate safer tackling by imposing superficial rules and fines. If you give competitors a battering-ram helmet, expect they will use it on occasion. The introduction of rugby's common-sense tackling rules and a return to lighter helmets with no face masks, or even no helmets at all, will reduce head injuries and change the game for the better. Because men are born for games, sometimes we need to be protected from our own violent, competitive drives. The NFL and NCAA have nothing to fear in these changes; they can still put a logo on a lighter helmet or hat. We know how important marketing is to them.

Rugby may also hold the "last frontier of innovation in football." The game has been spread out to the max—what else is left? The downfield option. By that I mean that someone is going to get really good at running what is now known as the Hook and Lateral, which is only used in desperation. The play is a pass to a receiver downfield, and when caught is lateraled to a trailing or crossing receiver. When someone gets really good at that and the initial receiver learns how to "option" (meaning to keep or lateral the ball depending on the defensive reaction) the first tackler he meets . . . look out!

QUARTERBACKS: STRIDE DON'T SLIDE

The NFL and NCAA now allow a quarterback or other runner to give up by going down; the ball gets spotted at the initial point the ball carrier's body hits the ground. This rule is another example of form over substance. Allowing a player to slide puts him in a vulnerable position with an increased risk of injury. The career-ending play of former St. Louis Rams quarterback Trent Green was a slide to "protect" himself. The idea that you protect a football player by taking them off their feet at the point of attack is a product of people who never played the game making the rules, or worse, former football players wanting to protect the status quo at all costs.

How many times do we need to see a tackler launch himself before the quarterback slides only to collide with the quarterback as he is sliding, causing a more serious injury to the protected quarterback? Then the commentators go nuts and call that tackler a dirty player. It's dangerous for the tackler too. How many awkward collisions do we need to see where the tackler contorts his body in completely unorthodox ways so as not to hit the sacred quarterback, only to find himself injured? The rule creates indecision on the runner's part and the tackler's part and decreases safety for all. This scenario plays out nearly every season and dishonors the game. Finally, a ball carrier giving themselves up is just plain unmanly. When I played, my job was to move the ball forward and put points on the board. I felt safest on my feet and on the attack. Eliminating the slide-protection rule and teaching quarterbacks, starting in high school, how to run with the ball so they can be tackled without getting hurt should be done. And while you're at it, teach them how to tackle in case they throw an interception! And speaking of passing, change the intentional grounding rule. Allow the quarterback to ground the ball if the ball reaches the line of scrimmage, or some other reasonable distance, without restricting it to a quarterback who moves outside the tackle position.

REPLAYS AND REORIENTED PRIORITIES

The NFL calls itself a family, but it seems to be more fixated on expanding replays to "get it right" than real changes to protect players. If it is a business and just entertainment, why is it so important to get every call right with replay? It's not that important, and it can't be done. Every year we see how they blow it even with replay. The replay delays ruin the rhythm and fun of every game. The NFL ought to focus on real rule changes to make the game safer and better. A fifteen-yard penalty for pass interference is fine. Let's not get carried away with longer and longer penalties. One foot in bounds for a legal catch. Multiple motion should be okay too. More offense is more fun, but let's get it without stopping defenders from being defenders.

PLAYERS MUST TAKE CARE OF THEMSELVES

More important than rules and equipment is how a player takes care of himself. I have to admit that some of my choices weren't the best for me or my health. With the Vikings, I had a mechanic help cut off my leg cast so I could play in a preseason game. I enjoyed celebrating with my teammates too. I had a black eye from Lonnie Warrick to prove it. The eye healed without lasting effect.

Some guys aren't so lucky. Art Scullion was a veteran on our Calgary Stampeders team. He was a great teammate and a tough Canadian lineman who loved to drink and carouse. His cure for hangovers was to dunk his head in our team whirlpool tub, even if it was being used by a naked Stampeder. Yes, football is a mug's game. Art broke his leg in a game and was in the hospital recuperating in a cast. I went to see him, but he was gone. Later, I heard that Art made a jail break from the hospital by climbing out of the second-story window and scaling his way down, cast and all. Art's broken leg never healed properly. His playing career ended in 1960. The bottom line is that a player needs to take care of his body and his mind, despite all the obstacles in the way, including themselves.

WOULD YOU LET YOUR KIDS PLAY?

Football is a dangerous game. I am often asked if I'd let my kids play. My answer is yes, but not before eighth grade. My son Will was a fullback and Special Forces player at Cal, receiving the Stub Allison award (then awarded to the most inspirational Cal player) in 2011. He had a great experience in Berkeley, and a great playing career despite suffering serious injuries. My grandson Frank enjoyed playing football in high school. He was a team captain and All-Leaguer and a scout-team player for Cal. I have mixed emotions because of the risks, but I'd be a hypocrite to keep them from playing. There are many good things about football—most importantly, providing an outlet for the violence that exists in the souls of men. Men are born for games. Whether or not a parent should let their child play is a personal decision with many variables. A parent should get informed on all the risks for their child and make the best decision for that child's best interests. Some children are meant to be football players, others aren't. Football isn't what's most important. The child's best interest is.

A TEAM IS A FAMILY . . .

. . . and a family is a team. I was a migratory child. I remember our struggles with poverty, addiction, and uncertainty. My father did his best, but it was my mother who held it together for us. My brother and all three of my sisters always supported me with maximum enthusiasm. Whatever setbacks and instability we endured, I knew I had a family that loved me. I was also a migratory football player. Football was all about family too. Coach Lewis was a second father to me, and every coach I had shaped who I was as a player and a man. The structure, discipline, and camaraderie of team life gave me direction and purpose, as I am sure it did for my teammates. Every person contributing to the team effort is important. I remember all the people who helped me throughout my life: my family, my teammates, and my friends. I am grateful. In the end, life is all about people, especially loved ones. If you have a family, you are blessed. If you have a team, you are blessed. If you have both, you have it all. Whether you're sharing a holiday dinner or some Jose Cuervo after a win, it's what we do as a team that matters. And speaking of Jose Cuervo, my beloved Golden Bears have still not won the Rose Bowl since the year I was born in 1938. Jose Cuervo and I are still on the outs. I said no roses, no cactus juice, and I meant what I said. It will taste all the better when the Bears do it. I know they will. No matter where I am when it happens, I am confident Jose and I will enjoy a tearful reunion. The Bear will not quit. The Bear will not die.

DELUSIONS OF DEMENTIA

The words "delusions of dementia" come from my father's interview with Elliott Almond, published February 5, 2016, in the *San Jose Mercury News*. Pop was diagnosed with Alzheimer's disease in 2014. During the interview, his second wife Jennifer and I provided support. We wanted to do the interview because we thought going public with his disease might help others impacted by brain disease as well as those concerned about the risks of playing football. During the interview, Pop admitted that he got lost driving to Oakland to visit a former teammate, and he can no longer drive himself. Another time he walked into a hardware store but couldn't remember what he came for. He couldn't remember the names of friends he'd had for life. He talked about his frequent headaches. Jennifer shared that Pop took Aricept to improve his mental functioning. On his bestial style of play, Pop admitted, "I've been called one half of a collision looking for another."

I remembered that in one game in the CFL, he said he got hit so hard that the left side of his body went numb and his left eye closed—yet his team would not let him off the field. The old-school football ethic dictated that he play through it. Even so, Pop's sense of humor was on full display. He told Elliott, "I've got delusions of dementia." Then he added, "I've got calendars on both my shoes."

"It's as frustrating as hell," he said. "I know what I want to say, but it won't come out. I can't remember what I had for breakfast—or if I had it." He warned readers that one big hit is enough to cause brain injury and said that he is saddened that many of his former team-mates are struggling with memory loss like he is.

Elliott noted that, according to the *New York Times*, ninety of the ninety-four brains of deceased NFL players studied at Boston University had Chronic Traumatic Encephalopathy, more commonly known as CTE. Equally disturbing, Elliott noted the federal Centers for Disease Control found that NFL players are four times more likely to suffer from Alzheimer's than the general population. I conceded that the Kapps were afflicted with "football disease," so strong was our family's love for the game. My wife Pat and I let our son Frank play in high school and at Cal, and my half-brother Will played at Cal, where he suffered three concussions.

Pop talked about his new therapy dog, a Labrador puppy, which the family gave him for Christmas. He named it Mike as a tribute to one of his favorite CFL teammates, Big Mike Cacic. Pop shared his participation in a neurological study at UCSF and said, "When I cash in, they will take the brain and study it." Even while coping with his illness, Pop was aware enough to help others and had no regrets about his choices. Pop told Elliott, "It's past the time of concern," adding, "I've been to the Rose Bowl, I've been to the toilet bowl, I've done it all." He shared his secret when he said, "My slogan for the last fifty years is stay tough and keep smiling. The smiling part is how you keep tough."

Of Pop, I emphasized, "He's not a beaten, broken man," meaning that he is not a victim. In fact, thanks to the advocacy of Jamie Webb, Pop has recently been provided significant NFL benefits for his care through the 88 Fund. We are most thankful for these benefits, even though we'd of course much rather have our father clearheaded.

FORTY FOR SIXTY FOREVER

Since Elliott Almond's story was published, Pop has inevitably declined. His short-term memory is gone and his long-term memory is unreliable. But he has remained a source of strength and learning for all of us. And through all this, Jennifer has been our leader. Her patience and care with Pop are inspirational and also a source of strength in themselves.

Pop always stressed leadership, loyalty, and toughness to me. They were connected. My mother Marcia earnestly supported every one of those teachings. He is a leader because he cares more about his family and his team than he cares about himself. He always loved a quote by Canadian poet Robert Service: "A promise made is a debt unpaid." He taught me to be loyal and tough by insisting that I follow through and by making decisions and sacrifices for the greater good, even if they are unpopular. To Pop, that included confrontation and even physical conflict. Most of my participation in conflict and confrontation involved defending people accused of serious crimes in a courtroom. Those instilled values steered me toward and prepared me for those courtroom fights.

When my siblings Emi, Will, and Gaby came along, Pop added *smarter* to his ethos of loyalty and toughness. His mantra to them was to be "tougher and smarter." As it did with me, *tougher* meant you had to be willing to stand up for yourself and others who are not able to do so—not only figuratively, but literally. He taught all his children to box, including his daughters. *Smarter* meant you needed to think about your actions because they had consequences. Although Pop stressed the importance of education, when he talked about *smarter* he meant thinking about how to act before you did so. I found myself using the same message to our kids. As we cope with Pop's decline, we realize all our actions have consequences and attempt to make the most of our opportunities together.

Most importantly, Pop preached to all of us to stay tough and keep smiling. This is my father's core. When my sisters Emi or Gaby would fall and skin their knees, Pop would exclaim, "What about the ground? Is the ground hurt?" It sums up his eternal optimism and his sense of humor. My brother Will said Pop would yell "Smile!" as he dropped him and his sisters off at school. He taught us all to love fiercely, let our love be known, and guard our loved ones with our life.

Feel no pity for the Kapp family, or for the Toughest Chicano himself. Pop gave us all the inspiration and tools to rally behind him, even as he now relies on us. And for those of you who don't hear the call of the ball, thrive on confrontation, or even play sports, Pop's wisdom was far broader than the games men were born for. As Will observed, "My dad epitomized the philosophy that you can be a badass and a romantic, an athlete and an artist, and incredibly fiery and gentle all at once." Joe Kapp wants everyone to live their best life, their way, for the good of all.

Our father, this man who insists on saying "we" passed for seven touchdowns in one game as if he did not have much to do with it, has left his family, teammates, players he coached, and fans with fundamental lessons. Maybe they are unorthodox lessons of selflessness because he seems to embody a paradox, illustrated in his clear recognition that football is a "mug's game." It's Pop having a laugh at his own expense to make his point: pro football is run and played by scoundrels and brutes, with a debilitating impact on the mind and body. Yet he was proud to play it with gusto, and even let his sons and grandson do the same. His ability to clearly see the price he paid and accept it without regret or self-pity defines him. He can acknowledge this paradox even while accepting it as part of the life he chose. Whatever you say about Joe Kapp, he is his own man.

The Kapp family, Ned Averbuck, and Robert G. Phelps all hope we have given you a better insight into the paradox of Joe Kapp. We sincerely thank all Joe's coaches, teammates, friends, and fans who have been an enormous source of love and support for all of us, especially as Pop battles his Alzheimer's disease. Likewise, know that Joe and the Kapp family offer you our love and support as you and your loved ones face your own inevitable challenges in life.

We all wanted Joe Kapp to have the last word in his own biography. Despite his inability to write for himself now, I found a letter penned by him on September 18, 1993. It is his memorial tribute to Coach Al Lewis, his high school coach and mentor. While he wrote it to remember Coach Lewis, it says so much about who Joe Kapp is, what he values, and his endless capacity for love, courage, and gratitude. As my father stands in the twilight of his life, his remembrance of Coach Lewis stands as a timeless reminder to all of us that mortality can't defeat the endless love and vitality of the circle of life.

Forty for sixty forever—you, me, we, us, together!

—J. J. Kapp

GOODBYE, COACH

By Joe Kapp

SATURDAY, SEPTEMBER 18, 1993
11:00 A.M.

I didn't hear the phone right. I could barely hear anything over the breathless giggles and shrieks of laughter from my three little kiddies as they mugged ol' Dad in the middle of our den floor. We were obliviously involved in our routine Saturday-morning pajama version of World Championship Wrestling. These weekly romps are obvious fun for kids, but even more special to me. I've been an athlete all my life, even played professional football, so I tend to relate to the world on a more physical basis than most people. To Will, Gaby, and Emi, our three-on-one weekend tickle fests are pure delight. To me, each hug, each stolen kiss on the cheek is one more precious memory to treasure.

It takes tremendous concentration to fend off a trio of energetic grade-schoolers determined to pin your shoulders to the ground. When the phone rang a second time, I heard it, but my hands were full of bare feet and tiny, flailing arms. My wife, Jennifer, picked up the phone in the kitchen. Buried under a Medusa-like crown of miniature arms, legs, tummies, and grinning faces, I didn't know how long she was on the phone and I didn't see her come into the den . . . but I felt her standing over us. When I looked up at her face, it was clear something awful had happened. For no apparent reason, the room was instantly silent.

"Joe," she said, almost whispering, "there's a call for you. It's Peggy Lewis."

I untangled myself from the kids, whose expressions were now a mixture of disappointment at the time-out and hopefulness that I'd quickly return, and started toward the phone. Within two steps, I already knew what this call meant. My legs felt weak. A minute ago, I was tossing my children in the air like Frisbees; now, as I reached for the phone, I felt like I was running underwater.

Peggy had been Al Lewis's wife for over fifty years. There could be only one reason she would have to call me at home on a Saturday morning. And I knew what it was.

Al Lewis had been my football and basketball coach at Hart High School. He was the strongest man I had ever known. Like every other athlete and student at Hart, I always referred to him as Coach Lewis. Never "Mr. Lewis" or just "Coach." That would've placed him in the same category as every other coach. It wouldn't have given him the respect he deserved. When I spoke to him directly, even after I reached my middle-aged self, I called him Coach Lewis—it never occurred to me to call him Al.

"Mrs. Lewis, this is Joe," I softly spoke into the receiver. "How are you?"

"I have bad news, Joe. He's had a turn for the worse. I thought you'd want to know," Mrs. Lewis said. She uttered the words without any discernable emotion. I'd seen her stoicism before, but it had never concerned matters this critical.

I don't remember what I said next, but I know it was more to encourage myself than it was to cheer up Mrs. Lewis. The entire conversation lasted barely a few moments, yet it had a devastating effect on me. Sure, I knew Coach Lewis was sick. I knew his illness was life-threatening. But, hey, we're talking about *Coach Lewis* here.

Nobody ever allowed themselves to believe anything could defeat that grizzled old competitor, least of all me. Coach Lewis could never die!

I first learned Coach Lewis's body had been invaded by this insidious monster more than a year ago. I guess I understood what was happening, at least intellectually, but I emotionally denied all negative reality. Not once did the notion that Coach Lewis would—or could—be defeated by this senseless killer ever enter my thoughts. "If any person in the world could conquer cancer, it would be Coach Lewis," I'd tell myself. And I believed it.

Throughout my lifetime in the arena—not just in sports, but at all levels of competition—I looked to Coach Lewis, who had so profoundly affected me as my teacher, mentor, and ally, to be my touchstone. No one was more responsible for influencing the direction my life would ultimately take. No one else had left such indelible fingerprints on my personal development. At the crossroads of my young athletic career, it was Coach Lewis who first saw the quarterback in me. I was an end. Tall for my age, with pretty good speed, it never occurred to me—or to any other coaches—that I'd ever be anything else. Coach Lewis was convinced I should be a quarterback, so naturally he convinced me too.

He didn't only teach teams how to play the game; he taught us why playing the game well, and by the rules, was important. He instilled old-fashioned notions about fairness, sacrifice, hard work, dedication, and commitment into each of his players. In today's age of "winning at all costs," those early lessons learned in the gym and on the practice fields at Hart High School from that unassuming Irishman are challenged as being tired and out of steam. Was Coach Lewis now wearing out just like this arcane philosophy? How could any sense be made out of this situation?

No! Coach Lewis is the fiercest competitor I've ever known. If he faced them, he'd run over Dick Butkus; he'd slam down on Wilt Chamberlain; he'd brush Hank Aaron off the plate. He'll surely know how to win this one. He may be wounded, but not wounded forever. His team will help! The family, doctors, nurses, and all us old athletes he coached, we'll use our skills and talent and cunning and strength to pull him through. And we'll pray. It's the fourth quarter. Mrs. Lewis just called with the two-minute warning. Coach Lewis is facing the game of his life.

TUESDAY, SEPTEMBER 21, 1993 7:30 P.M.

Young Brian Lewis tried to phone me at home. He left this message on my answering machine: "It happened. . . . Dad passed away today."

Standing alone in my small home office, the recorded words ringing in my ears, I felt like I was in an elevator falling forty stories. A part of me clung to the cruel possibility that some kind of mistake may have been made. It was torture to imagine the truth. I had to call his house. I wanted him to answer the phone himself.

I called and reached Mrs. Lewis.

"It's true, Joe," she said. "The Coach is dead."

Her voice was sad, tired, and in pain. But the words she spoke as we continued talking demonstrated an inner strength that could only exist in a woman who'd mothered six children and been married to a high-school teacher for half a century. Don't forget, she shared forty-eight winning and losing football seasons with Coach Lewis. That provides a unique understanding of life's ups and downs. Despite her formidable stamina, she sounded vulnerable. I knew tears were somewhere nearby, but she kept them harnessed. She sounded tough, just like him.

TUESDAY, SEPTEMBER 28, 1993
10:40 A.M.

The funeral services for Coach Lewis were starting in twenty minutes. I sat in seat 18A on Reno Airlines on flight 59 from San Jose to San Diego.

It had been a beautiful, peaceful flight over the Salinas Valley and the LA Basin, where I first met Coach Lewis. We had traveled these skies many times together. A lifetime—my life—was flooding through my mind as I looked down from thirty thousand feet over the State of California, the place where many opportunities were opened for me by my high school coach. He challenged me to be what I wanted to be. He motivated my mind to the possibility of going to college. He recommended me to Pappy Waldorf and Pete Newell at the University of California–Berkeley. He was a second father to me, there for me at the right time.

We were scheduled to land at 10:20 a.m. Frank Mattarocci, a former Cal teammate, was picking me up in one of his presidential limos in time for the 11:00 a.m. service in Ocean Beach.

But there was a problem on the runway. No planes were landing at the San Diego airport. We circled the airport fourteen times in twenty minutes. We were going to have to refuel soon. Then we were rerouted to Ontario.

As a captive of this stranded plane, I was helpless. I grew numb with unventable anger. My stomach churned from pent-up sadness and empty feelings of loss. I was overwhelmed by my lack of power over this situation.

How could I miss this appointment? Coach Lewis had taught me the respect for self and for others demonstrated by being on time. And here I was, missing the whole event. How could I do this to the Coach, Mrs. Lewis, and the Lewis family and friends? How could Coach Lewis forgive me for this? How could I forgive myself? I was suspended ten thousand feet over north San Diego County—consumed by grief, guilt, and regret—when I sensed something. I wasn't sure, but I thought I heard . . . I felt . . . Coach Lewis.

"What's that?" I muttered, not quite aloud.

"Hello, Bub!" came that voice, that familiar greeting. I'd know it anywhere. Coach Lewis always greeted me in person with "Hello, Bub."

My mind was playing tricks on me. Had sorrow shaken my sanity? "But I *heard* him," I insisted to myself. I didn't imagine it; I'd actually heard Coach Lewis speak to me.

"Sure you did, Bub." There it was again: clear, audible, undeniable. "Relax, Joe. Take it easy. It's great up here, don't you think?" he said soothingly.

"Coach Lewis!" I whispered. Was I really talking to Coach Lewis on this airplane? "What are you doing here? You're supposed to be at your funeral. Father Sproul is waiting for you. It's bad enough I'm not going to be there."

What moments before had seemed surreal and impossible suddenly felt comfortable. Doubts about my sanity, my belly full of frustrated anger, the brokenhearted sadness I had endured for the past eight days—it all evaporated at the sound of his voice. It felt completely reasonable that Coach Lewis had come to talk to me, to give me confidence and strength, to offer me alternate choices. That's what he had always done.

"Don't worry, Joe," he said. "I don't think anybody will miss me for a few moments. I knew you could use a little conversation right about now."

The drone of the plane's engines and the din of the other passengers' conversations disappeared. It was as though we were the only two people on the plane, in the world. As I peered out the window at the soft, patchy clouds of the California sky, I eagerly embraced the chance to listen again to my old friend's voice. The past year had been a horrific nightmare. Watching his body deteriorate under cancer's inexorable assault, seeing his strength sapped, hearing his voice weaken. But today there was renewed vigor in his words. His power was back. There was life in the sound filling my ears, and I wanted more. I closed my eyes and silently listened.

"You fought for me this past year. I appreciate that," he said warmly, with genuine sincerity. "But even the game of life has an end." He said this matter-of-factly, the same way he used to explain how to read a defensive safety's coverage. With pride, he added, "We played our best."

Strangely, I wasn't feeling sad anymore, even though Coach Lewis's words had such finality. It was the absence of his recent pain in his voice. It was the presence of his old strength. "There's so much I want to ask you, Coach Lewis," I said, anxious to speak before he had to go. "I tried to discuss some of them with you this past year, but the strength was missing from our talks. I came to visit you armed with my usual energy, hoping to share it with you to make you better, but as soon as we shook hands, I could feel the force of your spirit flowing into my arm and body. It was supposed to be the other way around; the flow should have been in your direction. You were supposed to take for once, not always be the one to give."

In a low, mentoring voice, Coach Lewis reminded me, "Joe, the harmony of balance and nature is a circle of giving and receiving. You learned to trust your offensive line to block, your ends to get open and catch the ball when you threw it, and yourself to be able to get the pass off. Didn't you find that the harder you worked, the more you gave to your teammates, the more you got back in return?" he asked. "When you've lived your whole life getting the best out of people by giving them your best, it's impossible to stop just because you've got less to give," he explained, almost chuckling.

It may have been due to the rarefied air at that altitude, but I completely understood, maybe for the first time, why it's so important to give your best at all times. Coach Lewis had been teaching all us gangly, raw, undisciplined athletes back at Hart High how to get the most out of life by always giving all we had. That would be enough.

"Coach Lewis," I asked, "what did you mean when you used to say, 'We'll play for money, marbles, and chalk'?"

"Ah, so you were paying attention sometimes, hey, Joe? That was my way of saying the stakes weren't the issue, but rather being ready and willing to compete is what's important," he said. "Competition measures the heart more than the body. It's when you learn the most about yourself, and you should respect your opponents for providing a means to test your creativity, preparation, skills, determination, stamina, and honesty."

Even as he spoke, my appreciation of all he had taught me, all I had learned and applied throughout my own life, began to grow. Choices I had made and later questioned became more just in light of this conversation. My favorite memories of sports competition involve triumphs of spirit rather than winning trophies. Losing never represents failure, if competition itself is to be valued. Only those who do not compete fail.

"I'm sorry I'm not going to be at your funeral, Coach Lewis," I said regretfully. "But I sure am glad you came to see me so I could say goodbye." My sadness was starting to return.

"What do you mean 'goodbye,' Joe?" he said with a tinge of *I know something you don't* in his voice. "I'm counting on you to keep my spirit around forever. Aren't you going to tell those three little rug rats of yours about your old high school coach?" he teased.

It was true. Coach Lewis had given me enough of himself to always stay alive through me. He knew his ideas and values would live on in his players and be passed down to theirs. He knew it years earlier, when I asked for his advice about accepting a scholarship to Cal, and when I sought his counsel before I sued the NFL for the right to freely negotiate a contract, and when I consulted him about taking the head coaching job at Cal in 1982. He knew now that I would always keep him alive in my heart, in the way I feel about my family, and most importantly, in the way I feel about myself.

Great teachers like Coach Lewis never die. They live forever in the lives of their players and their families. We remember and honor them because they represent so much more than words—they lived their own lives true to the values they taught through sports. We're influenced to imitate their model because they proved it works by how they lived. I've been undeservedly fortunate. I've had several Al Lewises touch my life: Andy Smith, Brutus Hamilton, Pappy Waldorf, Pete Newell, Russ Messner, Ed Nemir, and Gene Stauber. When I need someone to talk to, all I have to do is sit very still and listen.

Goodbye, Coach Lewis. I'll be talking to you.

ACKNOWLEDGMENTS

Over the years there were several sincere and committed people who attempted to help Joe write this book. We want to thank them for their time and earnest efforts: Jack Richards, Bob Tower, Dan Breining, and Bob Lowell.

Thank you to all the Wise Ink Creative Publishing staff and contractors for their hard work on this book: Amy Quale, Alyssa Bluhm, Patrick Maloney, Cole Nelson, and Graham Warnken.

We also want to acknowledge some people who have always been there for Joe, particularly as he has battled Alzheimer's disease. Thank you for the love and action of Marshall Shoquist, Bill McClintock, and Rick Wardenburg.

Thank you to Mary Susan "Susie" (Kapp) McDonald and Bill Cooper for their assistance as historians.

Thank you to Bill Austin, founder of Starkey Hearing Technologies, for making it possible for Joe to hear in his later years and for all of the work he's done helping former players.

Thank you to Herb Benenson for his assistance with the Play photograph. Thank you to Jim and Coleen Stinnett for permission to use the Play photograph.

Thank you to Minneapolis attorney and former NFL linebacker Bob Stein for his work on the concussion and NFL Films lawsuits for Joe and all the legal work he has taken on for former players.

Thank you to Minneapolis attorney Jeff O'Brien for all of the work on Joe's behalf, especially the tenacious support and belief in this book. And to Jeff's outstanding team: Joey Balthazor, Natalie Paule, Georgie Brattland, Kristoffer Wathne, and Paul Nguyen.

Special thanks to Dan "the Man" Casey for significant photo contributions to this book, including the cover photograph, and *always* being there for Joe and the Kapp family.

ABOUT THE COAUTHORS

JOSEPH JOHN "J. J." KAPP

J. J. Kapp is the only child of Joe and Marcia Day Kapp. After obtaining his bachelor of arts from Chico State University and his JD from Santa Clara University, he served as a trial attorney for the Santa Clara County (CA) Public Defender's Office from 1990–2017. He and his wife Pat have two children, Frank and Kelly.

ROBERT G. PHELPS

Robert G. Phelps is a screenwriter and filmmaker who earned an MFA in film and television at UCLA in 2013 after working for almost twenty-three years as an attorney in the Santa Clara County (CA) Public Defender's Office. He's written feature stories for the Los Angeles Angels, the Arena Football League's San Jose SaberCats, and *Parachutist*. He is the owner of Robert G. Phelps Productions LLC and can be reached at robertgphelps@gmail.com.

NED AVERBUCK

Born in New York, Ned Averbuck spent his childhood in East Los Angeles and obtained his bachelor of arts from the University of California. He is a lifetime high school and college instructor, and served as director of Pete Newell Basketball Academy from 1981–2012.

REFERENCES

Fimrite, Ron. "The Anatomy of a Miracle." *Sports Illustrated*, August 31, 1983.

Jenkins, Bruce. *A Good Man: The Pete Newell Story*. Lincoln: University of Nebraska Press, 2010.

Kapp, Joe. "A Man of Machismo." *Sports Illustrated*, July 20, 1970. www.si.com/vault/1970/07/20/611157/a-man-of-machismo.

Kapp v. National Football League, 586 F.2d 644 (9th Cir. 1978).

"Lay Those Elbows Down, Mike." *Sports Illustrated*, November 16, 1959. www.si.com/vault/1959/11/16/601092/lay-those-elbows-down-mike.

Mackey v. National Football League, 543 F.2d 606 (8th Cir. 1976).

Martin, Glen. "Kapp Redux: Revisiting Joe Kapp v. NFL in Light of the Kaepernick Case." *California Magazine*, November 6, 2017. www.alumni.berkeley.edu/california-magazine/just-in/2017-10-23/kapp-redux-revisiting-joe-kapp-v-nfl-light-kaepernick-case.